D1571030

The Vast and Terrible Drama

The Vast and Terrible Drama

American Literary Naturalism
in the Late Nineteenth Century

Eric Carl Link

The University of Alabama Press · Tuscaloosa

Designer: Daniel Urban
Typeface is Monotype Bulmer

∞

The paper on which this book is printed meets the minimum requirements of American
National Standard for Information Science–Permanence of Paper for Printed Library
Materials, ANSI Z39.48–1984.

Library of Congress Cataloging-in-Publication Data

Link, Eric Carl.
The vast and terrible drama : American literary naturalism in the
late nineteenth century / Eric Carl Link.
p. cm. — (Studies in American literary realism and naturalism)
Includes bibliographical references and index.
ISBN 0-8173-1385-0 (alk. paper)
1. American literature—19th century—History and criticism.
2. Naturalism in literature. I. Title. II. Series.
PS217.N42 L56 2004
810.9'12'09034—dc22   2003015077

In loving memory,
this book is dedicated to my father,
Rev. Louis P. Link

Contents

Preface

Naturalism is dead. Notwithstanding Paul Alexis's famous 1891 telegram to Jules Huret ("Naturalism not dead. Letter follows."), according to at least one periodical, by the turn of the twentieth century the only thing naturalism lacked was an elegy by Emmeline Grangerford. In 1900 an obituary entitled "The Passing of Naturalism" in *The Outlook* officially declared the literary movement deceased. Sadly, implies the eulogist, naturalism may never have lived at all: even the works of Émile Zola, in retrospect, turn out to be little more than moral tracts against a parade of vices. Zola's attempt to create a scientific literature—an experimental novel—was a failure. According to the eulogist, naturalism as a literary method proved to be "impracticable and untenable" and has thus been abandoned—and wisely so—by the younger generation of authors.[1] Someone should have told Dreiser, I suppose.

The writer for *The Outlook* declared naturalism dead because the fiction associated with the movement did not seem to fit the alleged principles upon which the movement was founded. In light of what we believe to be the achievements of certain works by Rebecca Harding Davis, Mark Twain, Frank Norris, Jack London, Edith Wharton, and Kate Chopin, just to mention a few of the more notable authors of the late nineteenth and early twentieth centuries, this seems a brash claim. Yet, the impulse behind such a claim warrants investigation, and in fact has resurfaced from time to time as critics have occasionally paused to scratch their heads and ask what literary naturalism, in the final analysis, is. The common answer that emerges from these collective musings is that naturalism is a branch of the realist movement, a branch informed by a reasonably well-defined set of philosophical attitudes regarding the relationship of humans to their environment. On occasion, however, a skeptic tolls the same bell as *The Outlook,* rejecting literary naturalism as a failed movement based on failed premises.

A recent example of such skepticism can be found in Sidney Gendin's 1995 article "Was Stephen Crane (or Anybody Else) a Naturalist?"[2] In what amounts to one of the more engaging and entertaining articles on the subject in recent years, Gendin, a philosopher by trade rather than a literary critic, begins with a standard definition of naturalism (derived from Lars Åhnebrink, and from Zola through Åhnebrink) and proceeds to demonstrate—using Stephen Crane's *Maggie: A Girl of the Streets* (1893) as his test case—that it is philosophically naïve to imagine that Crane, or anyone else, can accurately be labeled a naturalist. But what if we shift the definition of literary naturalism away from philosophy and toward methodology, toward the study of human documents and the photographic depiction of the sordid lives of the lower classes? This definition fails too, argues Gendin, as a work like *Maggie* demonstrates, with its dreamlike episodes and, at times, sparse textual detail based upon Crane's own objective observation of slum life. In the end, Gendin suggests, the only definition of naturalism that actually works is "the portrayal without false sentiment of certain classes of people. It neither presupposes, evinces or argues for any philosophical theory of determinism; it is art, not science; it never permits improbably happy endings; it is imaginative and may freely employ metaphors and similes; it is not pseudo-documentary. It is none the worse for any of this. *Maggie,* for one, is the better for all of this" (101).

It need hardly be observed that, while amazingly accurate in its way, the definition offered here by Gendin really says very little about literary naturalism. And yet, Gendin's observations regarding the difficulties encountered when one brings forward virtually any major work of literary naturalism, including *Maggie,* as a definitional test case are astute, and it is hard not to agree with Gendin that the standard definitions of literary naturalism should be "cast into the flames, never to be heard from again" (89). After all, does literary naturalism really do what Zola says it does? And who was paying attention to Zola anyway?

Let us return for a moment to our eulogist and grant—for the sake of argument—that naturalism is dead and in fact never lived. If we momentarily discount the context of Zola's theoretical writings, in what context, then, do we see Frank Norris's *McTeague* emerging? Or Rebecca Harding Davis's "Life in the Iron Mills"? Or Kate Chopin's *The Awakening?* Or Jack

London's *Martin Eden?* Or . . . fill in your own favorite here. Easy, one replies, they emerged within the dynamic of their cultural context. A reasonable answer, to be sure. Perhaps we might begin to paint our picture of the second half of the nineteenth century in America by looking at the table of contents of a few leading periodicals of the day. Here are a few titles:

"The Progress from Brute to Man"
—John Fiske, *North American Review* 1873

"Arthur Schopenhauer and His Pessimistic Philosophy"
—E. Gryzanovski, *North American Review* 1873

"Spencer's Evolution Philosophy"
—E. L. Youmans, *North American Review* 1879

"Malthusianism, Darwinism, and Pessimism"
—Francis Bowen, *North American Review* 1879

"Man and Brute"
—George J. Romanes, *North American Review* 1884

"Morality and Environment"
—Arthur Dudley Vinton, *The Arena* 1891

"Heredity and Environment"
—A. M. Holmes, *The Arena* 1894

"Society's Protection against the Degenerates"
—Max Nordau, *Forum* 1895

"Degeneration and Evolution"
—Max Nordau, *North American Review* 1895

"How Evolution Evolves"
—Stinson Jarvis, *The Arena* 1895

"Degeneration and Regeneration"
—H. T. Peck, *The Bookman* 1896

"Hereditary Influences and Medical Progress"
—J. J. Morrissey, *The Arena* 1897

"Evolution: What It Is and What It Is Not"
—David Starr Jordan, *The Arena* 1897

"Why Homicide Has Increased in the United States: Parts I and II"
—Cesare Lombroso, *North American Review* 1897/98

"Social Progress and Race Degeneration"
—Frank A. Fetter, *Forum* 1899

Given titles such as these, there is little doubt that scientific naturalism, at least, was a readily available influence for authors like Chopin and Crane. And from here we may begin to fill in the rest of the picture, taking note of immigration patterns, urban growth statistics, popular journalism from the 1890s, political movements, social trends, even aesthetic theories and art movements from the time. Indeed, this critical methodology has been the trend in recent years, and some of the best work to appear on American literary naturalism has emerged from this method. Of these studies, one of the best examples is Donna M. Campbell's *Resisting Regionalism: Gender and Naturalism in American Fiction, 1885–1915* (1997). Campbell broadens our perspective on the place of American literary naturalism within American literary culture in the late nineteenth century by looking at the cultural dialogue between regionalism and naturalism. Aside from the intrinsic value of studies such as this one by Campbell, their larger value rests in the fact that they free the study of literary naturalism from the critical box it is often placed in when it is treated as the lesser son of realism and when treatments of it degenerate into lamentations over their philosophical shortcomings (or on rare happy occasions, celebrations of their philosophical acuity).

One of my primary objectives in the present work is to continue this current trend in scholarship, and, with luck, to help broaden our perspective on the development of American literary naturalism in the nineteenth century. For all of the work that remains to be done on the intersection of naturalistic texts and social, economic, and cultural forces at work in the nineteenth century, literary naturalism is still proposed as an aesthetic movement. Thus, the main (although not the only) focus on the chapters to follow is on literary naturalism as an aesthetic movement—an art form, a way of writing. As a result, many of my concerns are definitional in nature. I return to the questions implied from the outset by the writer for *The Outlook:* what is literary naturalism, if it is anything, and in what context can we place it in the broader perspective of the nineteenth century?

Each chapter of this study—especially the first four—tackles a new set of problems and issues surrounding American literary naturalism. Therefore, this is not proposed as a typical book on the subject, in which a chapter or two of background or theory is followed by a series of author studies or textual close readings. In fact, there is very little textual analysis of an extended nature throughout the entire work. My aim is to take a broad perspective on literary naturalism and to try to suggest some ways in which we can discuss and interpret naturalistic fiction. If I have been successful, the perspectives and suggestions offered here will provide a number of avenues for ongoing scholarly effort. In other words, in this study I am concerned with definitional, descriptive, contextual, and theoretical matters and with matters that concern our understanding of literary naturalism as a whole, rather than with the idiosyncrasies of individual authors, and in my pursuit of certain holistic evaluations and definitions, extended critiques of single texts would probably detract more than contribute. More optimistically, my effort in this study has been to try to lay groundwork for further scholarship on the subject; there remains much work to be done in the future as individual works and authors are given thorough examination within some of the contexts discussed in this book.

When textual illustration is needed, I draw primarily from those works commonly discussed within the context of American literary naturalism: Rebecca Harding Davis, Stephen Crane, Frank Norris, Theodore Dreiser, Charlotte Perkins Gilman, Harold Frederic, Jack London, Edith Wharton, and others. The exception to this comes in the form of introducing into the study of literary naturalism—for reasons that should be apparent in context—texts that, to the best of my knowledge, rarely, if ever, show up in discussions of literary naturalism, such as *Elsie Venner* (1861) by Oliver Wendell Holmes and *Looking Backward* (1888) by Edward Bellamy. It is my opinion that studies of "literary naturalism" in the second half of the nineteenth century have perhaps suffered a bit by limitation to the tried-and-true works of Crane, Norris, and Dreiser. Fortunately, recent studies have begun to integrate works by Wharton, Chopin, Gilman, and Davis into their analyses. I hope to take such scholarship on the subject one step further by exploring the influence of naturalism upon utopian fiction, and by suggesting that naturalism is not a phenomenon restricted to the 1890s and beyond.

As the subtitle to this volume suggests, my interests in this text rest primarily on manifestations of literary naturalism in the late nineteenth and early twentieth centuries. Many recent treatments of American literary naturalism have traced it well into the twentieth century, where it found expression in the work of writers such as John Steinbeck, the later Theodore Dreiser, William Faulkner, Richard Wright, and James T. Farrell. Perhaps to some of these critics my approach will seem limiting. I hope not, however, for my intent, like theirs, is to extend our understanding of literary naturalism in America—I just pursue it in a different direction: while they push into the mid- and late twentieth century, I push back past the 1890s and into earlier decades of the nineteenth century. Moreover, with the First World War, the rise of modernism, and twentieth-century advances in science and technology, literary naturalism went through various transformations. Because this study focuses on the birth and early manifestations of literary naturalism, studies of its twentieth-century modulations lie outside its scope.

Four related issues are addressed in the course of this text. The first concerns the genre of naturalistic narrative. When American authors of naturalistic fiction in the latter half of the nineteenth century integrated naturalist theory into narrative form, they often did so by turning to the tradition of American romance. Rather than writing within the tradition and strict conventions of the realistic novel, Rebecca Harding Davis, Oliver Wendell Holmes, Frank Norris, Stephen Crane, Harold Frederic, and Jack London drew heavily upon romantic forms and conventions. These romantic tendencies become clear if the texts are placed in their critical, historical, and aesthetic contexts, and textual analysis underscores these claims.

The first issue, therefore, involves a reconsideration of the traditional association of literary naturalism and literary realism. Reading naturalistic narratives as romances—or as drawing, in part, on the romance tradition—provides an alternative perspective to studies that place naturalistic fiction within the tradition of the realistic novel. Still, to trace these connections is not to overlook their "novelistic" or "realistic" features. From the beginning of the nineteenth century forward, the American tradition of romance was never divorced from realistic impulses. Nevertheless, the lessons taught to the American naturalists by the literary realists, rather than dominating naturalist fiction and dictating genre and convention, were instead used by American literary naturalists to revise and revive a tradition of American romance that has its roots in the antebellum writings of Charles Brockden

Brown, Nathaniel Hawthorne, Edgar Allan Poe, and Herman Melville. To be clear, literary naturalism is not a retread of the antebellum romance tradition; rather, our understanding of literary naturalism is enhanced when we take a closer look at how literary naturalism manipulates in positive ways some of the tradition it inherits from earlier authors.

A second, and closely related, issue concerns aesthetic theory in the nineteenth century. How and why naturalistic fiction in America participates in the tradition of American romance (and romanticism generally) is made clear by an examination of the relationship between the specific aesthetic theories of the American literary naturalists and nineteenth-century theories of the novel and the romance. Pursuing these connections inevitably leads to a discussion of the relationships among realism, naturalism, romanticism, and idealism: each of these aesthetic orientations is discussed, to one degree or another, in this study.

The third issue grows out of the second. Beyond looking at the aesthetic traditions underlying the development of American literary naturalism, this study also examines pieces of the cultural/intellectual/historical context within which American literary naturalism operates. Diachronically, while some of the generic roots of American literary naturalism lie in antebellum conceptions of the romance, some of the intellectual roots of American literary naturalism can be traced back to the Enlightenment, out of which naturalist theory emanated. Synchronically, some of the key features of American literary naturalism can be illuminated by juxtaposing it with both realistic and idealistic strains of literature popular in the late nineteenth century, including, perhaps surprisingly, the wave of utopian fantasies popular in the 1880s and 1890s.

The fourth issue, a definitional one that encompasses all of the others, concerns the definition and description of the school of American literary naturalism. One of the problems over the years with the phrase "American literary naturalism" is that defining it has proven so difficult. After all, what *is* literary naturalism, and what does the American "school" of literary naturalism look like? These questions are the subject of the introductory chapter, "Defining American Literary Naturalism." Two main points are pursued in this chapter. First, I examine the relationship between the American school of literary naturalism and the French school. The argument developed here is that the theoretical writings of Émile Zola had limited *practical* impact on the development of *American* literary naturalism, and that the aesthetic practices outlined in *Le roman expérimental* do not, in general, correspond with those of American naturalistic fiction. The second main point in chapter 1 is that in order to define the phrase "American literary naturalism" accurately, one must first make some important distinctions among philosophical naturalism, scientific naturalism, and literary naturalism. To view literary naturalism as the transference into literary form of the assumptions of philosophical naturalism or of the experimental, observational practices of scientific naturalism is to define American literary naturalism in a way that does not accurately reflect the concerns of the texts themselves. Therefore, American literary naturalism must be defined in a different manner.

If I have succeeded, the present study is both synthetic and exploratory. It is synthetic because behind it resides a strain of earlier criticism that has noted the difficulty of too closely associating American literary naturalism with the realistic novel. It is exploratory because of its detailed examination of the continuities between the tradition of American romance and the school of American literary naturalism. The association of American literary naturalism and American romanticism has been a minor—but noticeable—theme during the past century. One of the objectives of this study is to bring this minor theme to the surface, through an examination of numerous historical documents from, primarily, the nineteenth century, and as a result, to offer to students and scholars of American literature another legitimate and relatively unexplored avenue for the study of American literary naturalism—an avenue different from a century of criticism that has seen naturalism as an artistic subset of literary realism and bound by the conventions of realistic narration. Noting the connections between American literary naturalism and the romance is not new, per se, but it is relatively unexplored. This study contributes to that exploration.

Within the broad field of American literary history, and nineteenth-century literary history in particular, the texts associated with the school of American literary naturalism are, to borrow a phrase from Edward Taylor, a rich "vein of excellence." The power of Norris and Davis, the artistry of Crane and Wharton, the imagination of London and Gilman, the sophistication of Frederic and Chopin, the relentless scope and drama of Dreiser—these authors contributed to American literature a body of work that still speaks to us today, texts that provide a powerful counterpoint to other literary trends in the late nineteenth century. Their narratives are at once vigorous and philosophical, imaginative yet reasoned, sometimes subtle, sometimes radiant. Perhaps the greatest tribute we pay to these authors is our continued attention; and in the end, this study is yet another tribute paid to this provocative body of work.

Acknowledgments

I owe a great deal of gratitude to many people who helped and encouraged me through the years while this study was in progress. Many thanks go to G. R. Thompson, who believed in this project from the start and who aided me in innumerable ways through his encouragement and insightful criticism. Without his support this project would not have been possible. Special thanks also go to Robert Paul Lamb for the countless hours he spent thoroughly critiquing the first draft of this manuscript, and to Wendy Stallard Flory, who not only read and critiqued an early draft of the manuscript but also was instrumental in helping to move an early version of this project toward a denouement.

My good friend Steve Frye of California State University at Bakersfield was a constant source of help and encouragement, and his commentary and critical insights, not to mention the long hours he invested listening to me work out the arguments of this book, proved invaluable. There are no better scholarly collaborators than Steve Frye. Thanks also go to Christine Harvey of U.C. Santa Barbara; her work on American literary naturalism and her helpful commentary on this manuscript were sources of inspiration. My ongoing discussions with Christine about American literary naturalism have helped sharpen some of the material in this text, and for that I am in her debt. Finally, my thanks to Donald Viney of Pittsburg State University for his very helpful suggestions regarding chapter 4 of this study.

I would also like to thank Hugh Shott, Elsa Ann Gaines, Lennet Daigle, Thomas Austenfeld, and my colleagues in the Department of Language and Literature at North Georgia College and State University, who supported this project in many ways. The librarians and staff of the Stewart Library at NGCSU were helpful at every turn, and their willingness to help me locate even the most obscure sources is much appreciated. Additional thanks go to the editorial board of the University of Alabama Press, and to Jill R. Hughes, whose skillful editorial assistance is much appreciated.

Finally, I would like to thank my wife, Laura, who spent many tireless hours proofreading this manuscript and helping me prepare it for the press; my children, Sarah, Nathaniel, and Natalie; and my mother, Marilyn Link. Their support and encouragement were (and remain) of incalculable value.

1

Defining American Literary Naturalism

In 1899 Frederic Taber Cooper contributed an article on the works of the novelist Frank Norris to *The Bookman*.[1] Printed on the first page of the article was a picture of Norris, a reproduction of a painting by Norris's friend Ernest Peixotto. A simple portrait, the painting portrays a young, solemn—though not overly serious—Norris in dress coat and collar, sitting in a dark chair and resting one hand against his chin. The angle of his head accents Norris's prematurely gray hair. The title of the article appears underneath the picture in capital letters: "FRANK NORRIS, REALIST." The article makes the striking assertion of the title a little less bold. Cooper finds Norris's work puzzling. On the one hand, Norris is "frankly, brutally realistic," and yet, "paradoxical as it may seem, he has an obstinate and often exasperating vein of romanticism running through all his work." The conclusion Cooper comes to is that Norris is a realist who, at times, perversely succumbs to romanticism. According to Cooper, romanticism is Norris's "pet failing," his "besetting sin."

Cooper's difficulty assessing the literary creed governing Norris's fiction isn't simply a matter of one critic's confusion or one novelist's literary failure. On the contrary, the literary incongruities discussed by Cooper strike right to the heart of late-nineteenth-century American literature. Norris's work is not only the product of a young author's powerful imagination, it is also the product of his age, and the puzzling character of Norris's fiction (as well as the fiction of contemporaries such as Jack London, Stephen Crane, Kate Chopin, Edith Wharton, and Harold Frederic) reflects the shaping influence of a whole century of competing literary creeds, theories, manifestos, and critical opinions.

These authors grew up in an America ripe with incongruities.[2] New discoveries in science and natural history conflicted with long-standing religious tradition. Industry and agriculture underwent unparalleled economic expansion and growth, but sometimes through the exploitation of the democratic and capitalistic values that such growth seemed to justify. It was not only a time of labor unrest, but also a time in which real wages grew and the cost of living went down. In 1886, when Chopin was thirty-five; Frederic, thirty; Wharton, twenty-four; Norris, sixteen; Crane, fifteen; and London, ten, agriculture in the Midwest was devastated by drought, there were more strikes than in any other single year in the nineteenth century, anti-Chinese riots broke out in Seattle, anarchists and police collided in Chicago's Haymarket Square riot, and Geronimo's capture in Arizona marked the end of the last major Indian war. In that same year, however, technology rolled on: important discoveries in metallurgy made it possible to extract aluminum from ore, and the alternating current system of electricity for commercial applications was introduced by George Westinghouse; meanwhile, the Statue of Liberty was dedicated on October 28 in New York Harbor. Although the "Gilded Age" was a time of political malaise, materialism, and commercialism, it was also a time of technological advancement and economic growth, through which the United States began to move toward center stage in the world theatre. A symbol of the complexities in American society might be found in the American city, balancing newly raised skyscrapers against burgeoning slums.

In many respects Norris, London, and Crane grew up in a scientific age. The intellectual imagination in the latter half of the nineteenth century was captivated by new scientific theories and philosophies from Charles Darwin, Herbert Spencer, John Fiske, William Graham Sumner, Thomas Huxley, Karl Marx, Charles Lyell, and Arthur Schopenhauer. One rarely opened an issue of the *North American Review* or the *Forum* without encountering long discussions of "Social Progress and Race Degeneration," "The Progress from Brute to Man," "Morality and Environment," "Heredity and Environment," "How Evolution Evolves," "Natural Selection, Social Selection, and Heredity," and virtually any imaginable combination of the above.[3] Collectively, these scientific theories marked the coming-of-age of the "naturalistic" shift in scientific thought that had begun with the Enlightenment. These scientific and philosophical theories increasingly sought to explain humankind and the natural world through reference to natural phenomena and physical laws. In this respect, at least at the academic level, the age of Norris, London, and Crane was a *naturalistic* age. Naturalistic fiction was certainly a product of this age. Still, the question for students of late-nineteenth-century American literature is what do we mean when we refer to Norris, London, Crane, and company as *literary naturalists?*

Literary naturalism is difficult to define. Variously defined over the years, literary naturalism is usually identified as generally dire in outlook, deterministic in philosophy, and aesthetically aligned with literary realism. Typically, such definitions are based on the theoretical writings of Émile Zola. As influential as Zola was, however, he was not the only critic in the nineteenth century who tried to define literary naturalism. Adding to the confusion experienced by the contemporary student of naturalism, many of these other critics and authors describe it in terms far different from Zola. The nineteenth-century definitional debate can be briefly illustrated by looking at an essay written by the Spanish author Leopoldo Alas.

In a preface to the second edition of Emilia Pardo Bazán's *La cuestión palpitante* (1883), Alas explicitly distances his definition of literary naturalism from Zola.[4] Two of Alas's six points are of particular importance. First, Alas argues that naturalism is not "subordinate to positivism, or limited in its procedures to observation and experiment in the abstract, narrow, and logically false sense in which such aspects of method are understood by the illustrious Claude Bernard. It is true that Zola in the worst of his critical works has said something to this effect; but he himself later wrote what amounted to a correction; and in any event naturalism is not responsible for Zola's systematic exaggeration" (268). By separating literary naturalism from Zola's aesthetic strategies in *Le roman expérimental* (1880), Alas allows more latitude in literary naturalism to explore hidden realities and nonempirically verifiable truths and premises. It also allows certain literary naturalists—the ones who do not wish to restrict their writing to documentation, observation, and experimentation—more freedom in shaping their narratives. Equally important about Alas's claim is that he believes *literary* naturalism must be distinguished from *philosophical* naturalism. Philosophical naturalism does indeed have a positivistic inclination in that it leans toward allowing only strictly empirical evidence to enter into truth-determining equations.

Alas further separates literary naturalism from Zola's "systematic exaggeration" when he asserts that naturalism is *not* pessimism. "It is true that Zola speaks on occasion . . . of what Leopardi called 'the utter vanity of everything'; but this does not occur in a novel; it is a critic's opinion. And although it may be demonstrated, though I doubt it, that the novels of Zola and Flaubert prove that their authors were pessimists, that does not prove that naturalism, a school, or rather a purely and exclusively literary tendency, is strictly bound to deterministic ideas about the causes and goals of life" (268–69). In this manner Alas allows for the possibility of a naturalistic narrative that is not pessimistic, or unremittingly deterministic, but that may conceivably exhibit or provoke a whole range of emotional and intellectual responses.

What is most striking about Alas's 1883 preface is that it seems at odds with the views of many twentieth-century critics who have defined naturalism as realistic fiction that incorporates a pessimistic determinism and whose form is dictated by a "Zola-esque" spirit of documentation and experimentation. A definition of literary naturalism based on Alas rather than Zola likely would maintain that naturalistic fiction should not be held to the strict mimetic/verisimilar standards of literary realism (especially in its positivistic manifestations), nor should one expect all naturalistic texts to be pessimistically oriented or be characterized by their incorporation of a strict determinism. It would be a liberating definition of literary naturalism, for sure, though we would still be pressed to say what literary naturalism *is*, rather than simply what it is *not*.

Of course, Leopoldo Alas should not be taken as the final authority in naturalist literary theory. In fact, Alas's countryman Don Armando Palacio Valdes asserted in 1889 that naturalism was indeed a type of realism characterized by a pessimistic determinism. Naturalism, Valdes writes, is "nothing else than a species of limited and pessimistic Realism" and is associated with "ideas of determinism and of pessimism."[5] Whereas Alas (largely a proponent of literary naturalism) attempted to minimize the importance of French naturalism in general, and the theoretical writings of Émile Zola specifically, Valdes (less sympathetic with literary naturalism than Alas) creates a definition that seems largely based on these same influences.

Historically, Alas's preface is significant because it provides evidence that some Continental writers felt that the school of literary naturalism was larger than the narrow confines of *Le roman expérimental*. Texts that did not necessarily conform to the formal strategies and philosophical orientations of Zola's positivistic and putatively objective realist strain of naturalism (as described in his theoretical writings) might still be considered naturalistic on other grounds. But granting a larger domain for naturalistic fiction does raise an important question: if the school of literary naturalism is not theoretically bound by the claims of *Le roman expérimental,* what are the boundaries of the school? And even more importantly for the present study is the corollary question: what are the boundaries or defining characteristics of the *American* school of literary naturalism? How one arrives at answers to these questions is the focus of the present chapter and requires, first, a look at the relationship between the French school and the American school, and, second, the drawing of certain distinctions among philosophical, scientific, and "literary" naturalism.

The French Connection

Critics of literary naturalism have been plagued by the problems that arise when an attempt is made to reconcile "American literary naturalism" with its European counterparts.[6] Why does the movement in America seem to encompass more diverse forms and treatments? Why did American literary naturalism remain a viable mode well into the twentieth century, while its European counterparts had all largely faded away, if not been completely abandoned, by the turn of the century? (Even Zola had turned to other projects by that time.) If we propose Zola's concept of the "experimental novel" as a leading influence on the American literary naturalists, then what are we to make of those American texts that diverge widely from the largely realist creed set forth by Zola? For instance, how do we account for the presence of a distinctly romantic symbolism (based largely in metaphysical and epistemological concepts regarding the relationship between man and nature) in *McTeague* (1899), *Sister Carrie* (1900), *The Red Badge of Courage* (1895), and, of course, in the korl woman of "Life in the Iron Mills" (1861), as opposed to the more common intratextual symbolism found in the works of literary realism (what Edwin Cady in *The Light of Common Day* referred to as the "imploding symbol" used by the realists to "intensify inwardly the total effect of a novel" but that did not "refer outside the novel to general meaning"[7]). Are these flaws in otherwise realistic novels, or do they represent a break on the part of the literary naturalists from the aesthetic creeds of William Dean Howells and Henry James? The answer to these questions is twofold: (1) the American tradition was not as closely linked to the French and European traditions as has been traditionally asserted; and (2) there is a discrepancy between naturalist theory and practice that has not been fully accounted for in studies of the school of literary naturalism.[8]

The tendency to try to account for American literary naturalism by linking it with the theories of Zola and with his school of fiction began early with the writings of critics such as Vernon Louis Parrington (1930), Oscar Cargill (1941), Malcolm Cowley (1947), and Lars Åhnebrink's *The Beginnings of Naturalism in American Fiction* (1950).[9] Available evidence, however, suggests that accounting for American literary naturalism in this manner tells only one part of a larger story. In fact, American literary naturalists, while not provincial, were hardly disciples of Zola. Of Norris, London, Crane, and Dreiser, only Norris seems to have eagerly read and studied the French naturalists. London was far less interested in French aesthetic theory than he was in philosophy and in the "business" of writing; Crane, though he probably read several of Zola's works in translation, claims to have found Zola's fiction "tiresome," and he openly distanced himself from the French author; and Dreiser declared in November of 1911 that he had "never read a line of Zola"—which (if true) would mean that Dreiser did not read any of Zola's fiction or theoretical writings until after he had published both *Sister Carrie* and *Jennie Gerhardt* (1911) and was well into writing *The Financier* (1912).[10] The implication is not that there is no connection between American literary naturalism and its French counterpart; it is merely that to define literary naturalism for American authors in the 1890s on the basis of Zola's theory and literary circle is to skew any historically accurate treatment one wishes to give American naturalistic narrative. In general, the connection between American naturalism and French naturalism is there, but it is blurry, primarily indirect, and needs to be treated as such.[11]

Theory versus Practice

One of the main problems with the French/American connection is that Zola's theory—around which so many definitions of American literary naturalism have been built—does not correspond with the practice of many literary naturalists, both in America and in Europe. Taken at its face value, Zola's *Le roman expérimental* describes an aesthetic practice that corresponds to the theory and practices of literary realists. It comes as no surprise that Zola saw Balzac and Stendhal as the pioneers of naturalistic fiction in France. Looking at *Le roman expérimental*—in particular, the essays "The Experimental Novel" and "Naturalism in the Theatre"[12]—one finds Zola championing narrative strategies typically associated with literary realism. In "The Experimental Novel" Zola emphasizes that material in a novel should be rendered mimetically through careful and purposeful observation, and that fiction should not depart from the laws of nature (166–68, 189, 191). In "Naturalism in the Theatre" he identifies several key features of naturalistic fiction. He claims that naturalism is a "return to nature" (from the realm of fantasy, or the romantic) that seeks "direct observation, exact anatomy," and "the depiction of what is" (200–01). Likewise, naturalistic fiction inquires into "nature, being, and things," without recourse to "fable" or the "imagination" (207). And like all good realists, the naturalist author is "impersonal" and "never intervenes" into his narrative through a process of selection or idealization (208–09). With these characteristics it is understandable that descriptions of literary naturalism built on *Le roman expérimental* would view literary naturalism as a type, subset, or extension of literary realism. As one reviewer wrote in 1881 regarding *Le roman expérimental:* "This medication [via Claude Bernard] of literature which Zola advocates is only of use so far as it is an appeal in favor of realism in literature."[13]

The problem arises when one actually tries to account for naturalistic fiction in light of Zola's theory. Zola's strict rejection of romanticism, his call for purely objective scientific documentation and observation, and his positivism do not characterize much naturalistic narrative, especially in America. One might allow for a more rigidly (and traditional) linkage between literary realism and naturalism in studies focused on a description of those French and European authors who are more directly tied into French aesthetic theory—such as early studies like Martin Schutze's "The Services of Naturalism to Life and Literature" (1903), and later studies like *Naturalism in the European Novel* (1992), edited by Brian Nelson; David Baguley's *Naturalist Fiction: The Entropic Vision* (1990); and Yves Chevrel's *Le naturalisme* (1982). But the same standard cannot be so rigidly applied to treatments of *American* literary naturalism. And even studies of the French and European traditions have noted the considerable discrepancy between Zola's own theory and practice, as well as between his theory and the works of his Continental contemporaries.

Thomas Hardy makes this point in his 1891 essay "The Science of Fiction."[14] After noting that Zola's theoretical writings in *Le roman expérimental* promote literary realism, Hardy points out that Zola's fiction is not realistic and that Zola himself is quite a "romancer." Hardy then takes issue with Zola's claim that the "novel should keep as close to reality *as it can,*" for this remark is open to a wide variety of interpretation. Even Alexandre Dumas and Ann Radcliffe, suggests Hardy, would concede this point. Hardy argues that the *as it can* "implies discriminative choice," and that once artistic choice is introduced into the equation, all hope for a mimetic realism is lost. In the end, Zola maintains "in theory what he abandons in practice," and, observes Hardy, this discrepancy in literary naturalism is not limited to Zola alone.

The theory/praxis incongruity was also noted by a critic for the *Westminster Review* in 1889.[15] The critic observes that Zola does not follow the aesthetic creed set forth in *Le roman expérimental,* and neither do other members of the naturalist school such as Joris Karl Huysmans and Guy de Maupassant. Noting that Zola has "made the grand mistake of confusing the functions of science and art," the critic argues that Zola's "system is unworkable—it is based on a radical error."

This incongruity between Zola's theory and practice helps explain the "romantic" and "poetic" liberties taken by Zola in novels like *Germinal* (1885). Like many great poems, *Germinal* is built around a central image. *Le Voreux* (a coal mine) dominates and permeates the narrative, acting as the axis around which the lives of Etienne and the other characters revolve and as a symbol for the swirling vortex of natural law within which the characters are entangled. In various passages throughout the narrative, Zola's romantic impulses and poetic sensibilities are revealed. "Le Voreux struck fear into him [Etienne]. Each squall seemed fiercer than the last, as though each time it blew from an even more distant horizon. No sign of dawn; the sky was dead: only the furnaces and coke ovens glared and reddened the shadows, but did not penetrate their mystery. And, huddled in its lair like some evil beast, Le Voreux crouched ever lower and its breath came in longer and deeper gasps, as though it were struggling to digest its meal of human flesh."[16] Even more difficult to reconcile with Zola's theory is Huysmans's "spiritualist naturalism" in *Là-Bas* (1891) and the mingling of naturalist theory and artistic decadence in *A Rebours* (1884). And then there is Paul Alexis's remarkable observation in 1891 that in naturalism, "romanticism, whence we all came, is still there, too near at hand. None of us has yet succeeded in purging his blood completely of the hereditary romantic virus."[17] Finally, to add to our amusement, there is the episode recorded in the journal of the Goncourt brothers in which Zola takes a rather cavalier attitude toward his own theoretical writings. According to the Goncourts, Zola once remarked, "I consider the word *Naturalism* as ridiculous as you do, but I shall go on repeating it over and over again, because you have to give things new names for the public to think that they are new." Furthermore, continues Zola, "I divide what I write into two parts. On the one hand there are my novels, on which I shall be judged and on which I wish to be judged; and on the other hand there are my articles for the *Bien public,* for Russia and for Marseilles, which are just so much charlatanism to puff my books."[18]

Thus, there is an observable discrepancy in Zola's theory of literary naturalism and the texts themselves, and there is notable disagreement in the nineteenth century over just what "literary naturalism" is. When one also considers the distance (literal and figurative) between the Continental school of literary naturalism and the American school, one can see how the close association of Zola's theoretical naturalism and late-nineteenth-century American narrative grows increasingly strained.

Of course, of the French naturalists, Zola was perhaps the most read and renowned in America, and what influence French naturalism had on American fiction was likely to be primarily grounded in English translations of Zola's *Rougon-Marquart* series, which began appearing in 1879 with the translation of *L'Assommoir.*[19] Zola's *Le roman expérimental* was not published in English translation until 1894, after both Norris and Crane had begun publishing.[20] (It is possible, though I believe unlikely, that Norris had read the volume in French prior to 1894.[21]) As far as the relationship between French and American literary naturalism is concerned, critics have done important work tracing these linkages. Still, these connections are strongest in Frank Norris, and, ironically, Norris rejected the idea that the naturalistic novel was an outgrowth of the realistic novel. In fact, Norris claims in "Zola as a Romantic Writer" that naturalism is a type of romanticism, not a type of realism, and that Zola is a writer of romances, not realistic novels. Within this context we note with interest that several recent critics have begun finding romantic elements running throughout Continental naturalism.[22]

I do not wish to claim an exaggerated provincialism for these American novelists. Indeed, as a group they were quite expansive in their thought and writings. Instead, I wish to suggest that connecting the French school of literary naturalism, specifically the theories of Zola, to the American school only *partially* (at best) explains the American naturalist aesthetic, and that a definition of American literary naturalism should not be based solely, or even primarily, on Continental theory. In order to more accurately define American literary naturalism, its American context needs to be more fully investigated. One must strike a balance between acknowledging debts owed to the Continental tradition(s) of "literary naturalism" and the American narrative traditions that provide a more immediate aesthetic context for the writings of Norris, Crane, London, and Frederic.

Philosophical, Scientific, and Literary Naturalism

If *Le roman expérimental* does not hold the key to defining American literary naturalism, then what does? To answer this question we must ask, What makes literature naturalistic? What texts and authors are being referred to with such a label, and on what basis? What makes texts as radically different as Jack London's *The Sea-Wolf* (1904) and Theodore Dreiser's *Sister Carrie* (1900) both naturalistic? Why is Frank Norris's *Vandover and the Brute* (published posthumously in 1914) perceived as a model of the genre, while his *Blix* (1899) is seen as only marginally naturalistic (if at all)? As one's definition of literary naturalism changes, so too do the ways one classifies such texts. If one's definition of literary naturalism focuses on the perceived pessimism of the work, or the work's plot of decline, then Wharton's *Ethan Frome* (1911) and Chopin's *The Awakening* (1899) stand next to *Sister Carrie* and *McTeague* as models of the genre, but London's *The Sea-Wolf* looks like an aberration. On the other hand, if one's definition focuses on those texts that promote a deterministic worldview, then a case could be made for including a few of Henry James's texts, but probably not Frederic's *The Damnation of Theron Ware* (1896). Or if one's definition focuses on the materialistic or nihilistic orientation of the text, then Twain's *The Mysterious Stranger* (1916) is a strong candidate, but texts like *The Octopus* (1901) and *The Pit* (1903) require qualification. Moreover, if we want to try to include earlier texts such as Oliver Wendell Holmes's *Elsie Venner* (1861) and Rebecca Harding Davis's "Life in the Iron Mills" (1861)—both with their unique blend of science and theology, both bearing the hallmarks of Hawthorne and the romance tradition, yet both looking forward to late-nine-teenth-century interests in social realism and emerging science—then we certainly have to reconsider definitions of American literary naturalism that follow the "pessimistic materialistic determinism" formula.

Philosophical Naturalism

One can go far toward answering the above questions by drawing some important distinctions among philosophical, scientific, and literary natural-ism. Philosophical naturalism is a worldview that precludes the operation of *super*natural forces and stresses the notion that all phenomena (includ-ing physical action, emotion, and morality) can be explained in terms of material causation.[23] For instance, when James T. Farrell, author of the Studs Lonigan trilogy and an artistic heir of Dreiser, states in 1954 "by naturalism I mean that whatever happens in this world must ultimately be explainable in terms of events in this world," he is essentially taking the position of a philosophical naturalist.[24] To define literary naturalism through philosophi-cal naturalism is to claim that a text is naturalistic insofar as it embodies this particular philosophical orientation.

In the nineteenth century, the French author Paul Alexis—a devotee of the Médan group—defined literary naturalism in this manner.[25] Trying to save the school from what seemed like immanent death, Alexis claimed in 1891 that naturalism would be the "literature of the twentieth century." He argued that naturalism is not a "special way of writing," but a "method of thinking, seeing, reflecting, studying, experimenting, a need to analyze in order to know."[26] Significantly, Alexis explains that because naturalism is a philosophical orientation and not a method of composition, naturalistic fic-tion can—and does—take a wide variety of forms; it is "broad enough to include all kinds of 'writing'" from the "impeccable lyricism of Flaubert" to the "grandiose abundance of Zola" (408). It can even, suggests Alexis, con-tain the "romanticism" found in Zola's *Germinal* (409).

Contrary to Alexis, most twentieth-century critics do not allow for "all kinds of writing," but tie naturalism to the novel of social realism and to re-alistic narration and narrative form in general. However, like Alexis, many twentieth-century critics have defined literary naturalism by claiming that a text is naturalistic insofar as it embodies a philosophical naturalism. Lars Åhnebrink, for instance, writes that naturalism is "a manner and method of composition by which the author portrays *life as it is in accordance with the philosophic theory of determinism.*"[27] Likewise, George Becker claims that "in essence and in origin naturalism is no more than an emphatic and explicit philosophical position taken by some realists"; that is, "it is pessimistic materialistic determinism" (Becker 35).

These representative definitions by Åhnebrink and Becker construct a school of literary naturalism out of those authors and/or texts that possess the common denominators of a deterministic philosophical orientation and a realistic aesthetic creed. Although critical explorations stemming from such a definition have uncovered some of the ideological underpinnings of certain texts, to define American literary naturalism through such a direct correlation with philosophical naturalism creates as many problems as it solves. For instance, what American author or text can one view as a model representative of the school? As though in response to this very question, Edwin Cady writes: "I am not aware of a work of fiction which will stand adequately and consistently for the naturalistic sensibility. There was only a sensibility to be fragmentarily, inconsistently, or occasionally expressed. Nobody, at least in American literature, could bear to be its thoroughgoing exponent" (51). The point Cady is making here, and it is one with which I strongly agree, is that in nineteenth-century American letters there are no authors who sought in their fiction to fixedly, if not didactically, incorporate an orthodox philosophical naturalism. Can one find many texts (let alone a "school" of fiction) in American letters that truly incorporate an unqualified "pessimistic materialistic determinism"? Or can one find a text in which all of the major elements in the narrative are explained in terms of material causation? Defined in this manner, one would have to dismiss from the school Frank Norris and Harold Frederic for their mystic strains, and their transcendent moralism, as well as Norris's manichaeism. One would have to dismiss Stephen Crane for the abundant spiritual and supernatural aspects of his epistemological explorations—especially as reflected in the *Black Riders* poems—a thematic concern that does not square with a committed positivistic stance. Jack London's improbable and fantastic narratives, particularly *The Sea-Wolf,* would drop out of the school, as would Holmes's *Elsie Venner* and Davis's "Life in the Iron Mills." Perhaps we are left with a school of one: Dreiser.

Yet, even the inclusion of some of Dreiser's fiction becomes doubtful (see the discussion of Dreiser in chapter 2). Thus, however neat and simple a definition of literary naturalism through a direct connection with philosophical naturalism may be, it does little to help us understand the formal and generic aspects of authors like Norris, London, Davis, Chopin, and Crane. What one can do, of course, is trace in naturalistic narrative influences arising out of philosophical naturalism. What one finds when tracing these influences is that they typically form only one component of a more complex narrative. What one will also find is that American literary naturalists often turned to romantic forms and conventions in order to incorporate elements arising out of philosophical naturalism into their narratives.

Scientific Naturalism

Occasionally theorists of literary naturalism have focused not so much on whether or not an author is operating from a particular philosophical orientation, but on the attempt of the given author to emulate in narrative form the techniques and procedures of scientific naturalists. Scientific naturalism can be defined simply as that method of exploration, experimentation, and investigation that focuses its attention on the natural rather than the supernatural. It is in this sense that one refers to Darwin as a naturalist; and in a broader sense scientific naturalists are that group of post-Enlightenment biologists, physicists, anthropologists, and physiologists who focused on empirical investigation of the natural world and increasingly turned their attention away from divine, mystical, or metaphysical explanations for material phenomena and sought phenomenological (i.e., empirical rather than intuitive) explanations instead.

This shift from the metaphysical to the phenomenological had its parallel in literature with the mid-nineteenth-century shift from romanticism to realism. There is a notable correspondence among (1) this "realistic" trend in post-Enlightenment science, (2) the development of the scientific method of investigation, and (3) literary realism's attempt to objectively document normative reality. It is this theoretical and historical connection between scientific naturalism and literary realism that sparked the dynamic of Zola's hypothetical "experimental novel." Explicitly locating its roots in the eighteenth-century Enlightenment shift toward a more empirical science, Zola designed the "experimental novel" as a method of transferring the techniques and procedures of scientific naturalism to the writing of literature.[28] Through direct observation of the natural world, the recording of "exact anatomy," and the study of "human documents," the experimental novelist would conceivably be able to contribute to a "scientific knowledge, of man in his individual and social action."[29] In a novel such as this, suggests Zola, "the imagination no longer has a function";[30] indeed, two of the chief characteristics of the experimental novel are its objectivity and impersonality.

The problems with trying to describe and define literary naturalism through too close a connection with scientific naturalism, as Zola did with his description of the experimental novel, are that, as noted previously, such a definition does not accurately describe the fiction itself. Equally important, it would seem that the principles valorized by scientific naturalism and by Zola in his theoretical writings have much more in common with literary realism than with literary naturalism. This confusion created an overlapping of terminology in the nineteenth century, because the term "naturalism" (with scientific naturalism hovering in the background) was often applied to the writings of literary realists, not the writings of "literary naturalists" as we currently think of them (Norris, Crane, London, and Dreiser). In the critical parlance of the late nineteenth century, the term "naturalism" when applied to literature is often used in conjunction with the term "realism" to denote the school of fiction that tries to mimetically and objectively re-create normative reality. In this sense, then, to say a work is "realistic" is to take note of its "naturalism." Used in this manner, "naturalism" and "realism" are relatively synonymous, thus the tendency for many twentieth-century critics to define literary naturalism as a type or subset of literary realism. Turning to Zola's theoretical writings and observing that he promotes, under the guise of "naturalism," many of the principles of literary realism seems at first glance to confirm the close relationship between literary realism and literary naturalism.

As sound as this logic appears, its fatal flaw is that when this application of the term "naturalism" is found in nineteenth-century criticism, it is principally used to describe not the fiction of Frank Norris, Stephen Crane, or Jack London, but the fiction of Henry James, William Dean Howells, and the school of realistic authors generally. For example, in 1884 Henry James referred to Howells as "the first American naturalist," indicating with this phrase that Howells was the first American practitioner of literary realism.[31] And, conversely, it is with this application of the term "naturalism" in mind, presumably, that James praises Zola as a (however narrow) practitioner of the realist school at the end of "The Art of Fiction" (1884). In a similar case, William Thayer in 1894 groups together Zola, Howells, and Tolstoy as representatives of the realist school and refers to Zola's *Le roman expérimental* as "the chief document of the theory of Realism."[32] When in 1903 H. B. Marriott Watson discusses the ongoing battle over the relative virtues of romance and realism in fiction, he refers to the "antagonism" that has "existed from time immemorial" between "romance and naturalism," using the term "naturalism" here to indicate the province of literary realism.[33]

It is with this sense of the term "naturalism" in mind that Edmund Gosse discusses late-nineteenth-century narrative in his essay "The Limits of Realism in Fiction" (1890).[34] In this essay Gosse equates the "experimental novel" with literary realism and suggests that James and Howells are the chief practitioners of the "experimental novel" in America (392). In fact, rather than interpreting naturalism as an outgrowth of realism—as so many twentieth-century critics have done—Gosse suggests the reverse: the "realistic novel" proceeded out of the "naturalist school" (392). In a similar vein, in his 1893 article "Realism in Literature and Art," Clarence S. Darrow draws some parallels between literary realism and the scientific method, and lists among the "great authors of the *natural school*" Tolstoy, Daudet, Howells, Ibsen, Flaubert, Zola, and Hardy; according to Darrow they are all "realists" who "worship at the shrine of nature."[35]

The connection between scientific naturalism and the realistic school of fiction also helps explain the claim made in 1883 by James Herbert Morse that both Howells and James operated out of a positivistic and "scientific critical spirit."[36] And it is similar reasoning that helps explain Hamlin Garland's reliance on evolutionary theory to help support his call for veritism (Garland's term for literary realism) in *Crumbling Idols* (1894).[37] Significantly, F. W. J. Hemmings in "The Origin of the Terms *Naturalisme, Naturaliste*" has shown that Zola consciously adopted (principally from Hippolyte Taine) and popularized the terms "naturalism" and "naturalist" for literature because he wished to associate his fiction with the positivistic orientation of philosophical naturalism and with the realistic orientation of scientific naturalism.[38]

Literary Naturalism

But what of the fiction of Frank Norris, Stephen Crane, Jack London, and Theodore Dreiser, as well as some of the works of Oliver Wendell Holmes, Rebecca Harding Davis, Harold Frederic, Edith Wharton, Kate Chopin, and Mark Twain? Occasionally in the late nineteenth century the phrase "literary naturalism" is used to describe something far different than the fiction of Howells, James, and Tolstoy. Pierre Loti may have been describing this "other" literary naturalism in his 1892 essay "The Literature of the Future."[39] In the opening paragraphs of this essay Loti distinguishes between the dying old naturalism—the body of fiction that grew up around Zola's theory— and the "new naturalism" that is "more lofty, more inspiring" and seems more of a piece with the renewed interest in symbolism, mysticism, scientificism, and other turn-of-the-century trends in literature.

Pierre Loti is mentioned at the conclusion of Edmund Gosse's 1890 essay. Here Gosse notes the downfall of the "realistic" naturalism, and writes, "M. Guy de Maupassant has become a psychologist, and M. Huysmans a mystic. M. Bourget . . . never has been a realist; nor has Pierre Loti, in whom . . . the old exiled romanticism comes back with a laugh and a song" (Gosse 400). Gosse's reference to the "old exiled romanticism" is almost certainly to the earlier nineteenth-century romanticism of which Victor Hugo was the primary representative in France. This is significant, for, as will be observed shortly, Frank Norris uses Hugo's romanticism to illustrate what he believes naturalism is. What is also notable about this passage from Gosse's essay is that literary naturalism as practiced in America looks as much like the psychological fiction of Maupassant, the mysticism of Huysmans, and the "old exiled romanticism" of Loti, as it does the fiction of Stendhal, Flaubert, and Balzac, all authors Zola sets up as exemplars of the experimental novel.

Later in the essay Gosse argues that "the limits of realism have been reached; that no great writer who has not already adopted the experimental system will do so; and that we ought now to be on the outlook to welcome . . . a school of novelists with a totally new aim, part of whose formula must unquestionably be a concession to the human instinct for mystery and beauty" (Gosse 400). Indeed, Gosse's words came just at the beginning of a massive romantic revival in the 1890s based on the renewed interest in the chivalric historical romance and the immensely popular romantic adventure tales of Rudyard

Kipling and Robert Louis Stevenson. Appearing in the midst of this romantic revival in the 1890s and 1900s was the work of some of the principal representatives of the "other" literary naturalism: Norris, Crane, London, Chopin, and Frederic. In their brand of "literary naturalism," direct ties with Zola's *Le roman expérimental*, the scientific method, and normative realism are severed. In place of these ties, these American "literary naturalists" created a form of literature that owes as much to the renewed interest in the romance in the 1890s as it does to the legacies handed down from the heyday of literary realism. Frank Norris describes this type of literary naturalism in his 1896 essay "Zola as a Romantic Writer." In a naturalistic narrative, writes Norris, "everything is extraordinary, imaginative, grotesque even.... It is all romantic ... closely resembling the work of the greatest of all modern romanticists, Hugo."[40] "Naturalism," Norris concludes, "is a form of romanticism, not an inner circle of realism." This brief but representative passage from Norris's own writings on the school of literary naturalism is clearly a departure from the antiromantic vituperation of Zola's theoretical writings, a departure based on Frank Norris's reading of Zola's *fiction* rather than on Zola's *theory* of literary naturalism.[41]

Direct reference to either philosophical or scientific naturalism is inadequate to describe the fiction of these "romantic" literary naturalists. Certainly, the relationship between *philosophical* and *scientific* naturalism is easy enough to see: there is an observable correspondence between the positivistic, phenomenological orientation of philosophical naturalism and the types of investigations pursued by scientific naturalism, with its valorization of the scientific method, direct observation of physical reality, and the pursuit of material explanations for natural phenomena. In fact, the discourses of philosophical and scientific naturalism tend to reinforce each other. As Enlightenment science revealed phenomenological explanations for the mysteries of nature, scientists and philosophers were given more impetus to shift from spiritualistic to positivistic orientations, which in turn resulted in a redoubled emphasis on scientific investigation and naturalistic explorations. Zola's theory as developed in *Le roman expérimental* describes a literary method that tries to legitimize novel writing as one branch of this increasing tendency toward scientific naturalism, coupled with a worldview compatible with philosophical naturalism. Literary naturalist praxis, however, does not carry out these theoretical intentions.[42]

Defining and describing the school of American literary naturalism requires a different emphasis.

There are two choices. One can continue to define literary naturalism through reference to philosophical naturalism, scientific naturalism, and Zola's theoretical writings (which will ultimately make Henry James and William Dean Howells more likely candidates for the school than Jack London and Frank Norris), or one can try to construct a better definition of "literary naturalism," one that accurately accounts for the fiction of authors like Norris, Crane, and London. This study proposes the second of these two options.

Norris, Crane, and London all used their fiction to explore popular scientific concepts of their day. When one speaks of a school of "literary naturalism" in American letters, one is really referring to those texts in the latter half of the nineteenth century (and into the twentieth) that incorporate at the *thematic* (as opposed to generic, philosophical, or methodological) level scientific or philosophical concepts arising from the work of the loose affiliation of nineteenth-century philosophical and scientific naturalists (like Charles Darwin, Herbert Spencer, and Auguste Comte) who capitalized on and extended the achievements of the Enlightenment. These American literary naturalists explored theories of evolution, atavism, degeneration, and natural law. They worked with concepts as specific as Thomas Malthus's 1798 population principle and as large and abstract as Herbert Spencer's "Force." It is *theme,* rather than genre, methodology, convention, tone, or philosophy, that qualifies a text for inclusion in the "school" of American *literary* naturalism.

The distinction between this and previous definitions may seem like a critical splitting of hairs, but it is actually crucial for an accurate understanding of American literary naturalism. Rather than attempting to transfer either philosophical or scientific naturalism into literary form, the American literary naturalists can be better understood as exploring themes arising out of the academic milieu of the day. This is the manner in which they responded to their scientific and philosophical environment. Their texts do not necessarily valorize philosophical naturalism, nor remain within the narrower and novelistic confines of literary realism. In fact, one of the benefits of this definition of American literary naturalism is that it frees the fiction from the "formal" constraints of former definitions and allows one to reconsider the genre/form of the texts themselves. Another benefit of this definition is that it does not predetermine the philosophical "message" of a given text or author. Consequently, it frees American literary naturalists from charges of failing to maintain a degree of objectivity or for failing to embody a strict determinism or philosophical naturalism. In this study, when a text is referred to as "naturalistic," the label simply indicates that it explores, *thematically,* elements of philosophical and scientific naturalism. When someone is referred to as a "naturalistic author," it simply indicates participation in the naturalistic school of fiction. Finally, the term "naturalist theory" in this study designates the amorphous set of concepts emanating from philosophical and scientific naturalism.

The body of naturalist theory is not a closed system, but a relatively broad and diverse coalition of theories and ideologies arising out of post-Enlightenment scientific and philosophical investigation. This body of theory grew in the early nineteenth century through the work of scientists and philosophers like Thomas Malthus, Charles Lyell, and Arthur Schopenhauer, and came to fruition in the mid- to late nineteenth century with the work of Charles Darwin, Herbert Spencer, Thomas Huxley, Auguste Comte, Hippolyte Taine, John Fiske, and William Graham Sumner.[43] The individual contributions of these philosophical and scientific naturalists to nineteenth-century intellectual thought have been discussed countless times by critics and historians and need not be described here. What is worth noting is that collectively these scientists and philosophers looked toward the natural world for explanations of the mysteries of the universe. They saw the world operating under the aegis of natural laws—laws of evolution, of cause and effect, of heredity, of atavism—and they increasingly saw man not as a special creation, but as simply one element of a mechanistic universe.

This body of theory had a major impact on nineteenth-century culture. As Charles R. Lepetit noted in 1900, it was the age's "general enthusiasm for science" that stimulated the development of literary naturalism.[44] James T. Farrell would express a similar idea in 1950: "Zola's attempt to embody scientific methods, procedures, and conclusions in the novel should be seen as an effort to incorporate in literature something of the developing mental climate of his own time" (146). All things considered, Zola probably would have agreed with Farrell. The experimental novel, Zola suggested, was an outgrowth of the "scientific evolution of the age";[45] and a review of *Le roman expérimental* that appeared in the *Atlantic Monthly* in 1881 agreed with

Zola that "the general turn of thought at the present day is in the direction of science."[46]

Although naturalistic narrative arose from the "scientific evolution of the age," when Zola makes the subsequent claim that "literary naturalism" was *the* "literature of our scientific age,"[47] he was talking about the realistic novel.[48] There may be a direct correlation between literary realism and philosophical and scientific naturalism, but there are nevertheless distinct differences between realistic narratives and naturalistic narratives. The principal difference arises from the defining characteristic of "naturalistic" narrative; that is, the artistic integration of naturalist theory as theme. This is the difference between a distinctly realistic text like William Dean Howells's *The Rise of Silas Lapham* (1885) and a distinctly naturalistic text like Frank Norris's *The Pit* (1903). While one can make some linkages between *The Rise of Silas Lapham* and contemporary scientific and philosophical thought, and while one can trace elements of late-nineteenth-century scientific and philosophical ideology that have filtered into Howells's tale of American business, Howells, unlike Norris, does not explicitly integrate naturalist theory into the narrative in such a way as to elevate it to thematic or structural significance.

Worth recalling is Charles Child Walcutt's observation in 1956 that the body of naturalist theory does not "control" naturalistic fiction, but merely affects it in a variety of ways.[49] It can enter a narrative through symbolism, as in the aquarium passage that acts as a thematic icon in Dreiser's Cowperwood trilogy. It can enter the narrative through characters who express or represent elements of naturalist theory. One sees this in London's Wolf Larson, Frederic's Dr. Ledsmar, and Holmes's Reverend Pierrepont Honeywood. Naturalist theory can also form the basis of plot, as in Frank Norris's "A Reversion to Type" and "Son of a Sheik," and in the more extensive treatments of degeneration in *Vandover and the Brute* and *McTeague*. Sometimes the naturalist theory is seen in a positive light, as in London's *The Star Rover* (1915); sometimes it is seen as harsh, violent, and oppressive, as in London's *The Sea-Wolf* and Norris's "A Deal in Wheat." This last point recalls an observation made by Leopoldo Alas: naturalistic authors—authors who incorporated some aspect or aspects of naturalist theory into their narrative—were not all pessimistic. Some, in fact, were resoundingly optimistic. Naturalist theory was used by American naturalistic authors in many ways—even, on occasion, to justify the possibility of a utopia.

2

The Naturalist Aesthetic

The expectations we bring to a text help shape the way we read and respond to it. This point was not lost on nineteenth-century authors, who at times took delight in manipulating their reader's genre expectations. Edgar Allan Poe was a master at this game, casting certain of his most fantastic gothic romances in the form of realistic reportage or autobiography. Such is the case in "The Facts in the Case of M. Valdemar," in which a gruesome tale of mesmerism and bodily decay is presented as a true account of an actual scientific experiment, and in *The Narrative of Arthur Gordon Pym,* in which an increasingly fantastic account of a trip to the South Pole is presented as an authorized account only *edited* by Poe. Herman Melville also had some fun with this type of ruse as early readers debated whether *Typee* was a romantic adventure tale of the South Seas or an autobiographical rendering of real events. Perhaps it was both.

Melville, of course, did draw heavily upon his own experiences when writing *Typee* and *Omoo,* however embellished the finished products may be. Writing his third novel, *Mardi,* was a different prospect altogether. In this work Melville set aside any pretensions about rendering experiences realistically or factually and let his imagination roam with abandon. In a letter to publisher John Murray dated March 25, 1848, Melville wrote that in *Mardi* he would "out with the Romance."[1] Melville makes it perfectly clear to Murray that *Mardi* is to be read as a *romance* rather than an autobiographical travel narrative or realistic *novel.* Melville emphasized this point in order to clarify for Murray what he should expect to find in the novel, thus preventing *Mardi* from being judged by the wrong genre conventions and literary standards.

The antebellum historical romance writer William Gilmore Simms made a similar point in his preface to *The Yemassee* (1835). "I have entitled this story a romance," Simms writes, "and not a novel—the reader will permit me to insist upon the distinction. I am unwilling that 'THE YEMASSEE' should be examined by any other than those standards which have governed me in its composition."[2] Simms's insistence in this passage emphasizes just how important certain nineteenth-century writers felt genre distinctions were. If we read *The Yemassee* expecting a *novel,* we will find the work seriously flawed—full of extravagant indulgences that cross the boundaries of realistic representation. If we read it as a *romance,* however, then *The Yemassee* will strike us, presumably, as one of the better historical romances written in antebellum America.

For many years, a theme running through accounts of late-nineteenth-century American literature has been that Norris, London, Frederic, Dreiser, and even Crane, wrote "flawed" narratives—fiction that is often labeled "powerful" though less than masterful, if not downright inartistic. The reasons critics have labeled such works "flawed" are various; for example, American literary naturalists are sometimes charged with failing to create a perfectly deterministic world or for failing to live up to the standards of realistic fiction as practiced by Howells and James. Or sometimes they simply write bad novels, as seems to be the case with Norris's *A Man's Woman,* to name just one of the lesser lights in the naturalist pantheon.

Staying with Frank Norris for a moment, one notes that he has been criticized for an overly formal style, the earnest (and sometimes condescendingly judgmental) tone of his authorial commentary, strains of anti-Semitism, and posturing that smacks of ill-conceived notions of Anglo-Saxon supremacy. Regarding those "flaws" that are attributable to common attitudes of the time (e.g., Norris's racial beliefs) or to artistic shortcomings (e.g., Norris's overly formal passages), we can do little; there is no special pleading that can erase racial stereotyping found in the pages of *McTeague* or *Vandover and the Brute.* And even if there were, this study is not concerned with acting as an apologia for the lesser (or even the greater) works of Holmes, Norris, Crane, London, Chopin, Wharton, or anyone else.

Occasionally, however, naturalistic narratives are regarded as flawed for reasons related to definitional concerns and matters of narrative genre, and it is these alleged "flaws" that we can address with some assurance. In other words, certain types of criticism leveled against naturalistic novels may be the result of critics bringing misdirected genre expectations to bear upon these texts. Taking Norris as an example again, his works are often considered flawed for being improbable, for not being realistic enough, and for being melodramatic. But what if we don't assume that Norris is writing within the tradition of the novel of social realism? What happens if we look at Norris's novels in the context of the American romance tradition? To change the definition of the genre of naturalistic fiction (along the lines proposed in chapter 1) is to change the expectations one brings to its texts. Surely, if we view certain naturalistic novels as participating in the tradition of American romance, they cannot be dismissed as flawed on the grounds that they fail to live up to the "standards" of literary realism as established by Howells and James, not to mention Flaubert, George Eliot, and Tolstoy. *The Scarlet Letter* is not flawed because an immense "A" glows in the sky, nor is Poe's "The Fall of the House of Usher" flawed because the house crumbles into the tarn; likewise, Norris's *Vandover and the Brute* cannot be assumed to be flawed solely on the grounds of his use of lycanthropy. One may find other flaws in *Vandover and the Brute,* but one must at least allow Norris, as Henry James argues, his donnée as a writer of romantic fiction. One may even argue that Norris's use of lycanthropy is inartistically or immaturely managed, but the lycanthropy device itself is surely fair game for the romance writer. As Hawthorne notes in his preface to *The House of the Seven Gables,* the romance writer "has fairly a right to present" his or her "truth" under "circumstances, to a great extent, of the writer's own choosing or creation," and even immoderate use of this liberty is not a "literary crime."[3]

In a similar vein, allowing that naturalistic narratives are first and foremost literary art rather than scientific tracts or dogmatic statements of naturalist theory suggests that a particular naturalistic text is not necessarily flawed because it does not incorporate certain scientific theories in a complete and/or orthodox manner. By gross analogy, such would be the equivalent of slighting Hawthorne because he did not explicitly foreground *The House of the Seven Gables* in an orthodox Hegelian historiography. Charles Child Walcutt finds naturalistic narratives flawed because there are recognizable discrepancies between the deterministic worldview Walcutt feels they are supposed to represent and the reformative elements one finds in the same texts.

Walcutt's criticism is a standard result when one does not maintain clear distinctions among philosophical, scientific, and literary naturalism. Instead of declaring a text flawed when we notice what appears to be a textual inconsistency, or contradictory philosophical or scientific strains running through a narrative, let us first ask ourselves why the author might have designed his or her text in such a manner. We may eventually conclude that certain texts here and there are legitimately flawed in some manner, but this should be arrived at only after other, possibly aesthetic, explanations have been pursued.[4] Some of these aesthetic explanations become evident once American literary naturalism is restored to its Anglo-American critical context. Ultimately, even if it still leaves certain mysteries intact, examining the aesthetic theories of the American literary naturalists will aid our efforts to read their works with the proper genre expectations in mind.

Literary Form in the Nineteenth Century

American literary naturalists, although hardly provincial, did not write fiction that necessarily embodied a strict philosophical determinism, nor did they re-create in narrative form the techniques and procedures of scientific naturalism in pursuit of Zola's phantom experimental novel. Instead, as noted in chapter 1, we are better served by defining American literary naturalism as the exploration of naturalist theory at the thematic level.

The purpose of this chapter is to examine the aesthetic context of American literary naturalism, with an emphasis on narrative form. In order to establish an interpretive context within which to examine the aesthetic theories developed by literary naturalists in America, the first half of the chapter focuses broadly on conceptions of narrative form in nineteenth-century American criticism. My method throughout this portion of the chapter is inductive rather than deductive; to this end I have presented a reasonable selection of significant essays written by nineteenth-century literary critics. I have tried not to burden the reader with too much raw critical data, but to include enough evidence to validate certain assumptions about nineteenth-century aesthetic theory.[5] The second half of this chapter looks directly at what Norris, Crane, and London had to say about their own aesthetic theories. The chapter concludes with some speculation on why the romance held such promise as a narrative form for American literary naturalists.

Bellamy, Holmes, Norris, and Literary Taxonomy

In an 1893 article in the *Dial* titled "The Persistence of the Romance," the critic Richard Burton writes, "The romance of the future will present such high interests keeping pace with the evolution of society; and its vantage-ground over the romance of years agone will be that it is firm-based on truth to the phenomena of life, and is thus, in the only true sense, realistic. Nobler in content, and persistent in type, the romance, broadly viewed, may be regarded as that form of literature which more than any other shall reflect the aspiration of the individual and the social progress of the state."[6] Burton's call for an idealistic romance that keeps pace with the "evolution of society" neatly describes Edward Bellamy's *Looking Backward* (1888). Bellamy's novel explores the "aspirations of the individual" and the "social progress of the state" in its portrayal of social utopia in the year 2000. Notably, Bellamy's text relies heavily on naturalist theory: his utopian society "evolves" out of the degenerate capitalism of the late nineteenth century. His reliance on evolutionary theory does not lead to determinism, however. In fact, Bellamy's socialistic utopia provides more, not less, freedom for the individual, and it provides the means for individuals to pursue their own interests and to make the most of their "aspirations."

The connection between utopian fiction and literary naturalism will be discussed in detail in chapter 3 of the present study. For now, what is worth noting is that Bellamy explicitly labeled *Looking Backward* a *romance.* In his preface, Bellamy—through the persona of a late-twentieth-century author—states that he has purposefully cast his work in the "form of a romantic narrative." This form was chosen, Bellamy notes, because it seemed the best method for incorporating the evolutionary and socialistic theory represented in the text. Certainly *Looking Backward* is a romance in the most basic sense. Set over a hundred years in the future, the book is broadly fantastic with doses of mesmerism, dream visions, and perhaps even faint echoes of Poe's "Ligeia" (the "rebirth" of Edith Bartlett in Edith Leete is loosely parallel to the much darker rebirth of Ligeia in Rowena).

Perhaps surprisingly, Bellamy was not the first to use the romance as a means of integrating naturalist theory into a narrative. In fact, it is becoming clearer in recent years that discussions of American literary naturalism that begin in the mid- to late 1890s are taking a limited view of what is almost certainly a more vibrant literary movement in America than traditionally believed. The American literary naturalism that is seen as realism infused with a deterministic philosophy and a pessimistic view of society is indeed a diminished, and unsustainable, literary movement, doomed to be taught forever at the tail end of classes that focus on the "Rise of Realism." But if we discard for a moment this limiting definition of literary naturalism and explore the implications of the definition offered in chapter 1, then the second half of the nineteenth century becomes a wider field for naturalism to roam in. (In chapter 3, for instance, I will suggest that the utopian fiction so prevalent in the 1880s itself bears some relation to the school of literary naturalism.)

Some critics have started to drift toward a broader conception of literary naturalism even within the context of a limiting definition, as the core trio of Dreiser, Crane, and Norris have been supplemented with texts by Wharton, Chopin, Frederic, Mark Twain, and even certain works by Henry James. But these authors all wrote in the 1890s, so there are no chronological difficulties there, at any rate. All are realist or postrealist. But then someone hints that Rebecca Harding Davis's "Life in the Iron Mills," although published in 1861, might bear some relationship to the school of literary naturalism with its gritty depiction of the lower classes and its focus on what Howells might call the "wolfish problems of existence." Is this a single aberration? No. In fact, Oliver Wendell Holmes's *Elsie Venner,* also published in 1861, has as good a claim (better, in fact, in my opinion) to kinship with the school of literary naturalism as "Life in the Iron Mills." Although not as dark as a *Sister Carrie* or *Vandover and the Brute* nor as optimistic as *Looking Backward, Elsie Venner* foregrounds perspectives on both freedom and determinism, particularly as they relate to questions of original sin, guilt, and morality.[7] In fact, as a novel of ideas that directly confronts issues of determinism arising out of nineteenth-century philosophy and science, *Elsie Venner* makes a nice companion to a novel like London's *The Sea-Wolf.* Moreover, and to the point of this chapter, like *Looking Backward, Elsie Venner* is explicitly presented as a romance: *Elsie Venner* is subtitled *A Romance of Destiny,* and in his first preface (1861) Holmes writes, "In calling this narrative a 'romance,' the Author wishes to make sure of being indulged in the common privileges of the poetic license. Through all the disguise of fiction a grave scientific doctrine may be detected lying beneath some of the delineations of character. He has used this doctrine as a part of the machinery of his story without pledging his absolute belief in it to the extent to which it is asserted or implied. It was adopted as a convenient medium of truth rather than as an accepted scientific conclusion." This "physiological romance," as Holmes describes *Elsie Venner* in his second (1883) preface, took its form not through direct imitation of a similar story—Holmes offers Hawthorne's *Marble Faun* (1860) as an example; instead, Holmes's "poor heroine found her origin, not in fable or romance, but in a physiological conception, fertilized by a theological dogma." One can't help but wonder if the same terminology couldn't as easily be applied to several of the "core" texts of American literary naturalism; certainly *McTeague*—with the title character's inherited "taint" cast in the language of original sin—could just as easily be the subject of Holmes's apt description. Significantly, Holmes found the best expression for this "physiological conception" (born out of naturalist theory) in the romance.

A generation later, in 1896 Norris would make the remarkable dual claims that Zola wrote romances and that naturalism is really a type of romanticism, not an "inner circle of realism." Norris's own fiction is highly romantic, as is much of the fiction of his contemporaries Crane, London, and Frederic. To understand why Bellamy and Holmes labeled their fictions *romances* rather than *novels,* why Norris would later argue that Zola's fiction was highly romantic, and why naturalistic fiction, as Norris claims, is an outgrowth of romanticism, one must begin with an overview of one of the central oppositions in nineteenth-century literary criticism: the novel/romance distinction.[8]

Novel and Romance

Throughout the nineteenth century authors and critics stressed the importance of proper generic classification. Certain literary forms carried with them assumptions that bore heavily on the way the author wished his or her text to be received by its audience. For narrative fiction the two principal taxonomic poles used by authors and critics were the *novel* and the *romance.* There were many subdivisions within these two broad categories (e.g., sentimental novel, domestic novel, picaresque novel, reform novel, Gothic romance, frontier romance, sentimental romance, historical romance, psychological romance, metaphysical romance, oriental romance, chivalric romance, and so forth). Nevertheless, the novel/romance dichotomy was the broadest of these generic distinctions, and nineteenth-century authors, reviewers, critics, and readers continually turned to this opposition as a way of foregrounding the interpretive approaches, narratological strategies, and reader contracts implicated by either pole of the dichotomy.

Perhaps the best-known expression of the novel/romance distinction in nineteenth-century American letters is that given by Nathaniel Hawthorne in his preface to *The House of the Seven Gables* (1851). Hawthorne writes: "When a writer calls his work a Romance, it need hardly be observed that he wishes to claim a certain latitude, both as to its fashion and material, which he would not have felt himself entitled to assume had he professed to be writing a Novel." The novel "is presumed to aim at a very minute fidelity, not merely to the possible, but to the probable and ordinary course of man's experience." Although the romance "sins unpardonably so far as it may swerve aside from the truth of the human heart," it has "fairly a right to present that truth under circumstances, to a great extent, of the writer's own choosing or creation."[9]

However astute, Hawthorne's distinction was given its "classic" status not by his nineteenth-century contemporaries, but by twentieth-century literary historians who have focused on Hawthorne as the premier nineteenth-century American romancer. In its historical and critical context, Hawthorne's preface, while clearly and succinctly stated, was neither the first, nor even the most developed, of the various recountings in American letters of the basic distinction between the novel and the romance. The critical tendency to distinguish between these two broadly distinct fictional genres can be traced back at least as far as William Congreve's preface to *Incognita* (1691), and can be seen throughout the English literary criticism of the eighteenth century, appearing, for example, in the criticism of John Hawkesworth, Hugh Blair, James Beatty, George Canning, and Clara Reeve.[10] Sometime around the turn of the century the distinction made its way from England to America, probably as a result of the popularity of European Gothic fiction, which coincided with the development of narrative fiction in America during the early national period. This transmission was aided in the early nineteenth century by the popularity of Sir Walter Scott, who, through his numerous critical works, contributed to the popularization of the basic distinction on both sides of the Atlantic. In the 1824 *Encyclopaedia Britannica* supplement, for example, Scott writes: "We would be ... inclined to describe a Romance as 'fictitious narrative in prose or verse; the interest of which turns upon marvellous and uncommon incidents'; being thus opposed to the kindred term Novel, which Johnson has described as a 'smooth tale, generally of love'; but which we would rather define as 'a fictitious narrative, differing from the Romance, because the events are accommodated to the ordinary train of human events, and the modern state of society.'"[11] Through the influence of Scott and other early Anglo-American critics, the basic novel/romance distinction was reiterated by literary critics from the turn of the century forward.[12]

Next to Hawthorne's preface to *The House of the Seven Gables,* the best known of nineteenth-century documents relating to the novel/romance distinction is William Gilmore Simms's "Advertisement" to the 1835 edition of *The Yemassee.* He writes:

> The question briefly is, what are the standards of the modern romance—what is the modern romance itself? The reply is instant. Modern romance is the substitute which the people of to-day offer for the ancient epic. Its standards are the same. The reader, who, reading Ivanhoe, keeps Fielding and Richardson beside him, will be at fault in every step of his progress. The domestic novel of these writers, confined to the felicitous narration of common and daily occurring events, is altogether a different sort of composition; and if such a reader happens to pin his faith, in a strange simplicity and singleness of spirit, to such writers alone, the works of Maturin, of Scott, of Bulwer, and the rest, are only so much incoherent nonsense.
>
> The modern romance is a poem in every sense of the word. It is only with those who insist upon poetry as rhyme, and rhyme as poetry, that the identity fails to be perceptible. Its standards are precisely those of the epic. It invests individuals with an absorbing interest—it hurries them through crowding events in a narrow space of time—it requires the same unities of plan, of purpose, and harmony of parts, and it seeks for its adventures among the wild and wonderful. It does not insist upon what is known, or even what is probable.[13]

Some of the interest in Simms's "Advertisement" lies in the connections he makes between the "modern romance" and the ancient epic.[14] A reviewer of *The Yemassee* for the *American Monthly Magazine* makes a similar association. The "romance of the nineteenth century," the reviewer writes, is "the peculiar literature of the age; filling that place which was occupied by the epic poem of heroic days, and by the comedy of a hundred years ago; it embodies the thoughts, and represents the customs of its own era, as they could not be represented by any other style."[15] Toward the end of this same paragraph, the reviewer notes that "the novels and romances of the present day are invariably composed" of poetry, excitement, metaphysics, and lively dialogue. Despite these similarities, however, the novel is concerned with "describing the customs, satirizing the follies, and giving a body to the spirit of the times," while the romance mingles "truth with fiction, painting the lights and shadows of history with the gayer colors of the poet's pencil." What is striking about this review is that it combines in one brief essay the ideas seen in the quotations from both Simms and Hawthorne. The critic combines the idea in Simms's essay that the modern romance is a substitute for the ancient epic with the notion expressed in Hawthorne's essay that the novel concerns the "ordinary course of man's experience," while the romance allows for a "latitude, both as to its fashion and material."[16]

Postwar Criticism and the Novel/Romance Distinction

The importance of the novel/romance distinction in American literary criticism did not diminish after the Civil War. What did change, however, was that responsible assessments of American fiction had to account for both romanticism and realism in their studies of the development of American narrative. One such assessment, by James Herbert Morse, was a lengthy historical survey published in *Century Magazine* in 1883.[17] Part 1, "The Native Element in American Fiction: Before the War," traces the development of American narrative from its inception in the romances of Charles Brockden Brown—who had a "peculiar gift to paint the night side of human experience"—through the more realistic fiction of Louisa May Alcott and Elizabeth B. Stoddard. During much of this period, notes Morse, "the novelist was left free to range to the utmost verge of the possible: for the national sentiment welcomed anything in romance that gave evidence of imagination."

After Brown's dark romances came James Kirk Paulding's allegorical romance *John Bull and Brother Jonathan* (1812), and the early work of Washington Irving and John Neal. It was, says Morse, with "the appearance of
Cooper [that] we began to hold up our heads among the romancers of the
world." The historical romances of Cooper, Simms, and Child, as well as
the work of Poe, John Lothrop Motley, James Hall, and others, held sway
until the appearance of Hawthorne, in whom "we have our first true artist
in literary expression, as well as the most completely equipped genius of
romance." In the mid-1850s, however, Harriet Beecher Stowe's fiction
"marked a new era in American novel-writing. Here we had the genuine
novel,—no mere romance, or allegory, or evolution from the inner consciousness, but a work saturated with American life,—not local, but spanning the
whole arch of the States." In part 2 of his study, "The Native Element in
American Fiction: Since the War," Morse begins to account for the emer-
gence of realism in American letters. He observes that American history still
contained vast possibilities for romancers in the tradition of Cooper and
Hawthorne, but "all the conditions of the times forced the romancer out of
the field and pushed the novelist in." These works, written "in the Howells
vein," attempted to satisfy America's "mania for facts,—the open, outward,
visible facts; facts in science, facts in religion, facts in history."

This novelistic "mania for facts" was quick to affect Hjalmar Hjorth
Boyesen. In one of his many articles discussing and defending the tenets of
realism, Boyesen remarks that the "latest development of the novel" breaks
with the romantic tendency to create idealized and improbable heroes and
heroines.[18] The protagonist in the later realistic novel is founded upon "his
typical capacity, as representing a large class of his fellow-men. This is the
great and radical change which the so-called realistic school of fiction has
inaugurated." The "novel," Boyesen writes, "is no longer an irresponsible
play of fancy, however brilliant, but acquires an historical importance in relation to the age to which it belongs." For Boyesen, "Thackeray, for instance,
is . . . a far greater novelist than Dickens, because he has, to a large extent,
chronicled the manners, speech, and sentiments of England during his own
day." Dickens, on the other hand, "had no ambition to be truthful. He had
the romantic ideal in view, and produced a series of extremely entertaining
tales, which are incidentally descriptive of manners, but caricatured, extravagant, and fantastic."[19]

Howells and James were no strangers to the distinction between the novel and the romance. As champions of the realistic novel, both James and Howells were intensely interested in the distinction and the language it provided for helping to differentiate their projects from the writings of antebellum romancers. Given the importance of the distinction, it is not surprising that in 1880 Howells chides James for misusing the terms in his *Hawthorne* (1879):

> No one better than Mr. James knows the radical difference between a romance and a novel, but he speaks now of Hawthorne's novels, and now of his romances, throughout, as if the terms were convertible; whereas the romance and the novel are as distinct as the poem and the novel. Mr. James excepts to the people in The Scarlet Letter, because they are rather types than persons, rather conditions of the mind than characters; as if it were not almost precisely the business of the romance to deal with types and mental conditions. Hawthorne's fiction being always and essentially, in conception and performance, romances, and not novels, something of all Mr. James's special criticism is invalidated by the confusion which, for some reason not made clear, he permits himself.[20]

As though in response, James, in "The Art of Fiction" (1884), would comment on the "celebrated distinction between the novel and the romance," arguing that it is a "clumsy separation," one that, despite its prevalence over the years, has "little reality or interest" for the writers of fiction themselves.[21] Whatever James's motives for denigrating the distinction in "The Art of Fiction," in the preface to the New York edition of *The American* (1907) he would present a more carefully considered discussion of the formal differences between the novel and the romance.[22] In this preface, James claimed that what one finds in *romance* is a rendering of experience that is "uncontrolled by our general sense of 'the way things happen.'" But, he said, no single or restrictive definition can apply; the "only *general* attribute" of romance that "fits all its cases" is "experience liberated." By this phrase he meant experience "disengaged, disembodied, disencumbered, exempt from the conditions" that one knows usually "attach to it," but that also "drag upon it." Such liberated experience "romance alone more or less successfully palms off on us."[23] According to James, the romance operates in "a medium which relieves it . . . of the inconvenience of a *related,* a measurable state, a state subject to all our vulgar communities." Furthermore, the romance arrives at the "greatest intensity" when the "sacrifice of community, of the 'related' side of situations, has not been too rash"; in fact, if possible the reader should be kept from "suspecting any sacrifice at all." In order to clarify this statement, James employs the famous "balloon" metaphor: the "balloon of experience" soars romantically into space but is tethered to the mundane plane of the earthly by "a rope of remarkable length," so that one "swings" suspended "in the more or less commodious car of the imagination." It is "by the rope we know where we are"; when the rope is cut, one is "at large and unrelated." The "art of the romancer" is "insidiously to cut the cable, to cut it without our detecting him."

Like James, Howells reflected upon the romance/novel distinction throughout his career in a variety of essays, lectures, and books. In one of these lectures, "Novel-Writing and Novel-Reading: An Impersonal Explanation" (1899), Howells writes: "there are several ways of regarding life in fiction, and in order to do justice to the different kinds we ought to distinguish very clearly between them. There are three forms, which I think of, and which I will name in the order of their greatness: the novel, the romance, and the romanticistic novel."[24] The "novel I take to be the sincere and conscientious endeavor to picture life just as it is, to deal with character as we witness it in living people, and to record the incidents that grow out of character" (3:218). For examples of this "supreme form of fiction," Howells lists, among others, *Middlemarch, Anna Karenina,* and *Pride and Prejudice.* The romance, Howells argues, "deals with life allegorically and not representatively; it employs types rather than characters, and studies them in the ideal rather than the real; it handles the passions broadly. Altogether the greatest in this kind are The Scarlet Letter and The Marble Faun of Hawthorne, which partake of the nature of poems, and which, as they frankly place themselves outside of familiar experience and circumstance, are not to be judged by the rules of criticism that apply to the novel" (3:218). The third form, the romanticistic novel, is a bastard form that professes like the "real novel to portray actual life, but it does this with an excess of drawing and coloring which are false to nature. It attributes motives to people which do not govern real people, and its characters are of the quality of types. . . . The worst examples of it are to be found in the fictions of two very great men: Charles

Dickens and Victor Hugo" (3:218). Howells would make this same point again in *Heroines of Fiction* (1901), in which he observes "there was the widest possible difference of ideal in Dickens and Hawthorne; the difference between the romanticistic and the romantic, which is almost as great as that between the romantic and the realistic." Whereas *romantic narrative* "as in Hawthorne, seeks the effect of reality in visionary conditions," *romanticistic narrative,* "as in Dickens, tries for a visionary effect in actual conditions," where it does not belong.[25]

In addition to delineating the three fictional categories of novel, romance, and romanticistic fiction, Howells wrote an essay in 1900 on the rise of the historical romance in the 1890s.[26] He begins his essay by noting that although the tendency in the fiction of the 1870s and 1880s was realistic (notably, Howells's phrase at this point is that the "natural tendency" in fiction prevailed), there was nonetheless a rising current of popular historical romance present during these decades. Now, in the 1890s, the tables have turned and there is a noticeable current of realistic fiction still discernible despite the "welter of over-whelming romance." What is curious about this revived historical romance, as described by Howells, is that it is a mingled or hybrid form; for unlike the old heroic romance, the heroic historical romance of the 1890s "pays its duty to the spirit of reality ... and its writers represent life as they have themselves seen it look and heard it talk" (937). Thus, despite the influx of realism and the critical debates over the relative virtues of romanticism and realism, at the end of the century the basic novel/romance distinction was still intact and remained a critically powerful tool authors and critics could regularly draw upon.[27]

What one notices in these representative samples of late-nineteenth-century criticism is the attempt to integrate into the novel/romance distinction the tensions arising from the realism/romanticism debate that heated up after the Civil War. As in antebellum criticism, later nineteenth-century critics continued to associate the novel, and realism, with the eighteenth-century productions of Henry Fielding, Samuel Richardson, Tobias Smollett, and Maria Edgeworth and the nineteenth-century productions of Howells and James. Likewise, the romance, and romanticism, was still identified with the gothic fictions of Matthew "Monk" Lewis and Ann Radcliffe, as well as the historical romances of Cooper, Simms, and Scott, and the work of Poe and Hawthorne toward mid-century.

The Transgeneric Romance-Novel

Howells's treatment of the late-nineteenth-century historical romance as a form that pursues romance while paying its duty to the spirit of reality echoes antebellum theories of the *modern* romance as a hybrid or transgeneric form. In fact, it is the transgeneric nature of the romance that made it perfectly suitable for American literary naturalism. The *romance* of the middle ages was a genre given to the use of the fantastic, the wildly imaginary, and the marvelous, as in *Sir Gawain and the Green Knight* and Spenser's *The Faerie Queene.* Opposed to the extravagance of the medieval romance was the early *novel*—as practiced by Fielding and Richardson—which avoided the extravagant and fantastic. In the late eighteenth and nineteenth centuries, the revitalized romance—often referred to as the "modern" romance—was thought of as a hybrid form that intermingled elements of the fantastic, marvelous, and uncanny with a novelistic concern for realistic detail, the ordinary, and the manners of society. Thus, the "modern romance" was *transgeneric:* it blended together the old romance and the novel, the ordinary and the extraordinary. In his "Custom House" introduction to *The Scarlet Letter,* Hawthorne writes that the province of the romance is a kind of "neutral territory" somewhere between the real world and an idealized or enchanted world; it is a territory "where the Actual and the Imaginary may meet, and each imbue itself with the nature of the other" (*Works,* 5:55). In like manner, William Gilmore Simms used the "neutral ground" metaphor to describe the domain of romance, and Henry James's preface to *The American* suggests a similar notion.[28]

As with the basic novel/romance distinction, the transgeneric feature of the modern romance was much discussed in nineteenth-century criticism. For example, preceding the *Seven Gables* preface by some thirty years are a pair of reviews that have formulations similar to what one sees in Hawthorne. In the *North American Review* in 1818, E. T. Channing wrote a review of Scott's *Rob Roy* in which he indicates that Scott's historical romances create a "union of the chivalrous and wild with the later habits of a busier and more worldly race."[29] In Scott's romances the earth "acquires a new and moral interest by its power of carrying us to something higher, and leading us to connect all that we behold here with our own minds and with God.— The romantic and poetical, both in the human character and the world which helps to form it, are naturally blended." Furthermore, "with his love of the picturesque and romantic, the author [Scott] unites a singular intimacy with men in the practical, common pursuits."[30]

Prior to the publication of Hawthorne's *Scarlet Letter,* a number of reviews and articles appeared that discussed the transgeneric nature of the modern romance. In 1829, in an essay titled "Present American Literature," a critic notes that in Scott's historical romances he "has taken the facts of history, and woven from them the beautiful fabric of poetry, and has given a more lasting and a deeper interest to its dry details, by connecting them in our minds with all the beauties and fascinations of romance."[31] In a short review of *The Five Nights of St. Albans, A Romance* that appeared in the *Knickerbocker,* a critic praises the "splendid romance" for achieving its success "with great force of expression, and by linking the unearthly with the natural, and freely drawing upon his own imagination and his reader's credulity."[32] And in a negative review of Bulwer's *The Pilgrims of the Rhine* in the *North American Magazine* for 1834, the writer notes that the romance is formed by the less than successful "intertexture of the supernatural with the merely common, of the ideal with the actual."[33]

Literary Realism and the Modern Romance

In the 1860s and 1870s, as critics debated the relative virtues of realism and romanticism in literature, the idea of the transgeneric intermingling of the actual and the imaginary in the modern romance evolved and expanded. Just as the novel form became increasingly associated with the domain of literary realism, so did the "actual" half of Hawthorne's transgeneric binary. At the same time, the "imaginary" aspects of the modern romance became linked with both wild productions of the imagination and an idealistic orientation in literary art. This association of the romance with idealism helped precipitate a shift in the way the novel/romance controversy developed in the first few decades after the Civil War.[34] Thus, in the second half of the nineteenth century one finds critics occasionally talking about the transgeneric blending in contemporary narrative of "idealism" and "realism," or of "romanticism" and "realism." Whereas, prior to the advent of literary realism in America the "actual" half of the modern romance was conceived of in terms of portrayals of "realistic" characters and settings and a concern for the "ordinary course" of human action, after the arrival of literary realism the realm of the "actual" becomes associated with a school of realistic fiction backed by a developed theory. Thus, a return to the "modern romance" in the late nineteenth century became in practice an attempt to blend literary realism with the "imaginary" (be it the fantastic, the symbolic, or the uncanny).

The passage by Richard Burton quoted earlier illustrates this impulse toward a mingling of realism with romanticism. Burton claims that the idealistic "romance of the future" will have a higher "vantage-ground over the romance of years agone" because "it is firm-based on truth to the phenomenon of life, and is thus, in the only true sense, realistic." What Burton seems to argue here is that the late-nineteenth-century romance is created through an intermingling of (1) a realistic concern for the phenomenon of common life and an attention to detail, with (2) the extraordinary and idealistic features of the romance. According to Burton, this blending of the techniques and devices of literary realism with a romantic spirit of idealism will lift latter -day realist fiction to a higher artistic plateau. Therefore, the modern romance as understood by Hawthorne and other antebellum critics was revised by postwar critics in order to accommodate the advent of literary realism and the renewed call for an idealistic literature that seems to have been born out of the utopian ideology implicit within some naturalist theory.

Recognition of this postrealist configuration of the modern romance was widespread among late-nineteenth-century literary critics. For instance, Julian Hawthorne, in "The American Element in Fiction," notes that Bret Harte's "touch is realistic, and yet his imagination is poetic and romantic."[35] Likewise, Henry A. Beers, in *Initial Studies in American Letters* (1895), observes that "the weirdly imaginative and speculative character of the leading motive" in Holmes's *Elsie Venner* "suggests Hawthorne's method in fiction, but the background and the subsidiary figures have a realism that is in abrupt contrast with this, and gives a kind of doubleness and want of keeping to the whole."[36]

On several occasions during the heyday of literary realism critics can be found calling for a "revival" of the modern romance, and doing so in ways that may prefigure Norris's own comments in "A Plea for Romantic Fiction."

For instance, in "The Real and the Ideal. A Hint from Nature," John Burroughs writes: "To cast an air of romance, or adventure, of the new and untried, over common facts and common life—to infuse the ideal into the real—that is the secret."[37] The transgeneric modern romance is also described by George Pellew in "The New Battle of the Books," where he observes "even in romances most remote from actual life there are occasional natural touches."[38] The postrealistic transgeneric romance is likewise discussed by James Sully in his 1890 essay "The Future of Fiction." Sully distinguishes between a "pre-scientific age" and the modern scientific age, the one given more to idealism, the other to realism.[39] This realistic tendency in the scientific age has resulted in the development of the novel form, for it is "preeminently the novel which depicts life as social life." Still, argues Sully, even in the "earlier and freer form of wild romance" one can find elements of realism. These earlier romances "discreetly kept the world of real experience within view." And this transgeneric impulse in the earlier romance Sully wishes to carry forward into the modern scientific age of the late nineteenth century. He writes: "We may reasonably insist that the novel, in growing more observant and more learned, shall not wholly separate itself from its parent stem, but retain a trace of the sweet and gracious complacency of the first romance." For an example Sully offers "Mr. Bellamy's little sketch."

One thing that the modern romance did for American authors and critics in the 1880s and 1890s was to provide some way for classifying the postrealistic romantic fiction growing in mass and popularity as the century came to a close. This new wave of romance had its roots in the antebellum romance, but it also moved away from it in some ways. Looking back over the nineteenth century, one critic, in an 1898 essay titled "The Revival of Romance," notes "the new romanticism . . . is not quite the same thing as the old, for it has learned something from the rival by which it has been for a time supplanted." Having learned some lessons from its realistic rival, he says, when we now speak

> of the prospective or accomplished revival of romance, we do not mean the sort of the thing that satisfied the eighteenth century. "The Castle of Otranto," and "Melmoth the Wanderer," will hardly serve as prototypes of the new product . . . but the romanticism that is now carrying

literature before it is a form of art that, like the giant of Greek fable, gains renewed strength from contact with the earth. The romancer is no longer privileged to live in the clouds, or to dispense with the probabilities, but he is nevertheless constrained to idealize and ennoble those aspects of life with which he is concerned, and to view them, not with the scientist, through a microscope, but with the philosopher, *sub specie oeternitatis* [*sic*].[40]

What this critic for the *Dial* observed was a revival of the hybrid romance-novel that not only characterizes some of the popular chivalric romances of the 1890s, as well as the romantic rags-to-riches tales of American success and progress, but also utopian fiction like Edward Bellamy's *Looking Backward*. This association was suggested by Katharine Pearson Woods in 1898: "Mr. Bellamy's great and distinctive merit is that by clothing the Ideal in the apparel of the Real he inspired us with a hope of its speedy attainment."[41] Howells had a similar response to *Looking Backward*. In an 1898 memorial essay for Bellamy, he writes: Bellamy "does not so much transmute our everyday reality to the substance of romance as make the airy stuff of dreams one in quality with veritable experience."[42]

One can also see a transgeneric impulse within the various calls in the late nineteenth century for an "imaginative realism." Dissatisfaction with surface realism, with realism that translates into a flat, analytic or documentary style of fiction, led to several invitations in the 1880s and 1890s for a new realism invigorated with more vision and imagination.[43] Sarah Orne Jewett, for instance, in an 1894 letter writes: "I am sure that one should always try to write of great things in a great way and with at least imaginative realism."[44] One also sees this in Edmund Gosse's plea in "The Limits of Realism in Fiction" (1890) for a "school of novelists with a totally new aim" from that of the realists. The "formula" for this new school must include "a concession to the human instinct for mystery and beauty."[45] And one sees the urge for a revitalized realism in Lewis E. Gates's *Studies and Appreciations* (1900). Perhaps best known as the influential Harvard professor under whom Frank Norris studied for a year and who was immortalized by Norris as the dedicatee of *McTeague,* Gates highlighted the need to fuse romanticism with common life in order to create a "renovating imaginative realism."[46]

The transgeneric features of the modern romance were what led Richard Chase in *The American Novel and Its Tradition* to define the generative dynamic of the "romance-novel."[47] Nineteenth-century critics used the hybrid nature of the modern romance to account for the occasional realistic or novelistic flourishes present in the romances of Sir Walter Scott, Nathaniel Hawthorne, and others. In the second half of the century, this notion was revised to account for the rise of literary realism. Thus, one finds critics noting the effect literary realism has had on the romances of the later nineteenth century. One sees in the second half of the century a type of modern romance that blends the techniques of literary realism with symbol, allegory, myth, the marvelous, the improbable, and often the epic and poetic in order to create a revitalized transgeneric romance that is both a continuation of the earlier romance tradition and a new form that takes advantage of the techniques of literary realism. One can see transgeneric impulses in the various calls for a literature that blends the divergent streams of realism and idealism, and, as shown, critics like William Dean Howells and Katharine Pearson Woods saw Edward Bellamy's *Looking Backward* as doing just that. For writers like Crane, Norris, and London, the romance-novel is the donnée of American literary naturalism, and one of the principle features of the naturalist aesthetic.[48]

The Naturalist Aesthetic

A brief 1899 essay in the *Dial* titled "New Phases of the Romance" by James O. Pierce not only captures the salient features of the modern romance, but also describes the development in the late nineteenth century of a new naturalistic romance-novel. For this reason Pierce's description of the naturalistic romance is a good introduction to the aesthetic theory developed by Norris and other practitioners of literary naturalism.[49] Starting at the end of the essay, we observe Pierce defining a key characteristic of the modern romance in this manner: "The Possible disputing ground with the Improbable, and pushing it to the rear,—this is always the basis of the marvellous, this is always involved in the romantic as its fundamental characteristic" (72). Pierce's romancer, he notes, is an "explorer" who is always "on the farther verge of neutral ground."

The body of Pierce's essay traces through the different phases of the romance tradition from the gothic romances of Horace Walpole through the works of Nathaniel Hawthorne, and then into the latter half of the century. He begins by confirming that there is a difference between the "old romance" and the "modern romance." "In the old Romance," writes Pierce, "realism had no proper place. The more unreal the events chronicled, and the farther removed from the actualities of life, the greater the credit to the imagination of the romancer." But the modern romance can be identified in some ways by its association with realism. There is "no necessity which compels the Imagination to bear false witness in order that it may be honored" in the newer romances. For instance, Sir Walter Scott's followers often incorporated "faithful representations of the characters and motives and deeds of past eras" in their historical romances.

With the arrival of Hawthorne, "an avenue was opened to new fields for the work of the romancer," for the "imagination now found its required material in the social life of a new world." In the old romance "the ancient, the unknown, the mysterious, the startling, were the elements theretofore conceded to be essential to romantic fiction. Hawthorne found, in the simple life of New England, sufficient of these elements to constitute real Romance" (70). In *The Blithedale Romance,* Hawthorne "opened up for the present age a new phase of romantic literature," which Pierce labels the "Romance of Real Life" (70).

Continuing past Hawthorne and into the second half of the century, Pierce notes "at the very time of this exaltation of Realism, there comes a revival of the Romance." One branch of this romantic revival is in the historical romance so popular in the 1890s, but another mode of romance includes naturalistic fiction:

> We have still another school, who aim to show us the romantic features of the everyday life around us; who find the romantic in the midst of the real; in a word, who transmute the Novel into the Romance. Their tales may or may not be labeled romantic, but such is their character. Those elements of the adventurous, the marvellous, or the mysterious, which the romancer is accustomed to seek afar off, among groups of people little known, or in past epochs, these writers find in their own time and among their own acquaintance. The marvels of the present day in science, in the arts, in psychology, and in occult learning and

the dreams of the mystic, the ambitions of the philosopher, and the schemes of the social reformer,—all these are proved to have their romantic phases, which are illustrated for the reading world of to-day. (71)

"This new tendency of Romance," Pierce writes, citing Holmes's naturalistic romance-novel *Elsie Venner* as one example, competes with "Realism in its own field. The realists, to champion the superiority of the Novel, argue that 'truth is stranger than fiction.' But it is the truth that is stranger than fiction, in modern life, which furnishes the material for these new exploits in Romance" (71). The "extraordinary, the marvellous, the startling, which always distinguished the romantic," were never found, "in greater abundance or more ready to the cunning hand of the story-teller, than they are now in the everyday incidents of this wonderful era" (71).

Pierce was not alone in his belief that the intellectual and social milieu of the late nineteenth century provided a wealth of material for the romance. Many authors and philosophers in the late nineteenth century believed that naturalist theory did not exclude the extraordinary and marvelous, but opened up a whole new field for romantic exploration. According to John Herman Randall,

> The idea of "evolution" remained throughout the XIXth century basically a Romantic conception. In its origin, it started with the Romanticists, with Goethe, Herder, Schelling, and Hegel. It was forced on biology after it had been long dominant in history and the social sciences and theology. It was accepted by the cosmic evolutionary philosophers, not as a mere scientific, biological theory, but as a principle of cosmic explanation, as a new primary cause, the true form of God's will and providence—that is, as a new Romantic faith, the greatest and most seductive of the great Romantic faiths.[50]

Randall's observation here is corroborated by several nineteenth-century essays on naturalist theory. For instance, the romantic orientation toward evolutionary theory described by Randall can be seen in Oscar W. Firkins's 1889 essay "The Commonplace in Fiction." Firkins notes that though the "development of science" in "modern life" seemed destined to shatter that "fabulous world" of romance that had so charmed antebellum romancers, this was not to be the case. Firkins says that out of the modern focus on the commonplace, "science has evoked new wonders which take rank with those which it supplanted. This is so undeniable that we involuntarily borrow the old terms of magic and enchantment to describe its achievement, and our poets call its revelations fairy tales."[51] In a similar vein, Hall Caine in 1890 would write that "on every side, in every art, music, the drama, painting, and even sculpture, the tendency is towards Romance. . . . and I do not think I belie the facts when I say that the cry of the Science of this hour is also for Romance."[52]

Caine's provocative connection between science and romance had been suggested a year earlier by Midwestern author Maurice Thompson. Thompson might be best known today for his on-again, off-again friendship with William Dean Howells, whose treatment of certain aspects of Midwestern life, as Gary F. Scharnhorst has noted, bothered Thompson.[53] Thompson, an Indiana poet and author of sentimental and historical novels, at times had little to say in favor of realism, and at times had much to say about the power of the romance. Despite—or perhaps because of—the dim view Thompson had of certain varieties of realism (including some works by Zola and Howells), his 1889 essay "The Domain of Romance" (almost certainly unintentionally, given Thompson's own fictional proclivities) is one of the more fascinating and useful essays when trying to describe the peculiar project of the literary naturalists in the 1890s. So, although Thompson likely would have been disgruntled by the association, his 1899 essay can help us understand the development of the naturalist aesthetic.[54] After discussing in broad terms the realism/romanticism opposition, Thompson makes the following assertion: "Separating realism from romance, I shall presently show that the period between 1840 and 1880 is in fact the great period of romantic achievement in the field of creative thought." The wellspring of this romantic achievement is Charles Darwin. "From my point of view," Thompson writes, "no other name is so honorably or so intimately connected with nineteenth-century romance." To the dismay of the realists calling for a return to the everyday, "out of a mass of commonplace Darwin had wrung the romance whose significance filled the whole area of life." Thompson even suggests that Darwin's romance is transgeneric; and he suggests that Darwin's methodology may serve as a model for future authors. He writes: "I should think fiction-makers might profit greatly by Darwin's method. It was a double method; the microscopic analysis (the attention to the most commonplace details, the worship of facts, so boasted of by the realists) was one lobe, the other was stupendous synthesis" that casts over these details a grand romantic interpretive frame that is even more imaginative, suggests Thompson, than the tales of Edgar Allan Poe.

For sure, Thompson's view of realism is narrow and his view of romance idealized, yet taken at face value, his observations regarding the "domain" of the romance in the late nineteenth century do provide an interesting context for the work of the literary naturalists. Notably, Thompson concludes his essay with some speculation that there would soon arrive a new direction for the romantic spirit in literature, that Darwin himself may give way to "another epoch" in which a "social ideal is to be expressed" by a "coming romancer." This new romance writer will "interpret life in terms of democracy. Not Whitman's democracy of the nude, not the communist's low deal, not the anarchist's lawless brotherhood; but the democracy of love, virtue, charity, sobriety, equality." In retrospect, although the utopian fiction of the 1880s and 1890s takes a slightly different path than the one charted by Thompson, it does in one sense fulfill Thompson's prediction, and utopian fiction is certainly idealistic in orientation and romantic in convention (a topic to be further addressed in chapter 3).

Whether or not one agrees with Thompson's predictions is less important than noting that Thompson perceived naturalist theory—Darwin, in particular—either as romantic in and of itself, or as allowing for, or tending toward, a romantic treatment in fiction. Darwin's "double method" also describes fairly accurately the fictional method of many naturalistic narratives that not only pay close attention to minute detail, but also incorporate elements of naturalist theory that act as vast synthetic frames through which to interpret the smaller details of the narrative. One can view the American naturalistic narrative within the dual context of the nineteenth-century aesthetic tradition in fiction built around the novel/romance tradition, and a line of thought in the late nineteenth century that did not view naturalist theory as inherently irreconcilable with romance. Such a view gives us a critical and historical frame of reference for understanding the development of an American naturalist aesthetic.

Frank Norris and the Naturalistic Romance-Novel

Norris is to American literary naturalism what Howells is to American literary realism. Not only is he the one American naturalist who we can say with assurance had a detailed knowledge of the European tradition of "literary naturalism" and had studied the novels of Zola, but he is also the only major American author in the 1890s who expended considerable effort trying to develop a theory of literary naturalism. The heart of Norris's beliefs about literary genre can be found distributed throughout a small handful of essays. In an early essay, "Zola as a Romantic Writer" (1896), Norris counters critics who have continually read Zola's naturalism as a form of realism.[55] "It is curious," writes Norris, "to notice how persistently M. Zola is misunderstood. How strangely he is misinterpreted even by those who conscientiously admire the novels of the 'man of the iron pen.' For most people Naturalism has a vague meaning. It is a sort of inner circle of realism—a kind of diametric opposite of romanticism, a theory of fiction wherein things are represented 'as they really are,' inexorably, with the truthfulness of a camera. This idea can be shown to be far from right, that Naturalism, as understood by Zola, is but a form of romanticism after all" (71).

Norris was not alone in viewing Zola as a romantic writer. Howells, for one, condemned Zola's "realism" for not being realistic enough. "Strange as it may seem," Howells remarks, "if I objected to him [Zola] at all it would be that he was a romancist [*sic*]. He is natural and true, but he might better be more so. He has not quite escaped the influence of Balzac, who, with Dickens and Gogol, marked the inauguration of the realistic era by taking realities and placing them in romantic relations."[56] A similar remark was made by William Morton Payne in 1901: "As a matter of fact, M. Zola is of the romantic school by instinct, and [in *Travail*] has now given up the attempt to suppress his true character."[57] Wilbur Larremore argues in 1899 that Zola's "perversion" of realism is no more real than the fiction of Victor Hugo.[58] In another instance, George Merriam Hyde notes in 1895 that some believe Zola "excels 'by his epic qualities,'" and "is 'colossally fantastic,' not to say romantic."[59] And W. H. Mallock writes in 1890 that Zola's "realistic" school of fiction actually misrepresents life monstrously and distorts reality through exaggeration.[60]

Norris, Howells, Payne, Larremore, and Hyde base their classification of

Zola as a writer of romances on Zola's works themselves, not on his theory. It is possibly those critics who, basing their judgment on Zola's theoretical writings, subsequently label him as a realist that Norris is referring to in the above quotation. Those critics who try to reconcile Zola's theory with his fiction discover the discrepancy discussed in chapter 1 of this volume. Thus, for instance, a critic for the *Outlook* in 1900 attributes the "Passing of Naturalism" in part to the fact that Zola's fiction was "untrue to the theory under which it was supposed to be done."[61]

Sometimes critics who note the theory/praxis discrepancy do so, like Norris, by specifically pointing to the romantic elements in the French school of "literary naturalism." This is the case in a 1900 article by Charles R. Lepetit.[62] In "The Decline and Fall of the Naturalistic Novel in France," after noting that the naturalistic novel developed out of the age's "general enthusiasm for science," Lepetit suggests that one of the reasons for the decline of the "realistic" naturalistic novel (the hypothetical novel described in Zola's theoretical writings) is that there developed in the 1890s a newfound "mysticism and skepticism" that has worked its way into contemporary narrative (58). Some of this skepticism and mysticism has resulted from the recognition that no matter how far science "may extend the area of our vision, we still remain encircled by an impenetrable wall of mysteries" (58). Furthermore, the decline of the naturalistic novel was inevitable, argues Lepetit, because the aesthetic creed cultivated in *Le roman expérimental* was too restricted to description and observation, with no allowances for an authorial presence, and did not allow for a study of "a most essential element of interest—psychology" (584). Because Zola's theory was so restrictive, authors were forced in their fiction to go far beyond it. "The naturalists . . . could not always curb their aspirations to the exigencies of their doctrine. The restrictions imposed were too many, and some of them too despotic; . . . Even the Goncourts, two of the staunchest partizans of naturalism, were unable to check the flight of their fancy; their novels are quite romantic in plot, and not only unreal, but improbable. And Zola himself, the apostle of scientific exactness, who had no epithets strong enough to revile the 'dreams' and the 'lies' of Hugo's school,—Zola is an allegorist" (838). Furthermore, to talk of Zola's "accuracy of observation is to mistake him entirely: he is essentially a visionary" (838). Zola's "process of grouping the elements of his intrigues round an object . . . which becomes a *living* emblem or symbol, is the process of a poet," and in his fiction Zola has a tendency to "deform and exaggerate everything" (838–39). These "deformations" and "exaggerations" are far removed from the restrictive and realistic aesthetic theory of *Le roman expérimental.*

Norris's own theory of "naturalism" is a far cry from the theoretical writing of Zola.[63] Nevertheless, it is Norris's theory of naturalistic fiction that more accurately describes American literary naturalism in the late nineteenth century. Norris's beliefs about Zola's status as a romance writer, and of naturalism's link with romanticism, are intricately connected by Norris with the idea of literary form. The domain of realism lies in the "smaller details of everyday life, things that are likely to happen between lunch and supper, small passions, restricted emotions, dramas of the reception-room, tragedies of an afternoon call, crises involving cups of tea. Every one will admit there is no romance here" (Norris 71). Having set forth the domain of realism, Norris continues by connecting this domain with the *novel* form: "The novel is interesting—which is after all the main point—but it is the commonplace tale of commonplace people made into a novel of far more than commonplace charm. Mr. Howells is not uninteresting; he is simply not romantic" (71).

Zola, however, *is* romantic. Things do not have to be presented "as they really are" in a romance, and Zola's characters are far from ordinary or representational; they are extraordinary, living in a world unlike our own. Furthermore, argues Norris, "terrible things must happen to the characters of the naturalistic tale. They must be twisted from the ordinary, wrenched out from the quiet, uneventful round of every-day life, and flung into the throes of a vast and terrible drama that works itself out in unleashed passions, in blood, and in sudden death." There can be "no teacup tragedies here" (72). In the naturalistic romance of Zola, "Everything is extraordinary, imaginative, grotesque even, with a vague note of terror quivering throughout . . . It is all romantic, at times unmistakably so, as in *Le Rêve* or *Rome,* closely resembling the work of the greatest of all modern romanticists, Hugo. We have the same huge dramas, the same enormous scenic effects, the same love of the extraordinary, the vast, the monstrous, and the tragic" (72). Thus, "Naturalism," Norris concludes, "is a form of romanticism, not an inner circle of realism" (72).

In his "Weekly Letter" of August 3, 1901, Norris develops in some detail his transgeneric notion of the naturalistic romance-novel. Here he suggests that literary naturalism is the perfect union of realism and romanticism. It takes the best techniques from literary realism—its fidelity to detail, its accuracy in description—and uses these techniques to do what the romance does, that is, to search for deep and hidden truths. Closely aligned with this blending of realism and romanticism in narrative fiction are Norris's beliefs about what he calls "Truth" and "Accuracy." Norris elaborates at some length on the differences between these concepts in his essay "A Problem in Fiction: Truth versus Accuracy" (1901).[64] "Accuracy" in literature, a concept Norris associates with Howells and Tolstoy, is surface realism; it is getting the details right. Just because one is *accurate,* however, does not necessarily imply any degree of *truth.* "Truth" is the more variable term and for Norris means something more abstract, more universal, more closely tied to effect than is "Accuracy." One can achieve a degree of *truth* without necessarily being *accurate* in one's details. The more difficult of these two to achieve is Truth; Accuracy "is the attainment of small minds, the achievement of the commonplace."[65] To illustrate the differences, Norris turns to impressionistic painting. The blue streak of paint on the back of the horse is not accurate: the horse would not have had a blue coat in real life. But stand away from the picture and the "blue smear resolves itself into the glossy reflection of the sun, and the effect is true." For further illustration, Norris offers Sir Walter Scott's *Ivanhoe.* The poetic dialogue between Rebecca and the wounded knight is hardly accurate (nobody could really talk in such a rich and poetic manner in such a situation), but it is *true*: the scene, writes Norris, "is not accurate, it is grossly, ludicrously in-accurate; but the fire and leap and vigor in it; there is where the truth is. Scott wanted you to get an impression of that assault on the barbican, and you do get it." For Norris, accuracy is the handmaiden of realism. Truth is more akin (1) with romanticism, having its antebellum analog in Hawthorne's quest for the "truth of the human heart," and (2) with verisimilitude in narrative fiction (that is, truth is capturing in fiction what *seems* real or true, rather than capturing what *really is,* as in a more direct mimesis).

In the August third "Weekly Letter" Norris emphasized the truth/romanticism relation more so than the truth/verisimilitude connection. After recapping the distinctions between Truth and Accuracy in the first few paragraphs, Norris turns to the question of literary form and its relation to "truth." In order to discuss this relationship Norris turns to a version of the

standard novel/romance distinction as it had been handed down throughout the century. By what standard, asks Norris, shall we recognize "truth"
in a work of fiction? The reply:

> Difficult question. Standards vary for different works of fiction. We
> must not refer Tolstoy to the same standard as Victor Hugo—the one
> a realist, the other a romanticist. We can conceive no standard which
> would be large enough to include both, unless it would be one so vague,
> so broad, so formless as to be without value. Take the grand scene in
> Hernani. How would Tolstoy have done it? He would have brought it
> home as close to the reader as possible. Hugo has elevated it as far as
> he could in the opposite direction. Tolstoy would have confined him-
> self to probabilities only. Hugo is confined by nothing save the limitations
> of his own imagination. The realist would have been accurate. . . . The
> romanticist aims at the broad truth of the thing. (74)

Is this, then, the true difference between the realist and the romanticist?
"Is it permissible to say that Accuracy is realism and Truth romanticism? I
am not so sure, but I feel that we come close to a solution here." Perhaps,
suggests Norris in conclusion, "Truth" lies in the middle of realism and romanticism after all: "and what school, then, is midway between the Realists
and Romanticists, taking the best from each? Is it not the school of Naturalism, which strives hard for accuracy and truth?" (75). Thus, aside from providing some evidence that Norris was not ignorant of the critical distinction
drawn between the novel and the romance, in this letter Norris also described
the transgeneric features of the naturalistic romance-novel: it is a postrealistic
romance that strives for accuracy in detail, while at the same time pursuing
hidden truths buried beneath surface reality.[66]

Norris continued his exploration of the naturalistic romance-novel in "A
Plea for Romantic Fiction" (December 1901), which begins by making a clear
distinction between romanticism and sentimentalism. Fearing that the wave
of second-rate chivalric historical romances popular in the 1890s may have
altered the public's perception of the romance, Norris stresses that "the true
Romance is a more serious business" than the merely amusing sentimen-
talities of these popular historical romances.[67] The romance is "an instrument with which we may go straight through clothes and tissues and

wrappings of flesh down deep into the red living heart" of life (75). Norris then protests against the "misuse of a really noble and honest formula of literature." He writes: "Let us suppose for the moment that a Romance can be made out of the cut-and-thrust business. Good Heavens, are there no other things that are romantic, even in this—falsely, falsely called—humdrum world of today?" (76). Following this "plea" for a romantic fiction, Norris elaborates on the differences between realism and romanticism: "Now, let us understand at once what is meant by Romance and what by Realism. Romance—I take it—is the kind of fiction that takes cognizance of variations from the type of normal life. Realism is the kind of fiction that confines itself to the type of normal life. According to this definition, then, Romance may even treat of the sordid, the unlovely—as for instance, the novels of M. Zola. (Zola has been dubbed a Realist, but he is, on the contrary, the very head of the Romanticists.)" (76). "The reason why one claims so much for Romance," continues Norris, "and quarrels so pointedly with Realism, is that Realism stultifies itself. It notes only the surface of things." The domain of realism is in the "drama of a broken teacup, the tragedy of a walk down the block." The domain of the romance rests in "the wide world for range, and the unplumbed depths of the human heart, and the mystery of sex, and the problems of life, and the black, unsearched penetralia of the soul of man" (78).[68]

Norris's formula for naturalistic fiction is remarkable for several reasons, not the least of which is its resemblance to antebellum formulas for the transgeneric modern romance. What is *Moby-Dick*, we might ask, but a romance that not only explores the "black, unsearched penetralia of the soul of man," but also provides a wealth of detail and description about the activities aboard a whaling boat? Is not Hawthorne's central romantic creed his quest for truth residing in the "unplumbed depths of the human heart"? Indeed, Norris appears to position the naturalistic romance-novel within the broader tradition of the *dark* or *negative* romance. He celebrates, as did Melville in "Hawthorne and His Mosses" (1850), the "power of blackness," and he seeks through narrative those "occasional flashings-forth" of "intuitive Truth"—those "short, quick probings at the very axis of reality." What Norris championed as the naturalistic novel was the postrealistic American romance-novel—a hybrid form that floats between the tendency toward the actual or imaginary, between the tendency toward realism or romanticism, made "naturalistic" through its thematic incorporation of naturalist theory. For Norris, the romance-novel was the narrative form that more than any other allowed for the preservation and combination of both mimetic accuracy and philosophical, psychological, spiritual, or cosmological truth.

Frank Norris: Criticism and Fiction

In much of his fiction Norris seems to have conscientiously tried to implement the naturalist aesthetic developed in his criticism. Evidence for this can be gathered from the works themselves, from some of Norris's own statements about his fiction, and from some of the reaction to his work by late-nineteenth-century reviewers and critics. To begin with, in a well-known letter to Isaac Marcosson, Norris discusses the transgeneric characteristics of *The Octopus:* "[*The Octopus*] is mostly done now and I know when it slumps and I know when it strikes and I think the strikes are the most numerous and important. I know that in the masses I've made no mistake. You will find some things in it that for me—are new departures. It is the most romantic thing I've yet done. One of the secondary sub-plots is pure romance—oh, even mysticism, if you like, a sort of allegory—I call it the allegorical side of the wheat subject,—and the fire in it is the Allegory of the Wheat" (Norris, quoted in Marcosson 238). In this letter Norris describes a text with both realistic and romantic strands. The realist strand is most certainly the "Annixter" plot, in which the wheat farmers band together in an attempt to covertly break the railroad monopoly. This plot comes to a climax with the death of Annixter during the massacre that occurs after the rabbit hunt. The romantic (or even mystic) strand is the "Vanamee" plot that traces Vanamee's quest to recover his lost love, taken by the "Other." These realistic and romantic strands are balanced against each other in the text through the artist/observer Presley and the wheat, with its sociological and symbolic implications. Notably, the British novelist Arnold Bennett referred to *The Octopus* as "romantic-sociological" and heralded it as "almost the only novel yet produced that deals with the activities of modern American life in a manner at once large, serious, and romantic. It is like nothing else, and it succeeds where M. Zola had again and again failed."[69]

In like manner, several of Norris's contemporaries point out the romantic elements in Norris's fiction while making the subsidiary claim that Norris was not a mere imitator of Zola. Hamlin Garland notes that *McTeague* "is without direct prototype. You may say it reminds you of Flaubert in treatment or of Zola in theme, but in reality it is without fellow. Its originality is unquestionable."[70] *The Octopus,* argues Garland, is more in the style of Zola, but it has a "Wagnerian" element that "gives unity to the structure of the novel and produces a most vivid and powerful impression." William Dean Howells also played down the Norris-Zola connection.[71] Howells notes that while Norris "seemed to derive his ideal of the novel from the novels of Zola," Norris's works "owe nothing beyond the form to the master from whom he may have imagined it." In other words, Norris's novels owe no more to Zola "than to the other masters of the time in which Norris lived out his life all too soon." Ultimately, "neither in material nor in treatment are his novels Zolaesque, though their form is Zolaesque, in the fashion which Zola did not invent, though he stamped it so deeply with his nature and his name." This form that Zola and Norris shared, notes Howells, is the epic form, the same form that sixty years earlier William Gilmore Simms had seen as the precursor to the modern romance. Indeed, the one "fault" Howells finds in both Zola and Norris is that they are guilty of an "occasional indulgence of a helpless fondness for the romantic." Of this Norris is guiltier than even Zola. In Howells's view, Norris "quite transcended Zola in the rich strain of poetry coloring his thought, and the mysticism in which he now and then steeped his story."[72]

A similar reaction to Norris's work came from Frederick Taber Cooper in 1899. For Cooper, Norris was a realist who "paradoxical as it may seem . . . has an obstinate and often exasperating vein of romanticism running through all his work."[73] Norris's is a "realism with a half-unconscious symbolism underlying it." Meanwhile, Ernest Peixotto declared that Norris was a "romanticist under the skin," and that "beneath all this outer skin of realism, [is] the romantic spirit that colored all his early life and his earliest works, and therein lies the basic difference between him and some of his most-brilliant successors."[74] Although Peixotto probably does not have a critical understanding of the *romance* or *romanticism* in mind here, a reviewer for the *Critic* in 1900 seems to have a more detailed understanding of the basic novel/romance distinction in mind when he or she writes: "It may be that there are people so misguided as to apply to 'A Man's Woman' that much-abused adjective, 'realistic.' It is the last word in the world to describe what Mr. Norris has done. He has created an improbable man and an impossible woman, put them into an unimaginable situation, and then breathed life into them."[75]

This assessment of *A Man's Woman* might also be used to describe what Norris was doing in *Moran of the Lady Letty*. Norris writes in a letter: "When I wrote Moran, I was, as one might say, flying kites, trying to see how high I could go without breaking the string."[76] Although Norris leaves us to speculate about exactly what he means in this passage, it seems reasonably clear that he is referring to the way in which *Moran* stretches probability to the utmost verge of plausibility, to soar as far into the romantic as possible without "breaking the string" and crossing over into the realm of melodramatic self-parody. One of the remarkable aspects of Norris's statement is that his "flying kites" metaphor not only foreshadows Henry James's "balloon" metaphor in the preface to *The American,* but it also strikes the same chord as James O. Pierce's observation that the romance writer is an "explorer" who is always "on the farther verge of neutral ground." Even more remarkable, this idea of the modern romance writer as seeking the farthest boundaries of probability can be traced back to the eighteenth century. In 1778 Clara Reeve argued that the modern romance should keep "within the utmost *verge* of probability" (Reeve's emphasis).[77] In *The Old English Baron,* Reeve tells us, she has blended a "sufficient degree of the marvellous" with "enough of the manners of real life" to keep her romance just within that utmost verge of probability. In America, similar sentiments can be found in Hawthorne, Melville, and in Poe's "The Philosophy of Composition" (1846).[78] For instance, James O. Pierce cites Hawthorne to the effect that "In writing a romance, a man is always, or always ought to be, careering on the utmost verge of a precipitous absurdity, and the skill lies in coming as close as possible without actually tumbling over."[79]

Finally, regarding the aesthetic blending in literary naturalism of "truth" and "accuracy," or romanticism and realism, Norris's *Blix* stands as an interesting case in point. This prose idyll is a thinly veiled roman à clef in which Norris tells two tales. One tale is of the love that grows between the protagonist, Condy Rivers (the Norris figure), and Travis Bessemer (the "Blix" of the title). The other tale concerns the development of Condy as a writer. Condy's writing career, we are told, began with an "inoculation of the Kipling virus." Condy soon "suffered an almost fatal attack of Harding Davis," and he was even "affected by Maupassant."[80] As a result, Condy "'went in' for accuracy of detail" (114). This penchant for realistic technique does not mean that Condy rejected the *romance,* however. On the contrary, much of Condy's fiction is highly romantic, such as his gothic and grotesque tale "A Victory Over Death" and his novel *In Defiance of Authority* (which bears a resemblance in type to Norris's highly romantic *Moran of the Lady Letty*). Late in the text Norris notes that not only were Condy and Blix entranced by the "uncharted world of Romance," but they also "were a Romance in themselves" (227). This latter comment suggests self-reflexively that the romance of Condy and Blix is contained within the *romance* called *Blix.* Significantly, this reflexive dual perception is intricately tied to naturalist theory, for the "romance" of both Blix and *Blix* emanates from the perception, in reality and in the imagination, of the great, primal forces operating throughout the world.[81]

Jack London and Idealized Realism

Compared with Norris, other American literary naturalists seem relatively uninterested in developing or recording their own aesthetic theories. Harold Frederic, for instance, said very little about aesthetic theory. In one of his letters, Frederic mentions having taken "two liberties with fact, in the interest of romance" in his novel *In the Valley* (1890).[82] A letter to Hamlin Garland, however, makes it clear that Frederic was an admirer of Howells, and he claims that he will be a "Howells man to the end of the war" (455). What "war" Frederic is referring to is open to speculation, although it seems likely that he is referring to the so-called realism war in the 1880s and 1890s, a conflict between proponents of literary realism and, often, sentimentalized versions of the romance that were popular throughout the nineteenth century. Even so, declaring himself a "Howells man" may not indicate that he is trying to follow in Howells's footsteps, for in a subsequent letter to Howells himself, Frederic notes that Howells had never told him whether he "hated 'Illumination'" as much as he feared (475). *Illumination,* the alternative title of *The Damnation of Theron Ware,* was certainly not in the same mode as *The Rise of Silas Lapham* or *A Hazard of New Fortunes* (1889); *Illumination* is much more in the mode of Hawthorne's *The Marble Faun.* This same point had been stated more explicitly by Frederic in an earlier letter to

Howells: "I am the richer for having come to know you—and the stronger for having gained a closer insight into your belief and feelings. It by no means follows that I see all things as you do, or that the work I am going to do will wholly please you, but I am sure both the vision and the performance will be helped by the fact of my knowing you" (269–270). Still, trying to draw firm conclusions about Frederic's aesthetic theory from such scant evidence is impossible. What seems more likely is that Frederic wrote with an understanding of current aesthetic debate, but did not write under the pressure of trying to advocate a particular mode. In fact, Frederic wrote both novels and romances; for all of the romance of *The Damnation of Theron Ware*, *Gloria Mundi* (1898) is essentially a novel of manners.[83]

Like Frederic, the few glimpses we get into the aesthetic theories of Crane, London, and Dreiser are sprinkled throughout their letters, narratives, and other incidental writings. None of these authors wrote enough on the art of fiction that we can construct with confidence their particular aesthetic theory, and some naturalistic authors, such as Crane, may have written their fiction without particular regard to any formulated theory of fiction. Taken as a whole, however, the incidental comments on fiction and narrative strategies made by several American literary naturalists generally confirm Norris's belief that the province of literary naturalism is in the realm of the modern romance.

Although he referred to himself on occasion as a realist, Jack London's "realism" has much more in common with the American *romance* than it does the American *novel*. Even when in the first chapter of *The Road* (1907) London writes, "I quite believe it was my tramp-apprenticeship that made a realist out of me. Realism constitutes the only goods one can exchange at the kitchen door for grub," his declaration jars with the rest of the chapter. In this chapter we find the narrator telling a purely invented sea adventure tale of "my life on the hell-ship *Glenmore*." The stories he weaves for the woman in Reno and her son are imaginative and certainly embellished for effect, and the end result is that the woman's son sees embodied in the narrator "mystery, and romance, and adventure."[84] In this case, then, *realism* is not incompatible with romantic form or a pervading romantic spirit. Indeed, the overall effect seems of a piece with late-nineteenth-century theorists who, like Norris, called for a blending of realistic "accuracy" with a romantic spirit or romantic "truth."

London's occasional references to himself as a realist probably do not indicate that London saw his fiction as participating in the tradition of Howells and James. In fact, in his 1901 review of Norris's *The Octopus,* London remarks that "one feels disposed to quarrel with Norris for his inordinate realism."[85] With this critique of Norris (however ironic in hindsight), London implies that his preferred method of fiction is much more selective than the "inordinate" detail of *The Octopus.* Also interesting about this review is that London finds in *The Octopus* not just realism, but also "something more than realism," and to illustrate this "something more" London quotes an extended passage from Norris's text that exhibits the poetry, myth, and romance underpinning *The Octopus.* This blending of realism and "more than realism" that London observed in Norris has much in common with what London would soon describe as his own fictional method: *idealized* realism.

London discussed his embellished realism in several of his letters. In one of these he begins by discussing the need to be selective in the presentation of realistic detail in order to develop the "distribution of light & shading" in a work (thus allowing the "true picture" to emerge from the mass of detail—compare to Hawthorne's comments on light and shade in the preface to *The House of the Seven Gables*). Then he notes that one of his critics "does not understand that mine is not *realism* but is *idealized realism;* that artistically I am an emotional materialist. My speech, in short, is alien to him."[86] Along these lines, his wife, Joan, would later write of London that his "materialism incarnated his idealism, and his idealism consecrated and transfigured his materialism."[87]

This blending of the actual and the imaginary is often discussed by London as a merging of the natural and the supernatural. In another letter, he writes: "I early learned that there were two natures in me. This caused me a great deal of trouble, till I worked out a philosophy of life and struck a compromise between the flesh and the spirit. Too great an ascendancy of either was to be abnormal, and since normality is almost a fetish of mine, I finally succeeded in balancing both natures. Ordinarily they are at equilibrium; yet as frequently as one is permitted to run rampant, so is the other."[88] A decade later London would explore these same sentiments in his autobiographical roman à clef *Martin Eden* (1909). Eden discovers that there are two "schools of fiction. One treated of man as a god, ignoring his earthly origin; the other treated of man as a clod, ignoring his heaven-sent dreams and divine possibilities." Eden, however, felt that "both the god and the clod schools erred" through "too great singleness of sight and purpose." Rather than align himself with either the purely idealistic school or the purely materialistic school, Eden tried to work out a compromise position. As London writes, Eden's "work was realism, though he had endeavored to fuse with it the fancies and beauties of imagination. What he sought was an impassioned realism, shot through with human aspiration and faith."[89] Like Hawthorne, Eden sought that neutral ground where the actual and the imaginary can interpenetrate.[90] For Eden, this fusion of the actual and imaginary was not a rhetorical "trick," however artistic, but was more akin to what Henry Wadsworth Longfellow wrote of Hawthorne's *Twice-Told Tales:* "Perhaps there is no one thing for which he [Hawthorne] is more remarkable than his power of finding the elements of the picturesque, the romantic, and even the supernatural, in the every-day, the common-place, that is constantly going on around us."[91] The ability to find the romantic in the elements of everyday life was a skill actively pursued by London. In an early letter to the editor of the *San Francisco Bulletin,* London notes that in his travels he has learned "to seize upon that which is interesting, to grasp the true romance of things, and to understand the people I may be thrown amongst."[92] With this skill London can "dream romances" for others in order to earn his "bread & butter."[93]

Stephen Crane's Accurate Romanticism

As with Zola, there appears to be a marked discrepancy between Crane's professed theory of fiction and the fiction itself. Crane wrote very little about the art of fiction. His two brief articles relating to fictional theory have been used at times to help position Crane within the realistic school, but the reportorial nature of these pieces make such claims only speculative.[94] The earlier of these articles, "Howells Discussed at Avon-by-the-Sea" (1891), really only tells us that Crane was aware of both Garland and Howells and to a limited extent was likely aware of the current debates in literary circles regarding aesthetic theory. The more provocative article, "Howells Fears the Realists Must Wait" (1894), makes it clear that Crane was reasonably well versed in Howells's theory of fiction. But the claim that this article is evidence that Crane was himself a realist in the Howells tradition is purely speculative. The majority of this article consists of Howells's thoughts on the novel. "It is the business of the novel," Howells is recorded as saying, "to picture the daily life in the most exact terms possible with an absolute and clear sense of proportion." The interview ends with the following exchange:

> "Mr. Howells," said the other man suddenly, "have you observed a change in the literary pulse of the country within the last four months. Last winter, for instance, it seemed that realism was almost about to capture things, but then recently I have thought that I saw coming a sort of a counter-wave, a flood of the other—a reaction, in fact. Trivial, temporary, perhaps, but a reaction, certainly."
>
> Mr. Howells dropped his hand in a gesture of emphatic assent. "What you say is true. I have seen it coming. . . . I suppose we shall have to wait." (617–18, Crane's ellipsis)

Does Crane feel this recent reaction against realism is good or bad? What kind of fiction does Crane have in mind when he refers to the backlash against realism? Could he be thinking of something other than the boom in historical romance in the 1890s? When he refers to the recent near-victory for realism, is this a subtle reference to his own *Maggie,* which would have been published at about that time?

Answers to these questions can only be speculative, but reading these two articles as generally corroborating the view that Crane believed himself a member of the realistic and novelistic school is given credence in a few incidental references to his own fictional theory found in his letters.[95] For example, in one letter Crane refers to Howells and Garland as his "literary fathers" (1:62). Later in the same letter Crane writes:

> You know, when I left you, I renounced the clever school in literature. It seemed to me that there must be something more in life than to sit and cudgel one's brains for clever and witty expedients. So I developed all alone a little creed of art which I thought was a good one. Later I discovered that my creed was identical with the one of Howells and Garland and in this way I became involved in the beautiful war between those who say that art is man's substitute for nature and we are the most

successful in art when we approach the nearest to nature and truth, and those who say—well, I don't know what they say. They don't, they can't say much but they fight villainously and keep Garland and I out of the big magazines. Howells, of course, is too powerful for them. (1:63)

Again, then, Crane identifies himself with Howellsian realism. The "clever school" of literature that Crane saw himself as rejecting after some earlier experimentation (probably referring to the Sullivan County Sketches) is most likely the decadent school of literature, for it is they who were known for their "witty expedients."[96] A similar sentiment is expressed in two other letters. In one Crane writes: "I decided that the nearer a writer gets to life the greater he becomes as an artist, and most of my prose writings have been toward the goal partially described by that misunderstood and abused word, realism" (1:232). In the other Crane notes that "it has been a theory of mine ever since I began to write, which was eight years ago, when I was sixteen, that the most artistic and the most enduring literature was that which reflected life accurately. Therefore I have tried to observe closely, and to set down what I have seen in the simplest and most concise way" (1:230). Furthermore, writes Crane, "I have been very careful not to let any theories or pet ideas of my own be seen in my writing. Preaching is fatal to art in literature. I try to give to readers a slice out of life; and if there is any moral or lesson in it I do not point it out. I let the reader find it for himself. As Emerson said, 'There should be a long logic beneath the story, but it should be kept carefully out of sight'" (1:230). While in this letter Crane clearly identifies himself with the realist camp, the latter passage does have noteworthy precedents in antebellum criticism. Crane's warning against "preaching" in literature recalls Poe's "Heresy of the Didactic." His comment on the submerged logic of a story echoes both Poe's and Hawthorne's belief that the "meaning" of a story is often presented to the reader through indirection, suggestion, and irony. As Hilda remarks to Kenyon in Hawthorne's *The Marble Faun,* the "highest merit" of literary art lies in its "suggestiveness." Of course, not to bend the argument too far in a potentially unwarranted direction, Crane's refusal to overtly moralize was a hallmark of the better works of the realists, and Crane's position does seem, to one degree or another, to parallel similar positions taken by Howells, James, and others.

As has been made clear by a century of criticism that has struggled to

contend with the "impressionistic" style of Crane's best works, despite the
fact that Crane associated himself with the realistic school of fiction, particularly the realistic creeds of Howells and Garland, his fiction does not
follow in the tradition of the Howellsian novel. Broadly speaking, then, we
note a shift when comparing Crane's work to his professed creed. The discrepancy between Crane's theory and praxis was noted in part by Robert
Stallman in 1951 when he wrote that there was "an ironic contradiction between his theory of creation and his art. It was Crane's theory that the closer
his contact with reality the greater the artist. Yet his art was at its greatest
when he wrote at some distance from the reality he had experienced."[97]
Crane's fiction, argues Stallman, might be better described as a "perfect
fusion of realism and symbolism based on realism"; and in this manner
Stallman comes close to describing the postwar romance-novel. Other critics have at times remarked how one Crane text or another does not quite
follow the form of the realistic novel. In 1902 William Dean Howells com-
plained that *The Red Badge of Courage* did not meet the realistic standard of
texts like *Maggie* and *George's Mother;* in *Red Badge* Crane "lost himself in a
whirl of wild guesses at the fact from the ground of insufficient witness."[98]
Sixty years later Larzer Ziff discussed the "romantic," "chivalric," and "biblical ideals" that form the backdrop of Crane's *Maggie,* and noted that the
"grotesque setting" of *Maggie* was not so much realistic as a "symbolic extension" of the "inner chaos" of Maggie's world.[99] Like Ziff's reading of
Maggie, Edwin Cady's reading of *The Red Badge of Courage* emphasizes the
mixture in the text of realism, romanticism, naturalism, and impressionism.[100]

In fact, Crane's theory notwithstanding, some (though not all, for sure)
of Crane's fiction is written not in the tradition of the realistic novel, but in
something approaching the tradition of the modern romance. In some ways,
works like *Maggie* and *The Red Badge of Courage* participate generally in the
tradition established by Brown, Poe, Hawthorne, and Melville, and continued in the second half of the century by other naturalistic authors like
Holmes, London, and Norris. From the wildly fantastic Sullivan County
Sketches and the Gothic elements in stories like "An Experiment in Misery"
and "The Fire," to the surreal dream-vision sequences of *Maggie* and the
symbolic and allegorical underpinnings of works like *The Red Badge of Courage,* "The Open Boat" (1894), and "A Dark-Brown Dog" (1901), Crane's
fiction repeatedly turned to the aesthetic possibilities of certain conventions
of romantic fiction.

In the end, it is reasonably clear that Crane associated himself with Howells's and Garland's cries for a realistic attention to detail and an accurate representation of external reality. Yet, his pervasive use of romantic irony and his suggestive symbolism positions him, to a degree, in the tradition of Hawthorne, Poe, and Melville as well. Thus, when Crane writes "we are the most successful in art when we approach the nearest to nature and truth," perhaps we can loosely interpret this as a call for an "accurate romanticism": a declaration of the importance of realistic accuracy, coupled with a search for truth that often directed Crane toward naturalist theory and toward a plumbing of the depths of human nature in the manner of Norris, London, Melville, and Hawthorne.

Theodore Dreiser on Knowing *Why*

Like Jack London, Theodore Dreiser had much more to say about sociology, philosophy, and politics than he did aesthetic theory, and, overall, he said nearly as much about his own aesthetic theories as Crane did—which is to say, very little. Clearly, compared with some of the other American literary naturalists, Dreiser's narratives seem the least like romances, the most like novels. And, indeed, Dreiser, more than any other literary naturalist (save, perhaps, Wharton), appears to have had a truer novelistic sensibility. Like Crane, however, Dreiser occasionally referred to himself as a realist, although he just as often decried terms such as "realism" and "naturalism" altogether. For example, in a 1930 article, "On the New Humanists," Dreiser reflects on his association with literary realism:

> Personally I appear to be charged with being a realist. I accept the insult but with reservations. For I fear I do not run true to type—do not march with any clan. Rather I see myself as a highly temperamental individual compelled to see life through the various veils or fogs of my own lacks, predilections and what you will, yet seeking honestly always to set down that which I imagine I see. I am told by some that it agrees with what they see. By others not. But what I think I see is beauty and ugliness, mystery and some little clarity, in minor things, tenderness and terrific brutality, ignorance sodden and hopeless and some admirable wisdom, malice and charity, honesty and dishonesty, aspiration and complete and discouraging insensitivity and indifference.[101]

The difficulty for the literary historian in defining Dreiser's own aesthetic creed is substantial, and perhaps impossible (or even partly irrelevant, in a sense, for in the end it is the novels themselves that we desire to understand and interpret). Still, critics have made valiant efforts, as illustrated by essays such as R. N. Mookerjee's "Dreiser's View on Art and Fiction" and Donald Pizer's "'True Art Speaks Plainly': Theodore Dreiser and the Late-Nineteenth-Century American Debate over Realism and Naturalism."[102]

If we turn our attention to the novels themselves, we discover that works such as *Sister Carrie* and *The Financier* implement a romantic symbolism that seeks to embody and reveal the abstract, hidden forces in nature in a way more reminiscent of the romantics than the realists. Significantly, Dreiser himself seems to have recognized this romantic element in his fiction. As Malcolm Cowley records (while quoting passages from Drieser's *A Book about Myself* [1922] and *Dawn* [1931]): "Dreiser in his autobiographical writings often refers to his own romantic temper. 'For all my modest repute as a realist,' he says, 'I seem, to my self-analy[z]ing eyes, somewhat more of a romanticist.' He speaks of himself in his youth as 'a creature of slow and uncertain response to anything practical, having an eye single to color, romance, beauty. I was but a half-baked poet, romancer, dreamer.'"[103]

Perhaps we can observe Dreiser's debt to the romance tradition of the early to mid-nineteenth century in his use of symbols. In several of his major novels, Dreiser abandons the intratextual realist symbol for the larger romantic symbol, with its universal and/or metaphysical implications. The difference between the "realist" symbol and the "romantic" symbol is that the realist symbol is generally confined within the text and does not point beyond the text to "deeper" or more universal truths.[104] The romantic symbol, on the other hand, typically points beyond the text in its efforts to represent a greater Truth. For example, in Mary Wilkins Freeman's story "A New England Nun," the canary that flutters wildly when Joe enters the cottage is clearly a symbol for the anxiety Louisa feels about Joe disrupting her cloistered environment. This is the extent of the "symbolism" one typically finds in the realistic novel: a completely intratextual symbol that points toward nothing outside of the story but instead captures in an image an analog of some element in the story itself. Such symbols provide texture within the text and are useful for strengthening themes, building associations, and so forth. The same canary-in-a-cage image is used by Frank Norris in *McTeague*. Norris's, however, is a more romantic symbol, for McTeague's canary symbolizes not only McTeague, but *all* of humankind, seemingly trapped like the canary within the confines of natural law and circumstance. Thus, Norris's symbol points outside of the text, or seen another way, it is a device for bringing an abstract concept into the concrete world of the narrative. Dreiser's symbols are more like Norris's, less like Freeman's.[105] For example, early in *The Financier* (1912) young Frank Cowperwood becomes interested in an aquarium at a local fish market. In the tank are a lobster and a squid. Each day Frank and others gather to watch the battle between these two creatures: the lobster attempts to kill and eat the squid; the squid desperately tries to avoid the lobster's claws. In a way, we are told, Frank "was witness of a familiar tragedy in connection with these two, which stayed with him all his life and cleared things up considerably intellectually."[106] As the struggle proceeds, the squid, with only defensive weapons, inevitably begins to lose the battle. "Young Cowperwood put his nose to the glass. He looked solemnly at the lobster. He stayed as long as he could, the bitter struggle fascinating him. He liked to study the rough claw with which the lobster did his deadly work. He liked to stare at the squid and think how fateful was his doom" (12–13). The whole thing "made a great impression on him," for it "answered in a rough way that riddle which had been annoying him so much in the past: 'How is life organized?' Things live on each other—that was it. Lobsters lived on squids and other things. What lived on lobsters? Men, of course! Sure, that was it! And what lived on men? he asked himself. Was it other men?" (13–14).

Thus, the symbolic struggle between lobster and squid does more than simply represent Cowperwood's struggle for survival in the world of finance; it symbolizes the struggle for survival engaged in throughout nature, of which Cowperwood's story is one example. This theme is underscored in another of Dreiser's major romantic symbols in the novel: the black grouper. At the conclusion of the novel, Dreiser appends a brief discussion—titled "Concerning Mycteroperca Bonaci"—of the deceptive powers of the black grouper, a fish whose powers to deceive illustrate the "genius of nature." The fish's power is so cunning as to border on the "spectral" and "unnatural." Dreiser uses the black grouper as a means to ask a difficult metaphysical question about the nature of God: what does it say about the character of an alleged supernatural being that it would create an animal whose very nature requires "subtlety, chicanery, trickery"? Dreiser asks: "Would you say in the face of this that a beatific, beneficent creative overruling power never wills that which is either tricky or deceptive? Or would you say that this material seeming in which we dwell is itself an illusion? If not, whence then the Ten Command-ments and the illusion of justice? Why were the beatitudes dreamed and how do they avail?"[107] With such a question, the black grouper stands as a living symbol of an unsettling theological conundrum, and as a whole the parable of the black grouper serves as a masterful commentary on the main line of the preceding narrative concerning Frank Cowperwood.[108]

Dreiser's urge to use his symbolism to explore the universal and the meta-physical as opposed to the local and the phenomenal may be a symptom of his desire (as seen, for instance, in the description of the black grouper) to know not just the *how* of things, but the *why*. Dreiser wrote about his dilemma in his 1929 essay "What I Believe": "I have pondered and even demanded of cosmic energy to know *Why*. But now I am told by the physicist as well as the biologist that there can be no *Why* but only a *How*, since to know *How* disposes finally of any possible *Why*. Yet, just the same and notwithstand-ing, here I sit at this particular moment, pen in hand and scribbling briskly concerning something about which finally I know nothing at all, and worse yet, about which no one can tell me anything, and yet wishing to know *Why*."[109] Focusing on tensions of this sort in Dreiser's work, Richard Lehan contextualizes Dreiser's major fiction within what Lehan refers to as Dreiser's "romantic dilemma" centered on his "inability to reconcile his romantic aspirations with his belief in a world of physical limits."[110] Perhaps it is the creative alembic of Dreiser's "romantic dilemma" from which Dreiser's own brand of dark romanticism emerges, and which manifests itself in Dreiser's symbolically charged naturalistic novels.

Postscript: Why Romance?

Norris's theory of literary naturalism, as well as the incidental comments on fiction by other American literary naturalists, make clear that rather than rejecting romanticism and the romance form, many of these authors posi-tioned their fiction, to varying degrees, within an ongoing romantic tradi-tion. Even Crane, who did not explicitly position his own work within the tradition of the modern romance, wrote some fiction that falls within the broad tradition of American romance. The question that remains—a question Dreiser would appreciate—is *why* did American literary naturalists turn to the *romance* rather than the *novel* for narrative form?

One answer to this question may lie in some of the broad cultural forces at work in the late nineteenth century that helped push authors like Norris, Crane, and London toward romantic form. The novel of social realism had not won the day in the hearts and minds of the reading public in the 1890s. Dime novels, sentimental novels, crime fiction—all were popular in the late nineteenth century. There was also a resurgence in the popularity of the romance during that time. With the successes of authors like Anthony Hope, Robert Louis Stevenson, George du Maurier, Lew Wallace, H. Rider Haggard, and other Anglo-American writers, the reading public devoured the sentimental, historical, and chivalric romances rolling off the presses on both sides of the Atlantic. So decisive was this swing of the literary pendulum back to the romance and romanticism in the 1890s and 1900s that in 1912 William Dean Howells, with bitter reluctance, was forced to the conclusion that his "long fight" for literary realism "had been a losing fight," for the "monstrous rag-baby of romanticism is as firmly in the saddle as it was before the joust began, and . . . it always will be, as long as the children of men are childish."[111]

Is it unreasonable to assume that the American literary naturalists of the 1890s were likewise caught up in this shift back to the romance and romanticism and away from the realistic novel? For some time now critics have noted that American literary naturalists were fairly in unison in their rejection of the popular cut-rate romanticism of the late nineteenth century; but to make this observation and leave it unqualified is potentially misleading. It is true that in general the American literary naturalists were exasperated by the steady stream of second-rate sentimental and historical romances that poured from the presses in the late nineteenth century, but they were not opposed to the romance, or even for the most part to romanticism. It is for this very reason that Norris makes such a point at the beginning of "A Plea for Romantic Fiction" of distinguishing between sentimentalism and romanticism: by making this distinction Norris is able to reject the popular second-rate romances without rejecting romanticism or the romance form. Just as the naturalistic authors were tired of the endless supply of chivalric romances trailing behind the clouds of Ben Hur's glory, they were equally tired, as Norris points out, of the staid and whitewashed efforts of the Howellsian realists.

It is not entirely accurate to claim that the American literary naturalists rejected the "excesses" of romanticism.[112] In fact, as Norris argues, in one sense it is the "excesses" of romanticism that appeal to the naturalistic author the most. These "excesses" allow for the building of "vast and terrible dramas." Moreover, the literary naturalists, like Howells, James, and others in the second half of the century, appreciated serious literary art, whether novelistic or romantic. In fact, at a time when the American literary world had almost entirely forgotten Melville, London stands out as a champion of Melville's fiction. Norris, London, and Crane were all admirers of Poe, and everyone was aware of Hawthorne's achievement. With the triple impact of the tidal shift toward the romance and romanticism, the dissatisfaction felt by Norris and others with the creative constraints placed on them by Howellsian realism, and the high regard American naturalistic authors held for such antebellum romancers as Hawthorne, Poe, and Melville, it is not surprising that they occasionally turned to romantic forms for their own art. Even James, we recall, wrote *The Turn of the Screw* and "The Jolly Corner."

Still, although these cultural forces played a role in their tendency toward the romance, it is probably the formal aspects of the romance that held the greatest appeal for the school of naturalistic fiction in America. Norris believed that the romance allowed for exploration of the extraordinary, the grotesque, the strange, and the unusual. It allowed the naturalistic author to narratize the "terrible drama" of life and to allow that drama to be resolved in heightened or idealized violence, passion, and bloodshed. The romance allowed the author to introduce into these dramas "enormous scenic effects" (as in *The Octopus*), a "love of the extraordinary" (as in *A Man's Woman*), the "vast" (*The Pit*), the "monstrous" (*McTeague*), and the "tragic" (*Vandover and the Brute*).

London also expressed his belief in the aesthetic power of the "terrible" and the "tragic." In his 1903 essay on the subject, he notes the paradox that people both love and hate horrific fiction like that of Poe and Ambrose Bierce.[113] He suggests (using the concept of evolution as a backdrop) that the "horrific" appeals to some primal instinct in man, and he goes on to suggest that all great fiction has at its base either a sense of the dreadful or of the tragically dramatic. He would repeat these beliefs in a letter in 1910: "The question at issue is really literature. What constitutes a short story, or the stuff of a short story? Go over the great short stories that are classics, and you will find that they deal, ninety-nine times out of a hundred, with the terrible and tragic."[114]

As Norris made clear, the romance allowed for the free reign of the creative imagination, while the realistic novel is regrettably confined to "probabilities." It was largely because the romance allowed for a latitude, as Hawthorne would say, in "fashion and material" that American literary naturalists in the nineteenth and early twentieth centuries turned to the romantic form. This freedom of conception and construction in the romance allowed for the narratization and exploration of naturalist theory to an extent not allowed in the *novel*. The romance allowed authors like Norris, Crane, and London to incorporate into their fiction the often abstract and hidden forces that naturalist theory revealed operating in nature. To do so they necessarily turned toward symbol, allegory, myth, and other narrative modes common to the American romance. Thus, in American literary naturalism, naturalist theory is elevated to the status of myth: it performs the function of providing a metaphysical backdrop upon which to build narratives of human experience and interaction, much in the manner of any idealist philosophy, the transcendentalists of the early nineteenth century included.

To borrow a phrase used by Richard Chase, America in the nineteenth century can be largely characterized as a "culture of contradictions."[115] For Chase, the American imagination was fired by the aesthetic possibilities of alienation, contradiction, and disorder.[116] The tendency in American fiction toward the romance is an outgrowth of these concerns, as the romance, rather than the novel, provided the flexibility needed to aesthetically frame the contradictions, the disorder. From Charles Brockden Brown through Herman Melville, antebellum romancers constructed narratives that explored the epistemological and metaphysical vagaries of nature and the human soul. In the latter half of the nineteenth century, Crane, Norris, and London were impressed by a similar epistemological uncertainty, a similar concern for disorder, moral and physical degeneration, and contradiction. The roots of these mysteries lay in Norris's "unplumbed depths of the human heart," and the instrument for bringing them to the surface was, more often than not, the modern romance.

3
Naturalism and Utopia

Viewing literary naturalism as the thematic exploration of naturalist theory has the surprising result of joining together two seemingly very different literary types. Just as Frank Norris in *Vandover and the Brute,* Stephen Crane in *Maggie,* and Theodore Dreiser in *Sister Carrie* all explore naturalist theory, so too—to an extent—do Edward Bellamy in *Looking Backward,* William Dean Howells in *A Traveler from Altruria* (1894), and Charlotte Perkins Gilman in *Herland* (1915). These idealistic utopian novels, from one perspective, are as much a product of the late-nineteenth-century naturalist paradigm shift as *McTeague, The Sea-Wolf,* and *The Damnation of Theron Ware.* As radically different as *Looking Backward* is from "The Open Boat," elements rising out of philosophical and scientific naturalism play a central thematic role in each of these narratives.

Certainly in terms of their participation in the school of "literary" naturalism, one principal difference between a text like *A Traveler from Altruria* and *McTeague* lies in how the naturalist theory is used in the narrative. For instance, the theory can be used to thematically justify or contextualize a plot of *incline* or a plot of *decline.* It can aid in the presentation of an optimistic or pessimistic interpretation of man and experience. The theory can be accepted, questioned, or rejected. For sure, reading *Sister Carrie* against *Herland* or *The Awakening* against *Looking Backward* suggests the provocative ways in which utopian fiction and the texts traditionally associated with literary naturalism operate in what we might call a cultural dialogue. Seen in this light, a work like "Life in the Iron Mills" becomes a study in compromise, balancing the bleakness of a harsh factory environment against the promise of faith and charity.

At risk of overusing what has proven a useful taxonomic system during the last fifty years, one does notice that lumping together certain late-nine-teenth-century utopian novels with the classic texts of American literary naturalism suggests a loose division between a "light" or "positive" literary naturalism and a "dark" or "negative" literary naturalism. Positive literary naturalism is substantially idealistic, progressive, and often utopian, as in Bellamy's *Looking Backward.* In contrast, negative literary naturalism typi-cally questions the often monological, millennialist, and optimistic assump-tions found in positive literary naturalism.[1] Norris's *McTeague* and *Vandover and the Brute,* Crane's *Maggie* and *The Red Badge of Courage,* and Dreiser's *Sister Carrie* can best be characterized as examples of negative literary natu-ralism. Positive literary naturalism, on the other hand, seems to have found its primary outlet in the wave of utopian fiction that flooded presses during the 1880s, Bellamy's *Looking Backward* being both the model and most re-nowned example. These positive and negative orientations, however, are only broad distinctions useful for critical taxonomy. Often a text will exhibit both positive and negative orientations. Texts like Norris's *The Octopus* and *The Pit,* as well as Dreiser's *Jennie Gerhardt* (to a lesser extent) and London's *The Sea-Wolf,* are neither wholly negative nor wholly positive, but blend positive and negative tendencies within the narrative, as in the juxtaposition of the Vanamee and Annixter plots in *The Octopus,* the dialogues between Maud Brewster and Wolf Larson in *The Sea-Wolf,* or earlier, in the blend of faith and failure in "Life in the Iron Mills."

The roots of both positive and negative literary naturalism are contained within naturalist theory itself. The darker Malthusian current running just below the surface in the "natural selection" paradigm of Charles Darwin stands in stark contrast to the progressive and utopian evolutionary theory of Herbert Spencer and his American disciple John Fiske. Spencer's "uto-pian" theory of evolutionary progress implied that humankind simply had to submit itself to the cosmic process that was ever urging onward toward greater and higher goods and not fret over the minor "adjustments" nature had to make along the way.[2] Spencerian evolutionary thinking claimed that evolutionary forces were gradually producing more complex and stable or-ganisms, and this process opened up the possibilities for social, biological, moral, and environmental perfection.[3] Spencer and like-minded theorists in the nineteenth century, in a sense, created a metaphysic of evolution that layered Darwinian thinking with a progressive or optimistic teleology.[4] The darker implications of naturalist theory are revealed when one focuses not on the "progress" of evolution, but on those moments of "adjustment" along the way. This focus exposes the violent and brutal implications of Spencer's "survival of the fittest" model, and Darwin's paradigm of natural selection itself highlights the endless struggle, the violence, the accidental and chance elements inherent in the operation of natural law.

In 1900 Henry C. Payne wrote: "Now, perception and feeling reach both ways, and every state of mind and every act is determined by negative as well as positive compulsions. This needs not to be proved, for experience every-where witnesses to it. It is shown in the equally imperative 'do' and 'do not' of every civil, moral, and religious code, in the divergent perceptions and sentiments of good and evil that determine all conduct, in every fear that waits upon every hope, in every hope that waits upon every fear."[5] One way to view nineteenth-century American literary history is to see American literature as reacting with and against these "negative as well as positive compulsions." American literature since the Enlightenment can be seen as a vast cultural exchange, with "positive" and "negative" voices engaging in a dialogue through the medium of literature. Throughout the nineteenth century, "negative" orientations challenge that seemingly narrowed focus positive orientations have on the *good*. Negative orientations expose the *evil* with which good is metaphysically, and often hopelessly, tangled.

American literary naturalism has a place within this nineteenth-century cultural dialogue. Building off of the premise that, to an extent, American literary naturalism is the intellectual offspring of Enlightenment science and antebellum romanticism, this chapter begins with a look at how Enlightenment thinking and literature contains both "positive and negative compulsions." Attention is then turned to a discussion of positive and negative romanticism. To explore this nineteenth-century dialogue is to examine the intellectual genesis of American literary naturalism itself.

Literary Chiaroscuro

To trace the roots of naturalist theory to the Enlightenment is not new. Zola himself did so in *Le roman expérimental,* and contemporary critics since Horton and Edwards (1952) and Walcutt (1956) have followed suit. In the

Enlightenment, through the diverse work of scientists and philosophers such as Isaac Newton, René Descartes, John Locke, James Hutton, Carolus Linnaeus, Jean-Jacques Rousseau, and Georges Buffon, a biblically based cosmology and theory of man gave way in academic circles to a more rationalist, humanist, positivist train of thought that in its concern with the empirical world was largely secular. In *The Democratic Enlightenment* Donald Meyer notes that the movement found its roots in the scientific revolution of the seventeenth century, which allowed for the possibility of a science of humankind: a social science.[6] As Meyer observes, there are a number of assumptions central to Enlightenment doctrine: first, Nature's workings are not unknowable or mysterious; man possesses a potential mastery of matter. Second, the political and social aspects of the universe are ultimately "testable"; that is, they can be experimented with and even altered. Third, human behavior exhibits predictable traits and patterns, and these patterns are universal and general. Fourth, Enlightenment thinkers rejected the notion of a God-centered universe in favor of one that is oriented toward humankind. By rejecting a Judeo-Christian providential historiography, they were better able to claim that society is knowable, changeable, and possibly perfectible. With the rejection of Calvinistic notions of natural depravity came the belief that human nature is fundamentally good, not evil.

For American thought, perhaps one of the Enlightenment's greatest legacies was a post-Calvinistic notion of progress. The belief of many at this time was that man—through application of his rational mind and a scientific exploration of nature—can know, change, and ultimately perfect the individual, government, and society. This movement toward perfection is in large part inevitable, because man inherently desires to improve his condition. Moreover, because man is fundamentally good, he will be concerned with the improvement of society as well.[7] This optimistic, progressivist orientation can be seen in the writings of Thomas Jefferson and Thomas Paine, as well as in John Wise's and Jonathan Mayhew's political sermons, and it certainly played a role in the drafting of the *Declaration of Independence*. Its classic statement in eighteenth-century American literature can be found in Benjamin Franklin's *Autobiography* (1771–1788).

Certain contemporaries of Benjamin Franklin were more willing than Franklin to expose the "negative" side of Enlightenment doctrine.

Crèvecoeur's *Letters from an American Farmer,* far more than Franklin's *Autobiography,* challenges the idealistic impulses contained within "positive" Enlightenment theory. The twelve letters that comprise the text operate at two levels: on the surface Crèvecoeur's farmer/narrator, James, paints an idyllic picture of agrarian nationalistic prosperity; beneath the surface James paints a portrait of political upheaval, violence, and discord. Norman Grabo puts it this way: "St. John's sketches distribute themselves according to two thematic emphases: first, the confident celebration of Arcadian possibilities under a political system that was essentially mild and enabling; second, the horror that accompanied the irrational repudiation of that system. Put somewhat differently, St. John's sketches depicted both the American dream and its brutal subversive nightmare."[8]

These dual principles are explicitly foregrounded at the beginning of the second letter, where James observes, "Good and evil, I see, are to be found in all societies, and it is in vain to seek for any spot where those ingredients are not mixed."[9] Later, the attempt at a detailed, optimistic and nationalistic portrait of how a community is born and flourishes in America (in letters 3–8) stands in stark contrast to letter 9 on Charles Town. Here James comments at length on the terrible practice of slavery, concluding the letter with a brutal anecdote about a slave in a cage who is eaten alive by predatory birds and insects. James observes the apparent paradox that Charles Town, situated on the richest land, practices slavery, is morally deficient, and does not boast the most industrious and prosperous laborers; while, on the other hand, people who live in harsher climates (the Nantucketeers, for example) often exhibit stronger moral character and are more prosperous and industrious. If moral development is directly connected to the landscape, Charles Town should house the most moral and prosperous Americans. This letter is thus tied to the introductory letter, where the moral new world is set up against the corrupt old world. Notably, Charles Town, suggests James, is the most "European" of all American cities. This darker current running through the ninth letter is continued in the tenth letter, "On Snakes; And on the Humming-Bird," in which James presents descriptive anecdotes about the violence in nature, centering on warring snakes and hummingbirds.

In the final letter, "Distresses of a Frontier Man," the dark and subversive element in the letters comes to its thematic conclusion. The outbreak of the Revolutionary War destroys the idealized fabric of James's existence and shatters the society on which he depends. James and his family are forced, like Huck Finn, to "light out for the Territory ahead of the rest" and seek refuge in an Indian village in the remote wilderness. This flight into the frontier presents a skeptical challenge to the tributes to westward expansionism and American exceptionalism residing in the more positive Enlightenment doctrines of Franklin and Jefferson. In this respect, we can see Crèvecoeur's *Letters from an American Farmer* as embodying a darker thematic strain that calls into question Enlightenment optimism regarding the progress of humankind.

Positive and Negative Romanticism

One of the first modern critics to develop a theory of romanticism that divides it into positive and negative streams was Morse Peckham, in his essay "Toward a Theory of Romanticism" (1950).[10] Peckham first emphasizes how romanticism marked a distinct change from traditional philosophical orientations that had been in place since the time of Plato. Peckham writes, "the shift in European thought was a shift from conceiving the cosmos as a static mechanism to conceiving it as a dynamic organicism" (9). It was a shift from viewing the universe like a watch (mechanical, uniform, rational, changeless) to viewing it instead like a tree (organic, imperfect, changing). According to Peckham, there were two sides to this dynamic organicism: positive romanticism and negative romanticism. For Peckham, the shift from classicism to romanticism is embodied in the romantic artist who passes from a trust in the universe (classicism) to a period of doubt and despair of any meaning in the universe (negative romanticism), and then to a reaffirmation of faith in cosmic meaning and goodness (positive romanticism). The transition from the first stage to the second is analogous to a spiritual death; from the second to the third, a spiritual rebirth (16–17). The rebirth into positive romanticism is the affirmation of an optimistic dynamic organicism. It is the "record of a process; it affirms the unconscious mind and the creative imagination; it affirms the principle of the living universe; it affirms diversitarianism; and it is a fully developed symbolism, an organic symbolism in which the shooting of the [Ancient Mariner's] albatross is without symbolic power unless it is thought of in terms of the power and the interrelations of the various symbolic units" (21). Negative romanticism, on the other hand, is the expression of the attitudes, the feelings, and ideas of a man who has abandoned static mechanism but has not yet arrived at a reintegration of his thought and art in terms of dynamic organicism. Peckham writes:

> As various individuals, according to their natures, and their emotional and intellectual depths, went through the transition from affirming the meaning of the cosmos in terms of static mechanism to affirming it in terms of dynamic organicism, they went through a period of doubt, of despair, of religious and social isolation, of the separation of reason and creative power. It was a period during which they saw neither beauty nor goodness in the universe, nor any significance, nor any rationality, nor indeed any order at all, not even an evil order. This is Negative Romanticism, the preliminary to Positive Romanticism, the period of Sturm und Drang. (21–22)[11]

Upton Sinclair discusses his own literary philosophy in terms that sound similar to the move from classicism to positive romanticism that Peckham describes. In his 1906 essay "What Life Means to Me," Sinclair not only describes his conversion to socialism in a manner that suggests the dialectical move (in Peckham's view) from a negative orientation to a higher, positive orientation, but he also discusses his art in terms of the modern romance.[12] Sinclair records how the illusory optimism of his youth was shattered with the dual realization that writing popular dime novels no longer satisfied him artistically because they could not express the deeper burdens of his soul, and that the publishers of his fiction were not interested in his more artistically satisfying work. In this "nightmare" realm Sinclair saw the world as "a place where wild beasts fought and tore one another without purpose and without end" (592). After his discovery of socialism, however, Sinclair experienced an intellectual and artistic rebirth. With this rebirth, Sinclair writes, "[I] learned to identify my own struggle for life with the struggle for life of humanity" (592). This higher vision enabled Sinclair to discover his "own place in the world, and the purpose and meaning of my experience" (592). Thus, Sinclair moved through both positive and negative naturalistic orientations. In his "nightmare" phase he interpreted experience negatively, which revealed the violence and brutality of nature. In his socialist phase he interpreted experience positively, which exposed the utopian possibilities lying within experience, and the inexorable evolutionary movement toward a more perfect society.

The first product of his positive orientation, Sinclair notes, was *The Jungle* (1906). This book was "the result of an attempt to combine the best of two widely different schools; to put the content of Shelley into the form of Zola— a method which I believe will come more into favor as the revolutionary Socialist movement finds its voice" ("What Life Means" 594). Although Sinclair does not elaborate further on what he believes is the hybrid nature of *The Jungle,* it seems reasonable to suggest that Sinclair saw his text as combining Shelley's romanticism and mystic idealism with Zola's social texture and attention to detail. If this is the case, then Sinclair, like Norris and London, saw his works as participating generally in the tradition of the modern romance.

The cultural dialogue between positive and negative romanticism is illustrated in one of the more influential texts of the first half of the nineteenth century: Thomas Carlyle's *Sartor Resartus* (1833–1834). In fact, Peckham develops his theory of romanticism largely with the aid of the three central chapters of Carlyle's book—"The Everlasting No," "The Center of Indifference," and "The Everlasting Yea"—which detail Teufelsdröckh's spiritual death and rebirth. Teufelsdröckh's journey, argues Peckham, is analogous to that of the romantic artist who passes through a stage of negative romanticism (the Everlasting No and the Center of Indifference) en route to a spiritual/aesthetic reaffirmation of positive romanticism (the Everlasting Yea).

Perhaps the classic expression in antebellum American letters of a positive romanticism comes from Ralph Waldo Emerson. For Emerson, art— "nature passed through the alembic of man"—was subsumed completely, as René Wellek writes, "into a monistic world view in which it functions as a language of ciphers revealing, in fluid transformations, the essence of a nature that is divine and good and luminously beautiful."[13] The poet is exalted by Emerson as both genius and prophet. His imagination, relying on inspiration and intuition, submits to the streams emanating from the Oversoul, and thus "creates works of organic, healthy, proportionate beauty reflecting and embodying the central Idea of the universe."[14]

In contrast to Emerson's positive romanticism is the tradition of negative romanticism: a tradition that in America includes Charles Brockden Brown, Edgar Allan Poe, Nathaniel Hawthorne, and Herman Melville. The differences in these two traditions of American romanticism can be illustrated in the contrast between Emerson's affirmed correspondential symbology and Edgar Allan Poe's dark, negative romanticism. Like Emerson, Poe's poetic is formed around an idealistic metaphysic (for Poe, the transcendental realm of supernal beauty), but unlike Emerson, Poe does not place much faith in one's ability to achieve a metaphysical or artistic apotheosis. According to Poe, the artist does not have ready access to the universal or transcendental realm.

For Poe, the aim of poetry is a momentary glimpse of supernal beauty. He believes that poetry—the "rhythmical creation of beauty"—can be built rationally (unlike Emerson's heavy reliance on Intuitive Genius) by the artist, and that the poem should be geared toward a unity of effect. The guiding force behind the creation of a poem, Poe argues, should be its "music," while the guiding principle of the tale should be a carefully constructed plot. Although both metaphysics are idealistic, Poe's separation of the romantic artist from the supernal realm lays the metaphysical foundation for his negative romanticism. Rather than being built around a direct correspondence with the ideal, Poe's art is instead built around "indefinite" sensations—the Theory of the Vague—as described in his "Letter to B—." Poe's negative romanticism translates into the multivalent and ambiguous symbolism and abrupt, or "negative," closure of *The Narrative of Arthur Gordon Pym* (1838), as well as into the dark, ambiguous gothic of "Ligeia," "The Fall of the House of Usher," and "Silence—A Fable."[15] As with Poe, Brown, Hawthorne, and Melville raise metaphysical and epistemological questions that undercut or skeptically frame transcendental idealism and American exceptionalism exemplified in Emerson and Whitman.

In American literature, at any given point, light and dark valences undoubtedly operate simultaneously.[16] One can see these valences in the contrasting orientations of Franklin and Crèvecoeur, of Emerson and Melville, and in American naturalistic narrative through a comparison of texts as dissimilar as Bellamy's *Looking Backward* and Dreiser's *Sister Carrie*. And perhaps one can even see these opposing orientations in American realism: Edwin Cady has applied Peckham's dialectical paradigm to American literary realism, locating positive and negative strands in Mark Twain, William Dean Howells, and Henry James.[17]

Realism and Idealism

Before exploring American literary naturalism within a positive/negative framework, it will prove useful to briefly examine another binary opposition central to late-nineteenth-century aesthetic theory and philosophy: the conflicting aesthetic and philosophical implication of realism versus idealism.[18] In the 1890s the realism/romanticism and novel/romance debate took on a slightly different appearance, one that helps to clarify the generic characteristics of American naturalistic narrative.[19] In a March 1890 article titled "The Relation of Art to Truth," the English critic W. H. Mallock begins his essay by pointing to the "one particular question" that has obsessed both European and American critics and writers: that of the "rival claims of realism and idealism in literature; or the relation of art, and particularly of artistic fiction, to truth." "Artistic fiction," writes Mallock, "means the romance or novel; and novels and romances are now read by everybody." The question, Mallock says, is "Should fiction, to be good artistically, be realistic, or idealistic?" First, "should the artist be realistic, or the reverse, in dealing with manners, scenery, and circumstance?" Second, "should he be realistic, or the reverse, in dealing with the human character?" In answer Mallock writes:

> The extreme of realism is wrong for this reason: it endeavors to represent manner and circumstances precisely as they are perceived by our own ears and eyes. Now what our own ears and eyes perceive of things, is the surface; and the surface, though it expresses what lies below the surface, also obscures it. . . . The extreme of idealism is wrong for the opposite reasons. If, instead of describing exactly manners and places that exist . . . a writer introduces us to what is altogether a dreamland . . . belonging to no place or period, and suggesting no place or period, the characters fail to have for us either existence or human interest; or, compared with what it otherwise might have been, the interest is indefinitely attenuated.[20]

Mallock eventually suggests that literary art must avoid the extremes of realism and idealism and should blend the two in such a way that truth is preserved. By "truth" he means something that is not purely realistic but nevertheless is bound by "what human nature may be, or may make of itself; just as an architect, in designing a cathedral, may make his designs unlike anything that has been, or has ever been dreamed of, but he must make them in strict accordance with the structural capacities of his material, which have been the same since time began" (46).

By proposing that literary art seeks to represent what human nature "may make of itself," Mallock seems to suggest that literary art focuses its attention on the optative. Thus, his theory of art is weighted toward the preservation of a progressive, if not boldly optimistic, philosophical orientation. If this is indeed Mallock's position, then his theory would privilege a positive rather than a negative orientation in naturalistic fiction. In this Mallock was hardly idiosyncratic. One can find numerous critics arguing that fiction, particularly idealistic/romantic fiction, should point humanity toward a more elevated state. F. Marion Crawford, for example, writes in his monograph *The Novel: What It Is* (1893) that "the realist proposes to show men what they are; the romantist [*sic*] tries to show men what they should be."[21] Crawford's definition of the novel as an "intellectual artistic luxury" and a "pocket stage" may strike us as highly simplistic; nevertheless, his use of the basic realism/romanticism, novel/romance distinctions in his monograph demonstrates the type of critical transformation noted so clearly by Mallock; that is, the adaptation and incorporation of the standard novel/romance distinction in the growing debate between realism and idealism.[22]

Howells's opinions regarding the proper domain of realistic fiction were not quite as optimistically oriented as those of Mallock and Crawford. While Howells encouraged American authors to focus their literary endeavors upon the "smiling aspects" of life, he was also one of the first, and most emphatically enthusiastic, American champions of Zola's works—not to mention Crane's *Maggie* and Norris's *McTeague*—all of which deal with what Howells would call in *Literature* (1899) the "wolfish problems of existence." Perhaps the crux of the matter is to be found in *Criticism and Fiction* (1891).[23] Here, Howells's call for a sanitized American realism seems to have been prompted by two concerns. First, when Howells refers to the "smiling aspects of life," he is doing so in the hope that American realists will create an American literature that is a faithful representation of American reality. Because "the strength of the American novel is its optimistic faith," and because we live in a nation with so "few shadows and inequalities in our broad level of prosperity," American novelists "concern themselves with the more smiling aspects of life, which are the more American" (58–74). Howells's logic here is simple enough: if the reality of American life is characterized more by "smiling" than by "wolfish" aspects of life, and if a truly American novel will reflect as faithfully as possible American life, then the American novelist should focus on the lighter rather than the darker side of life.

Howells was also concerned that American authors maintain a ready awareness that their fiction will be read by impressionable young women. Because in the nineteenth century young women read novels perhaps more than any other group in America, the American novelist had a responsibility to monitor the type of fiction produced and placed in their hands, a point not lost on Howells's Fulkerson in *A Hazard of New Fortunes,* who notes that women comprise 75 percent of the reading public.[24] Fulkerson seeks to use this fact in a targeted marketing campaign. But for Howells and some of his contemporaries, of course, the main concern is that too much literature emphasizing the seamy side of reality could give a young person a false view of American reality.

This position has less to do with the generic boundaries of realistic fiction than with social responsibility. Howells would still maintain that the domain of realism, the raw material that the realistic novel can draw upon, is not circumscribed by moral precepts, but is ultimately only bound by *what is real.* It is from this perspective that one can understand his advocacy of such wolfish fictions as *Maggie* and *McTeague.* At times, Howells could be emphatic about this broad domain for realism. Although virtually "every novelist" would agree that his art would improve if he could divorce it from an almost obsessive compulsion to "treat freely the darker aspects of the favorite passion," nevertheless, writes Howells, "as I have shown, the privilege, the right to do this, is already perfectly recognized" (*Criticism and Fiction* 74). The notorious "smiling aspects of life" phrase is thus not Howells's definitive statement on the material that can be used by the literary realist; it is a view of what the central characteristics of American reality are, a version of American exceptionalism.

Even so, the realism/idealism debate was not a purely American phenomenon. For instance, in 1893 the French author and critic Paul Bourget wrote that "among the philosophic terms commonly employed by the critics and the public on the appearance of literary works there are few which are more frequently used, or which have given rise to more discussion than 'Idealism' and 'Realism.'"[25] The broad, international association of the novel with realism, and the romance with idealism, is perhaps stated most succinctly by

Hjalmar Hjorth Boyesen in his article "The Great Realists and the Empty Story-Tellers" (1895), where he writes: "Who that has read Rousseau's 'Confessions' will fail to remember the emphatic avowal that he was unfitted for life by the reading of novels? To be sure, the novels he read were of a highly romantic, or, as it is euphemistically called, 'idealistic,' kind, which represented a condition of things that never was on land or sea."[26] "The most modern novel," Boyesen argues, "which should not be confounded with the romance—has set itself this very task of exploring reality, and gauging the relative strength of the forces that enter into our lives and determine our fates." Eliot's *Middlemarch* and Thackeray's *Vanity Fair* are good examples of the "modern realistic novel," because they deal "so searchingly with typical persons and conditions" and thus scrupulously exclude "everything that does not appertain to the experience of the average human being, in the sphere of society with which it deals." Boyesen is "distinctly conscious of being indebted to Thackeray" for having led him out of the "moon-illumined magic night" of "German romanticism."[27]

These essays by Mallock, Bourget, and Boyesen attest to, among other things, the way in which after the advent of realism the novel/romance distinction was being subsumed within the developing realism/idealism debate (itself a modification of the realism/romanticism polemic). The significance of this development for a fuller understanding of naturalistic fiction in America is readily observable. The spirit that underlies calls for a literary idealism (or, in other terms, a positive romanticism) in literature is akin to the spirit that lies behind positive naturalistic fiction. As one critic suggested in 1893, "Romanticism is to idealism in the novel what the garment is to the soul."[28] That is, a spirit of idealism manifests itself in the production of romanticism in literature. In the late nineteenth century, the renewed spirit of literary idealism formed the ideological basis for the production of utopian fiction. In fact, one can view literary idealism in the late nineteenth century as one of the bridges between American transcendentalism and utopian interpretations of naturalist theory.[29] Literary naturalism can be seen as the subversive, ironic, skeptical questioning of the idealistic foundation around which positive naturalistic fiction is built, thus giving rise to a darker romanticism in naturalistic fiction. What is also interesting, particularly in the article by Mallock, is the attempt by certain critics to reconcile realism and idealism and to create a theoretical basis for a fiction that would remain faithful to the tenets of literary realism and yet still try to idealize, or poetically elevate, these fictions, in order to create a higher, transgeneric fictional form.

Naturalism and Utopia

When tracing the genealogy of optimistic orientations, one could begin with the utopian millennialism of colonial New England. As a Calvinistic cosmology gave way in the eighteenth century to Enlightenment philosophy, this stream of thought changed into a progressivist, reason-based metaphysic that claimed the power of humankind to understand, change, and improve its condition. In the early nineteenth century, this Enlightenment orientation evolved into a positive romanticism that found its greatest expressions in the transcendentalists. From a cosmological perspective, the connection between Jeffersonian Enlightenment philosophy and transcendental philosophy is surprisingly close. As Henry Steele Commager has pointed out, both "assumed a universe governed by law and intelligible to reason; both taught that God, or Providence, was benevolent, Nature beneficent, Man and Society perfectible. To both, Man was the focus of the universe, and to both, the laws that controlled Nature and Society guaranteed, in the end, the infinite happiness of mankind."[30]

With the impact at mid-century of Darwin, Spencer, and other philosophical and scientific naturalists, this trend in American thought changed yet again into an evolutionary idealism and a renewed utopian millennialism, which subsequently gave rise (in late-nineteenth-century fiction) to an optimistic strain of naturalistic fiction in America.

Utopian thinking and utopian fiction were widespread in the second half of the nineteenth century. According to Jay Martin, utopian fiction in this period was vitalized by rapid cultural change, materialism, mysticism, and a progressive millennialism.[31] This revitalized millennialist utopianism was largely stimulated by the utopian possibilities in evolutionary optimism, particularly as advanced by Herbert Spencer and John Fiske. Significantly, some of these utopian narratives, such as Bellamy's *Looking Backward,* draw upon evolutionary naturalist theory as a basis for their utopian vision.[32]

In *Looking Backward* Bellamy creates a fictionalized utopia that comes to fruition as a result of an inevitable evolutionary process. In a sense, one can view Bellamy as reacting against the darker aspects of social Darwinism and

applying the more progressive features of Spencerian thinking, with its belief in the gradual evolution of more stable, complex, biological and social
forms. *Looking Backward* might be even more interesting as a cultural document because it turns certain 1880 status quo arguments against their de-
fenders. Laissez-faire supporters turned to Spencer and Darwin to argue for
the status quo: one must not tamper with the environment or one risks im-
peding the forward progress of evolution. This meant small government and
limited regulatory power. Bellamy created an imaginary world where the
forces of evolution have indeed worked, and what has been created is a so-
cial-gospel state with big government and heavy regulation. This irony aside,
in his postscript to the work Bellamy acknowledges the evolutionary paradigm around which the book is built. *Looking Backward,* he writes, is "in
all seriousness, as a forecast, in accordance with the principles of evolution,
of the next stage in the industrial and social development of humanity, especially in this country; and no part of it is believed by the author to be better
supported by the indications of probability than the implied prediction that
the dawn of the new era is already near."[33]

Part of Spencer's optimism rested in the belief that evolution held the keys
to the problem of evil and the moral development of man. As an organism
evolves, so too does the organism's moral sense. As evolution progresses and
the moral sense develops, evil is slowly but inevitably eradicated. Spencer
writes: "The ultimate development of the ideal man is logically certain—as
certain as any conclusion in which we place the most implicit faith; for instance that all men will die. . . . Progress, therefore, is not an accident, but a
necessity. Instead of civilization being artificial, it is a part of nature: all of a
piece with the development of the embryo or the unfolding of a flower."[34]
Onto this metaphysical evolutionary theory Bellamy grafts a specific teleological design. And he did so at just the right time, as Katharine Pearson
Woods claims in an 1898 article printed in the socialist organ *The American
Fabian.*[35] Bellamy's book, she writes, appeared "at a critical period in the
spiritual history of the race." The book "appealed to a widely spread, but
an only partially recognized sentiment," and it developed that sentiment "into
an Idea." That is, through *Looking Backward* and his other works, Bellamy
was able to shape a widespread ideology into a specific vision and thus give
shape and design to optimistic and progressive naturalist theory.

Bellamy would give explicit expression to this metaphysical evolutionary thinking not only in *Looking Backward,* but also in *Dr. Heidenhoff's Process* (1880), where he writes: "There is no such thing as moral responsibility for past acts; no such thing as real justice in punishing them, for the reason that human beings are not stationary existences, but changing, growing, incessantly progressive organisms, which in no two moments are the same."[36] In like fashion, in the utopian environment of *Looking Backward* crime has largely disappeared because the motive for crime has been eradicated. All remaining evil is largely the result of hereditary atavism and is restricted to a small handful of individuals, and those cases are treated in hospitals. Prisons are empty.[37] Notably, Bellamy's evolutionary utopia is essentially socialist and hence a departure from the laissez-faire capitalism ideologically supported by Spencer and William Graham Sumner.[38] Like Bellamy, Jack London often turned to a utopian vision founded on a socialist economy. Just as Bellamy's text rejects the darker implications of social Darwinism (when used as an ideological basis for capitalism), London, in his story "Goliah" (1910), uses the development of a socialist utopia as a basis for a direct refutation of the Malthusian doctrine that there is a direct connection between population growth and the world's ability to feed mankind. London writes: "The international government of the world was another idea that sprang simultaneously into the minds of thousands. The successful realization of this idea was a surprise to many, but as a surprise it was nothing to that received by the mildly protestant sociologists and biologists when irrefutable facts exploded the doctrine of Malthus."[39] In "Goliah," with the worldwide raising of the standard of living, the world's population does not rise, but falls. Moreover, as in Bellamy's utopian society, in "Goliah" crime is largely eradicated from society, and those few individuals who long for a predatory, brutal capitalism are treated in hospitals.[40]

A perennially popular topic in the nineteenth century, Malthus's population principle would be one of the subjects addressed in Bellamy's novel *Equality* (1897), a sequel to *Looking Backward.* Picking up where *Looking Backward* left off, *Equality* further explores Bellamy's evolved society. Evolution in this work is not only economic and social, but biological as well, as Bellamy depicts women as gradually evolving into a state of physical equality with men—the laws of nature themselves, suggests Bellamy, are inherently directed toward the realization of a utopian social vision.[41] Throughout *Equality,* Bellamy offers a scathing and relentless critique of capitalism, including the version of social Darwinism favored at the time by proponents of laissez-faire economic policy (see, for example, chapter 16 of the novel). Malthusian doctrines come under fire on a few occasions in *Equality*. In chapter 22, for instance, Bellamy suggests that the darker implications of Malthusian theory can be overcome with a rejection of traditional profit motives and a shift into a more socialistic economy. It is in the last chapter of the novel, however, that Malthus is discussed the most. In the conclud-ing—and, arguably, most interesting—chapter of the novel, "The Book of the Blind," Bellamy examines one by one a series of proposed counterarguments to the economic philosophy outlined in the previous chapters. The final argument—indeed, the subtitle of the final section of the novel—is called "The Malthusian Objection." The objection might be summarized as fol-lows: if a utopian society as described in *Equality* were to come into be-ing, and if, indeed, the social ills born out of the current capitalist system were to be eliminated as a result, then there would be no forces at work to keep population growth in check. The resulting population boom would quickly lead to horrific social problems, overcrowding, and starvation. The utopia, in effect, would be crushed under the by-products of its own suc-cess. Bellamy answers this argument by suggesting that advancements in culture and education within the utopia would supplant to a degree "the impulses of crude animalism" governing much of humanity under the capi-talist system (410). Thus, there is little danger of rampant overpopulation in his utopia. Indeed, in the final few paragraphs of the novel, Bellamy suggests that in his response to the "Malthusian objection" rests the re-pudiation of Malthusianism itself. Malthus and his followers never ad-equately accounted for higher intellectual activity among their representative populations.

Built around Bellamy's utopian vision, the "Nationalist" party of the Christian Socialists in the late nineteenth century helped revive and institu-tionalize the utopian millennialism that had been lying dormant since the utopian rationalists of the latter eighteenth century and the Puritan provi-dential historiographers of the seventeenth century. The Nationalists were dedicated to the principle of the "Brotherhood of Humanity," which distin-guishes "human nature from brute nature," and to the eradication of the "principle of competition," which is simply "the application of the brutal law of the survival of the strongest and most cunning."[42] With the eradication of competition (a product of capitalism and private property rights), humankind will be able to evolve to a higher stage. Thus, paradoxically, the Nationalist party believed that by eliminating the mechanisms through which evolution operates—natural selection, competition, and the survival of the fittest—society would be free to evolve to a higher, more perfect state. They took from evolutionary thinking the hope and belief that evolution was ameliorative and discarded from evolutionary thinking the darker elements that indicate the close connection between man and brute, the violence in nature, and the chance elements in random selection.[43]

One writer who became affiliated with the Nationalist movement was Charlotte Perkins Gilman, best known to today's readers as the author of "The Yellow Wallpaper." The renaissance Gilman has had in recent years as a result of that story has reintroduced to the literary community a series of her early-twentieth-century autobiographical, fictional, and nonfictional works that focus on her feminist critique of a variety of social and economic problems in America. Part of this body of work is comprised of several utopian novels written by Gilman between 1911 and 1916, the best known of which is *Herland* (1915). Written in the style of *Looking Backward* and a host of other utopian novels, *Herland* combines a series of philosophical dialogues with a loosely constructed travel/adventure narrative.[44] In brief, three male explorers—a wealthy adventurer, an idealistic doctor, and the narrator, a sociologist—venture into a lost country inhabited these past two thousand years solely by women, where they are taken prisoner, and after adjusting to the language of "Herland" (as one of the men calls the region) they spend the next year learning about the customs and conventions of the communal utopia based on principles of motherhood.

As several critics have demonstrated quite clearly, Gilman's *Herland* was heavily influenced by naturalist theory, especially theories of evolution and social Darwinism. In particular, Spencer's application of Darwinian evolution to social growth and development and Lester Ward's theories about the role of gender in the evolutionary process played a role in the shaping of Gilman's utopian vision.[45] Specifically, following the lead of Lester Ward, Gilman advocated a revised version of social Darwinism in which human cooperative enterprise allows for social reform and progress within a Darwinian framework. This "reform naturalism"—to borrow Gary Scharnhorst's apt and useful phrase—serves as a counterpoint to versions of social Darwinism used to justify laissez-faire economic policy and the type of predatory capitalism the Nationalist movement challenged. Thus, there is a connection between what I have called "positive" naturalism and "reform" naturalism: they both refer to a brand of narrative that envisions social progress within the framework of naturalist theory.

To illustrate how naturalist theory plays a central thematic role in the building of the utopian vision in *Herland*, a couple of passages stand out.[46] For instance, in one of the dialogues, the narrator attempts to explain to the citizens of Herland why there exists an impoverished class in the outside world: "I explained that the laws of nature require a struggle for existence, and that in the struggle the fittest survive, and the unfit perish. In our economic struggle, I continued, there was always plenty of opportunity for the fittest to reach the top, which they did, in great numbers, particularly in our country; that where there was severe economic pressure the lowest classes of course felt it the worst, and that among the poorest of all the women were driven into the labor market by necessity."[47] Naturally, this declaration by the narrator causes the women of Herland to inquire about the effect of this class system on population growth: do the poorest classes remain childless in order to prevent an increase in misery? Not so, replies the sympathetic doctor; in fact, there is a "law of nature," he explains, that demonstrates that "Reproduction is in inverse proportion to individuation" (200). The citizens of Herland are astonished at this claim—they are unaware of there being such "laws of nature" so stated. In fact, they have no such population problems, practicing as they do a type of selective and willed form of nondestructive population control that effectively answers the darker predictions of Malthus and, as the narrator points out, prevents the type of "struggle for existence" that allows for "no possibility for really noble qualities among the people at large" (205). Through wisdom and a desire to preserve and protect the better features of true *motherhood,* the women of Herland simply choose not to have more children than their resources can accommodate, an effective rebuttal of the more pessimistic implications of social Darwinism, for sure.

One can see this rejection or reinterpretation of social Darwinism not only in *Herland* and *Looking Backward,* but also in Howells's *A Traveler from Altruria.* An admirer of Bellamy's, William Dean Howells took note of the renewed millennialist hopes expressed in Bellamy's book. In 1898 Howells praised Bellamy as the "imagination which revived throughout Christendom the faith in a millennium."[48] Howells would try to promote a similar faith with his *A Traveler from Altruria*. As in *Looking Backward,* the harsh and brutal process of natural selection that forms the ideological backbone of America's capitalist economy is rejected. Offered in place of America's "the strongest survive" economy is the Christian socialism of Altruria. And like *Looking Backward,* the development of the Altrurian utopia is through an evolutionary process. This evolutionary process operates through a Christian sin-and-salvation paradigm.

> "I could not give you a clear account of the present state of things in my country," the Altrurian began, "without first telling you something of our conditions before the time of our Evolution. It seems to be the law of all life, that nothing can come to fruition without dying and seeming to make an end. It must be sown in corruption before it can be raised in incorruption. The truth itself must perish to our senses before it can live to our souls; the Son of Man must suffer upon the cross before we can know the Son of God."[49]

As illustrated by the development of whole political movements (like "Nationalism") ideologically connected to naturalist theory, there were optimistic strains of thought stemming from philosophical and scientific naturalism that had a profound impact on American thought. Bellamy's *Looking Backward* and Howells's *A Traveler from Altruria* bear witness that this naturalist theory found its way into a tradition of American fiction, giving rise to a strand of positive American naturalistic fiction. In contrast, one witnesses the negative naturalistic fiction working against this idealistic tradition. This is not to suggest that when the more "negative" authors wrote fiction they were necessarily (or consciously) working to subvert utopian narratives such as those by Bellamy and Howells. Rather, what the negative naturalistic authors did seem to work against were popular strains of literary idealism, of which utopian fiction is one particular manifestation.

The Night Side of Naturalism

When tracing through American letters the dark, subversive, skeptical orientations that counter more positive visions, one might begin in 1644 with the second book of William Bradford's *Of Plymouth Plantation.* Here one sees the first tensions in Puritan society, the despair felt by Bradford as he struggled to reconcile his idealistic vision of history with Puritan reality, in which wickedness would break forth and men like Thomas Granger would wreak havoc with community standards.[50] In the Enlightenment this darker current evolved in a work like Crèvecoeur's *Letters from an American Farmer* into a vision of America in which rationalist, ameliorative perspectives founded on concepts of American exceptionalism and the belief in the essential goodness of mankind are seen in conflict with human nature, war, slavery, violence, and tyranny. In the early nineteenth century, authors like Poe, Brockden Brown, Melville, and Hawthorne wrote fiction that called into question the positive romanticism of Emerson and Whitman. This tradition of negative romanticism implemented indirection, irony, ambiguity, and polyvalent symbolism to create narratives that undercut the perspectives of positive romanticism. With the rise and popularization of naturalist theory toward mid-century, negative romanticism evolved into a negative orientation in American literary naturalism. In the late nineteenth and early twentieth centuries, this negative orientation found expression in works by Crane, Norris, London, and others.

This darker vision did not appear in fiction alone. Henry Childs Merwin writes in an 1897 essay of "that most absurd of all dreams, the perfectibility of human nature."[51] In an 1883 article titled "Evil as a Factor in Evolution," C. T. Hopkins suggests that scientific advancement has only led to the further recognition that life is filled with dualisms, and he offers the possibility that, while *change* is the universal law of life, this constant change may not be "uninterrupted progress" but rather "an alternation of advance and retreat."[52] Mary Parmele, in her 1887 article "Relation the Ultimate Truth," begins by arguing that "we are in a world of illusions"; there is an elusive quality of life, for one perceives only surface reality; the only stable truth lies in "relation," which is powered by a mysterious and primal force.[53] "All that we call evolution or development," Parmele writes, "is simply a succession of changes in forms of relation." Even more significantly, we find philosophers such as August Weismann challenging Lamarckian theories of progressive development, throwing optimistic aspects of Spencerian thinking into doubt.[54]

Of course, to observe the dark side of naturalist theory one need only be confronted with the apparent incompatibilities of traditional moral systems with a harsh, random, indifferent universe and the apparent lack of human agency and will, as were Norris and Crane. These incompatibilities are reflected in accounts of characters like Curtis Jadwin in Norris's *The Pit* who are brought to madness and ruin because of the predatory laws of competition underlying social systems.

Just as certain social commentators in the late nineteenth century questioned or complicated ameliorative naturalist theory, the negative naturalistic authors simultaneously incorporated naturalist theory into their narratives and complicated the theory by exposing its dark, violent, and subversive currents. Contrary to optimistic Enlightenment thinking, the negative literary naturalists were often skeptical of man's belief in salvation through reason.[55] Like Hawthorne and Poe, Norris, for example, returns again and again to themes of guilt, madness, and evil. An apt metaphoric description of negative naturalistic fiction can be found in Richard Burton's 1901 essay "The Dark in Literature."[56] He writes: "But literature, and modern literature in special, makes room for other aspects of life besides the appealingly pathetic and the awe-inspiring. The ugly, and the brutal, and the foul are there in crowded cohorts and sickening display. The *night side of Nature and the devil side of human nature,* these are portrayed at full length" (my emphasis).

A similar metaphor was used at times to describe the fiction of negative romanticism. As James Herbert Morse wrote in 1883, it was Charles Brockden Brown's "peculiar gift to paint the *night side of human experience.*"[57] The connections between negative romanticism and negative naturalistic narrative are remarkable. Consider, for instance, how closely matched are the experiences of Carlyle's Teufelsdröckh (after confronting "The Everlasting No") and Norris's Vandover. Even the metaphors Carlyle and Norris use to describe their protagonist's perception of Nature echo one another. Teufelsdröckh says:

The speculative Mystery of Life grew ever more mysterious to me: neither in the practical Mystery had I made the slightest progress, but been everywhere buffeted, foiled, and contemptuously cast-out. A feeble unit in the middle of a threatening Infinitude, I seemed to have nothing given me but eyes, whereby to discern my own wretchedness. . . . it was a strange isolation I then lived in. . . . To me the Universe was all void of Life, of Purpose, of Volition, even of Hostility: it was one huge, dead, immeasurable Steam-engine, rolling on, in its dead indifference, to grind me limb from limb.[58]

Sixty years later, Vandover would stare out his window, having just discovered the loss of his artistic powers. Norris records his perceptions:

> It was Life, the murmur of the great, mysterious force that spun the wheels of Nature and that sent it onward like some enormous engine, resistless, relentless; an engine that sped straight forward, driving before it the infinite herd of humanity, driving it on at breathless speed through all eternity, driving it no one knew whither, crushing out inexorably all those who lagged behind the herd and who fell from exhaustion, grinding them to dust beneath its myriad iron wheels, riding over them, still driving on the herd that yet remained, driving it recklessly, blindly on and on toward some far-distant goal, some vague unknown end, some mysterious, fearful bourne forever hidden in thick darkness.[59]

Unlike Teufelsdröckh, Vandover experiences no rebirth into the Everlasting Yea, just a dark stasis in a position of degradation, degeneration, and despair. Unlike Presley in *The Octopus,* he has no final redemptive vision, no "transcendental" or intuitive awareness that evolution and determinism may lead toward perfection, utopia, or the good; instead there is the confusion and darkness of a "spiritual death," a de-volution, a dark and grotesque lapse into a brutish state without redemptive harmony.

To carry the machine metaphor of *Sartor Resartus* even further, Teufelsdröckh's perception of the "dead indifference" of Nature resembles other naturalist works like Crane's "The Open Boat" and his famous epigrammatic poem "A man said to the universe":

> A man said to the universe:
> "Sir, I exist!"
> "However," replied the universe,
> "The fact has not created in me
> "A sense of obligation."[60]

With Frank Norris's *Vandover and the Brute* caught in the maelstrom of the Everlasting No and much of Stephen Crane's work floating in the vast Center of Indifference, we find ourselves having to turn to authors like Edward Bellamy to give us a glimpse of the Everlasting Yea.

The key difference between positive and negative literary naturalism is depicted in the passage quoted above from *Vandover and the Brute*. When Bellamy looks at nature through the perspective of naturalist theory, he can identify ameliorative evolutionary processes at work, pushing mankind inexorably onward to higher states. When Norris's Vandover looks at nature, he sees the forces of nature driving life "recklessly, blindly on and on toward some far-distant goal, some vague unknown end, some mysterious, fearful bourne forever hidden in thick darkness." The same may be said of the difference between positive and negative romanticism: when Emerson feels the "currents of the Universal Being," he becomes "part or particle of God" and can identify in the Oversoul the great and good forces powering the machine of life. When Melville scrutinizes nature, unlike Emerson, he sees the power of blackness and the inscrutable pasteboard mask of nature. This ability/inability to resolve the subject/object opposition in positive and negative orientations points out another problem with too closely associating American naturalistic narrative and Zola's theory of "literary naturalism."[61] In "The Experimental Novel" Zola, like Melville and Norris, acknowledges that there is "an immense unknown which surrounds us." Zola, however, believes that the mask of nature need not remain inscrutable: the naturalistic author has the tools with which to "pierce it, to explain it, thanks to scientific methods."[62] Here Zola seems to have more in common with the positive orientations of Emerson and Bellamy than he does with Melville and Norris.

The differences between positive and negative literary naturalism can be further illustrated by reexamining the quote from Richard Burton's 1893 article in the *Dial* already taken notice of in chapter 1. Borrowing Burton's formulation, the positive naturalistic narrative often seeks to present in ideal fashion the "aspiration of the individual and the social progress of the state."[63] Or in Bellamy's words, *Looking Backward* celebrates "the progress that shall be made, ever onward and upward, till the race shall achieve its ineffable destiny."[64] What clearly sets apart positive from negative naturalistic fiction is that the positive naturalistic author often believes that this idealized state is obtainable, and that the evolutionary forces operating in both the individual and society are moving toward these ends. In a postscript to *Looking Backward*, Bellamy provides one illustration of the conflicting worldviews of negative and positive literary naturalists:

> All thoughtful men agree that the present aspect of society is portentous of great changes. The only question is, whether they will be for the better or the worse. Those who believe in man's essential nobleness lean to the former view, those who believe in his essential baseness to the latter. For my part, I hold to the former opinion. *Looking Backward* was written in the belief that the Golden Age lies before us and not behind us, and is not far away. Our children will surely see it, and we, too, who are already men and women, if we deserve it by our faith and by our works. (351)

The negative orientation complicates matters, sometimes rejecting the idea of societal or individual progress, as in Norris's "A Deal in Wheat." At other times negative literary naturalists complicate positive orientations by introducing into the equation variables that keep open multiple possibilities—for progress, for regress, for stasis—as in the contrasting philosophical orientations held in tension throughout texts like London's *The Sea-Wolf* and Norris's *The Octopus*.

Negative romantics and negative literary naturalists frequently confront similar issues and themes in their fiction. Hawthorne's psychological themes, his explorations of madness, guilt, and original sin in works like *The Scarlet Letter, The House of the Seven Gables,* and *The Marble Faun* reappear under slightly different guise in Holmes's *Elsie Venner,* Crane's *The Red Badge of Courage,* and in several of Norris's novels and short stories. The epistemological romances of Brown and Poe are revived and revised in several works by Crane and in Norris's story cycle "Outward and Visible Signs." In fact, an implicit crisis in epistemology is characteristic of much negative literary naturalism; as Don Graham notes, there is a "relativistic uncertainty" manifested in much naturalistic fiction.[65] Donald Pizer makes a similar point: "the major characteristic of the form of the naturalistic novel is that it no longer reflects this certainty about the value of experience but rather expresses a profound doubt or perplexity about what happens in the course of time."[66] One sees repeatedly a concern in negative naturalistic fiction with mystery, awe, the uncanny, and the inscrutable. Furthermore, in both negative romanticism and negative literary naturalism there is a focus on metaphysical themes. Works like *Moby-Dick, Elsie Venner,* and *The Sea-Wolf* address cosmological, spiritual, and philosophical questions. Negative romantics and negative literary naturalists also treat certain historical issues surrounding manifest destiny and American exceptionalism similarly. *The Scarlet Letter* and *The Red Badge of Courage* use the form of the historical romance in ways that complicate the more non-ironic, optative visions of history portrayed in works like *The Deerslayer.* One need only place a text like Mark Twain's *A Connecticut Yankee in King Arthur's Court* up against Bellamy's *Looking Backward* to see the stark contrast in dark and light treatments of history.[67]

In summary, then, two things become apparent. First, there is a vast cultural discourse in American literary history between shifting and contrasting philosophical orientations. This cultural dialogue is between a discernable dark, subversive, "negative" voice and a more progressive, positive voice in which one's potential to achieve an apotheosis, to some degree, is affirmed. This dialogue continues in the naturalistic fiction of the second half of the nineteenth century. Second, there are recognizable continuities between the psychological, epistemological, and metaphysical concerns of negative romanticism and negative literary naturalism, suggesting a native philosophical and cultural backdrop against which to witness the rise of literary naturalism in the late nineteenth century.

Postscript: Why Romanticism?

The previous chapter ended with some speculation regarding the question "Why Romance?" This chapter will end with some brief speculation regarding a related question: "Why Romanticism?" Heinrich Heine wrote that classic art portrays the finite, while romantic art suggests the infinite.[68] In a similar vein, literary realism could be said to attempt to represent the finite, and literary naturalism to suggest the infinite. Rather than focusing on the representation of reality, naturalism looks beneath the surface in an attempt to interpret reality. Above all else, "interpretation" may be the key concept linking naturalism and romanticism. Neither realism nor naturalism neglects reality; rather, both demonstrate an intense interest in physical reality. But in the last chapter, Frank Norris and (perhaps curiously) Maurice Thompson pointed out that naturalism seeks to push beyond physical (or social) reality. Norris observed that "Realism stultifies itself," noting only the surface of things, whereas the romance explores the "unplumbed depths of the human heart." Maurice Thompson would more closely tie this same sentiment to naturalist theory, noting, we will recall, that the method of Darwin was twofold, engaging in both a "microscopic analysis" of the facts and details heralded by the realists, and in a "stupendous synthesis" of the whole that casts these details into an interpretive frame. Indeed, rather than observing and recording outward reality, social or otherwise, as an aesthetic end in itself, the romantics and naturalists use their exploration of reality to explore philosophical and scientific theories that offer an interpretation of nature and experience. These theories were universalizing and expansive, and as a result, literary romantics and naturalists had to distort or heighten their portrayals of physical reality in order to introduce these theories into their texts. They had to rely on symbols and allegory, on the imaginative and the extreme.

What the scientific and philosophical naturalists did was offer an interpretation of reality, a paradigm that would help explain the mysteries of nature. Rather than rely on the "common sense" of perception, they either doubted the simplicity of perception like Berkeley and Hume, or were amazed, like Emerson, at the depth revealed in nature to one who looks deep enough. What Norris introduces into *The Pit* that separates it from a novel of social realism such as *The Rise of Silas Lapham* is a layer of speculation regarding the intangible forces that lie beneath surface representation. This deeper interpretive layer provides a method of giving meaning and/or order to human experience. In fact, to some degree, the dynamic of the naturalistic novel arises from the tension created between this deeper level and the forces of human aspiration in the experiential world. For these reasons, then, naturalism might have more in common with romanticism than with realism. Aesthetically, as seen in the previous chapter, the roots of American literary naturalism can be traced back as much—if not more—to the antebellum romance as to the novel of social realism, the donnée of the literary realists. Likewise, philosophically considered, the interpretive layers introduced into their narratives by the literary naturalists have a correlative in the interpretive gestures offered within literary romanticism. The interpretations are different, of course, and mark clear distinctions between the projects of the literary naturalists and the romanticists from the first half of the century, but noting the interpretive gestures of each gives us a point upon which to launch further investigation into the philosophical, structural, and technical projects engaged in by the American literary naturalists. Observe that by switching from a religious metaphysic to a scientific or pseudo-scientific metaphysic one can easily see the hereditary problem of *The House of the Seven Gables* in the atavistic regressions of Norris's *McTeague* and "A Reversion to Type."

Without relegating literary realism to a minor position within the framework of nineteenth-century literary history, the loose distinction between *representation* and *interpretation* may serve as a useful metaphor to consider the continuities between romanticism and naturalism. First, some clarification: certainly, it would be naïve to claim that a realistic text did not carry with it some interpretation of the world—this is inevitable. Moreover, the literary realists were certainly more sophisticated and aesthetically complex than mere documenters of the details of social and physical reality. The metaphor is useful only insofar as we treat the metaphysical themes and apparatus of the texts in question, and insofar as we understand that the interpretive layer in a work of naturalism or romanticism refers solely to the direct and often explicit foregrounding within the literary text of some metaphysical, epistemological, and/or psychological perspectives through which to interpret the events of the narrative. Put another way, the literary naturalists foreground an interpretive frame through which to view the events of the narrative; the literary realists foreground a representation of character, manners, and society with enough precision that an interpretation gradually emerges, with corresponding implications for understanding human social interaction and human psychology. Dreiser's suggestion noted in the previous chapter that he may have been a "romancer" all the time may reflect his recognition that he wasn't just "representing" character and action, but was interpreting these actions and characters through an explicit philosophical framework rooted in nineteenth-century scientific and philosophical naturalism. What Dreiser and the other literary naturalists did, in effect, was similar in type, if not in metaphysical perspective, to literary romanticism, which pushes beyond surface boundaries to reveal the metaphysical forces manipulating nature and human behavior. The connection between romanticism and idealism may help further develop this point. For instance, John Addington Symonds, in an 1887 article titled "Realism and Idealism," made the following distinction: "Realism is the presentation of natural objects as the artist sees them, as he thinks they are. It is the attempt to imitate things as they strike the senses. Idealism is the presentation of natural objects as the artist fain would see them, as he thinks they strive to be. It is the attempt to imitate things as the mind interprets them."[69] Although it is clear that Symonds's understanding of "idealism" is weighted toward the *idealistic,* it is also clear that he conceives of idealism as providing an interpretive framework through which the events of the narrative are filtered.

Juxtaposing Melville's *Pierre* with London's *Martin Eden* might help illustrate these continuities. Both of these texts are romantic *kunstlerromane* (novels concerning the growth and education of an artist) in which budding authors struggle with metaphysical and philosophical problems on their road to artistic success. Both texts follow their protagonists through extraordinary and heightened experiences, and both end with an isolated and alienated protagonist committing suicide in a moment of anguish. Many of the philosophical and metaphysical speculations in *Martin Eden* revolve around naturalist theory. Martin Eden's struggle to become a successful author (financially and artistically) is paralleled in the story by his gradual discovery of Herbert Spencer and other naturalist philosophers and scientists. Eden's death scene itself portrays a dramatic struggle of will versus will that typifies the deterministic themes running throughout the text: Eden's suicide by drowning is preceded by a pitched battle between Eden's will to live and his will to die.

Two other texts that might be profitably compared are Hawthorne's *Blithedale Romance* (1852) and Frederic's *The Damnation of Theron Ware.* These texts are psychological romances that explore the ambiguities of perception. Both Miles Coverdale and Theron Ware fall prey to limited and misapprehension, and in the end seem to have been completely baffled (along with the reader) about the events that transpired in the narrative. Just as Coverdale seems to have misinterpreted the true nature of the relationships among the other Blithedale inhabitants, so too does Theron Ware misinterpret the behavior and intentions of Father Forbes and Celia Madden; so much so, in fact, that his intellectual "illumination" becomes his damnation. What makes *Theron Ware* naturalistic is the fact that Ware's "illumination" comes about in part through his exposure to naturalist theory. Once he has been ushered into a realm of ideas for which he is ill equipped, Ware loses his own bearings amid the new intellectual pursuits before him, including higher biblical criticism, the arts, and nineteenth-century science. Although the characters and positions encountered by Ware—including, for example, Dr. Ledsmar, the pseudo-scientific "naturalist" conducting bizarre, vaguely Darwinian, experiments—are treated with a healthy dose of satire by Frederic, Ware abandons his faith in his profession and is eventually led toward a personal "damnation." Notably, regarding the representation/interpretation metaphor, the thesis of *Theron Ware* is that humans live according to the subjective "interpretation" that they cling to (religion, Darwinism, and so forth)—this is the very message of Sister Soulsby, whose evangelical prowess stems from her ability to manipulate the scenery behind the religious stage, to produce a religious "interpretation" of experience to give structure to the lives of the Methodist laypeople.

The Damnation of Theron Ware has been a focal point for some critical discussion over the past century about the very definition of literary naturalism. In several key articles and book chapters, critics have used Frederic's novel as a case study in the difficulty of making taxonomic claims about certain novels. Of these articles, two stand out. In 1939, Charles Child Walcutt published "Harold Frederic and American Naturalism."[70] In this article, Walcutt ultimately concludes that *Theron Ware* should not be classified as a work of literary naturalism, because the novel does not adopt a strongly materialistic and/or deterministic position, opting to allow characters to exert their will through ethical choices and judgments (with corresponding thematic overtures). A long generation later, Samuel Coale published a remarkable essay titled "Frederic and Hawthorne: The Romantic Roots of Naturalism" (1976).[71] Coale begins his essay by quoting Walcutt's earlier article, then he proceeds to demonstrate the close aesthetic ties between *Theron Ware* and the works of Nathaniel Hawthorne. Coale concludes that *Theron Ware* is not best classified as naturalistic, but as romantic. He writes:

> But the fact remains, Frederic was trying to forge a newer "romanticism" in *The Damnation of Theron Ware,* trying to penetrate the simplistic and iron forces of a naturalistic universe to reach the primal forces of the human psyche, that dark realm which has always been the

primal core of the best American literature. Perhaps *The Damnation of Theron Ware* reveals that there never really was a viable naturalist aesthetic at all, that the factual realism and accumulation of scientifically accurate force fields in the American novel were just not enough to get at the heart of the American experience. (44)

These analyses by Walcutt and Coale are both excellent. They are both exactly right: so long as we define literary naturalism as the adoption of a certain philosophical position (Walcutt) or a philosophically influenced realistic aesthetic creed (Coale), then, as discussed in chapter 1 of the present study, *Theron Ware* should not be classified as a work of literary naturalism. Yet, *Theron Ware* does engage themes arising out of late-nineteenth-century philosophical and scientific pursuits, including Darwinian evolution, atavism, and degeneration. Thus, if we adopt the definition of literary naturalism offered in chapter 1, *Theron Ware* becomes a poster child for understanding the possibilities and complexities of American literary naturalism. If we agree that an author can engage a theme within a work without necessarily promoting a unified worldview—particularly one governed by a strict materialism and determinism—then Walcutt's objection evaporates, and his article becomes an early argument for redefining a limited and limiting definition of literary naturalism in America. By the same token, liberating naturalism from its close association with realism tempers Coale's objection, and Coale's article becomes a powerful statement about the need to reevaluate the relationship between literary naturalism and the American romance tradition.

As in Frederic's *Damnation of Theron Ware*, many of Stephen Crane's tales explore the ambiguity of perception and the subjectivity of interpretation. The crisis in "The Blue Hotel" arises out of the difficulties the characters have interpreting each other's behavior, and the story ends with the cowboy and the Easterner debating the roles they may or may not have played in the Swede's death. In "The Open Boat" the correspondent, the cook, and the captain felt that they could be "interpreters" after hearing the "great sea's voice." What the sea said or what their subsequent interpretations were are not given. Other Crane characters are not even this lucky. Binks in "Mr. Binks' Day Off" finds himself at the end of the tale unable to speak the "unformulated question of the centuries." Likewise, the youth in "An

Experiment in Misery" finds the "roar of the city in his ear" to be a "confusion of strange tongues." As in many of Crane's stories, Poe's *The Narrative of Arthur Gordon Pym* employs what we might call a "negative" or "deconstructive" symbolism in order to foreground issues of perspectivity and the vagaries of interpretation. In Poe's *Pym* the title character stumbles across strange hieroglyphics carved into the mountains on the island of Tsalal, but these mysterious symbols are not given fixed meanings. This ambiguity is the essence of the "negative" symbolism of *Pym;* it is a symbolism that suggests meaning, but whose meaning is ultimately undiscoverable.

As René Wellek and others have argued, a symbolic reading of nature (and the corresponding use of symbols in an attempt to delve into nature) is a hallmark of romanticism. In "The Loom of Fiction," Roy R. Male notes—for Nathaniel Hawthorne's aesthetic vision—that the "full complexity of human life is best approached through metaphor, symbol, and myth; that mechanical, mathematical, and static concepts are incapable of grasping the rhythmic unity of living things; and that man and his artistic achievements must be considered as an integral part of this unity."[72] These observations are central to understanding literary romanticism, but might also prove useful to understanding literary naturalism. The symbolic texts of the literary naturalists may, in part, be explained by noting how symbol and myth provides an artistic means for exploring that "full complexity" of human life. "Naturalism," Norris wrote, "is a form of romanticism, not an inner circle of realism."[73] Indeed, for the naturalists, it may not be that "mechanical" and "mathematical" concepts are incapable of grasping the "unity of living things," but instead that enough mystery remains in our "scientific" understanding to warrant an artistic creed that pushes beyond social documentation and the direct observation of daily life.

4

The Forms of Determinism

In Frank Norris's satiric allegory "The Puppets and the Puppy" (1897), a Lead Soldier, a Doll, a Mechanical Rabbit, a Queen's Bishop (from a chess set), and a Japhet manikin discuss determinism, free will, sin, moral responsibility, and death.[1] The story begins with the Lead Soldier remarking: "Well, here we are, put into this Room, for something, we don't know what; for a certain time, we don't know how long; by somebody, we don't know who. It's awful!" (175). This initiates a discussion about the plausibility of the existence of the Boy (who represents God in the allegory). The Doll believes that the Boy exists, as do the Mechanical Rabbit (though he seems less sure), Japhet, and the Lead Soldier. But the Queen's Bishop dissents: "There is no Boy, except that which exists in your own imaginations," but "there is, perhaps, a certain Force that moves us from time to time—a certain vague power, not ourselves, that shifts us here and there." All of the chessmen, claims the Bishop, believe in this "certain Force." The Force is not omnipotent, for even it is subject to certain natural laws. The Force "can move us only along certain lines. I still retain my individuality—still have my own will. My lines are not those of the knight, or the pawn, or the castle, and no power in the Room can make them so. I am a free agent—that's what is so terrible" (176). The Bishop, then, sees himself as caught in a dreadful paradox: he is both subject to the manipulations of natural law and a free agent.[2]

In response to the Queen's Bishop, the Doll argues that all of the Bishop's "science and learning" does not necessarily mean that he has all of the answers. The Doll then reasserts a belief in the Boy and joins with the Lead Soldier and Japhet in claiming to be made in the Boy's image. This chorus is supplemented by the Mechanical Rabbit, who adopts a modest teleological argument for the existence of the Boy—somebody must have "wound up" the Rabbit, for how else would he have come by this "strange power of playing upon these cymbals?" (176). Japhet then turns their attention to the mystery of death, or being "Thrown-away." Japhet believes he will be transformed into rosewood and take his place eternally in a "Noah's Ark of silver." The Lead Soldier believes that upon being Thrown-away he will be melted and recast, ad infinitum, with each incarnation an improvement over the previous one. The Queen's Bishop, claiming that Japhet and the Lead Soldier are deluded by "Dreams! dreams! dreams!" suggests that upon being Thrown-away he will rot, decay, and be absorbed into the elements. The Doll finds the Bishop's position unthinkable, for this would constitute a dissolution of personal identity. For the Doll, the body may disintegrate, but personal identity—what the Doll refers to as the internal "Not-Me"—shall persist. Finally, the Mechanical Rabbit asserts, decisively, that "when I am Thrown-away that's the end of me—it's annihilation" (178).

The conversation then turns to various conceptions of sin and moral responsibility. Again it is the Lead Soldier who broaches the question by asking why "Falling-down" (i.e., "falling" or "lapsing" into sin) was "brought into the Room" (178).[3] All of the toys seem to agree that "it is wrong to Fall-down," for it "displeases the Boy" (or in the Bishop's case, Falling-down displeases the "Force that moves us"). The Mechanical Rabbit can understand how it is "horribly and fearfully wrong" for the Lead Soldier to Fall-down, for in his falling he "drags with him the whole line of other soldiers." In the manner of original sin, the Lead Soldier's Falling-down "does not stop with himself—it communicates itself to others. It is a taint that progresses to infinity" (178). But, argues the Rabbit (in a manner similar to Crane's cowboy at the end of "The Blue Hotel"), why is it wrong for him to Fall-down, to transgress? After all, he hurts no one but himself. To this, the Queen's Bishop (like Crane's Easterner) responds by noting that the Rabbit would be held just as morally responsible for Falling-down as the Lead Soldier, for his Falling-down would disrupt the "vast, grand plan of events." No one can know the intricate network of causal links that governs the "vast, grand scheme of the Room." Falling-down, argues the Bishop, reverberates throughout this network and inhibits the development of the "magnificent, incomprehensible aim of the Room" (179).

Agreeing that Falling-down should be avoided is one thing, accepting moral responsibility for Falling-down is quite another. The Lead Soldier asks of the other puppets whether a soldier whose standard had been bent by the Boy can be held responsible for Falling-down. And what of those soldiers who never were able to stand upright because of some flaw in their construction: should they be held responsible? These unfortunate soldiers were "doomed before they were cast, and were Thrown-away afterward" (179). These examples pose, as Japhet announces, a "dreadful problem!" and he notes that any day, without warning, the Boy might decide to pull off his standard, causing him to Fall-down and subsequently be Thrown-away. After Japhet's announcement each of the puppets in succession notes that he did not ask to be lathed, made, whittled, molded, or stuffed. The Lead Soldier argues that if he had been given any choice in the matter, he would have chosen to be molded in the form of a mounted general, not a mere private. The fact that he is a private is due to "accident alone" (179–80). At this point, Sobby, the Boy's fox-terrier puppy, unpredictably bounds into the room, tears apart the Rabbit and the Doll, chews the head from Japhet and knocks both the Lead Soldier and the Queen's Bishop down the register. The Bishop "disappears, muttering, vaguely, something about the 'vast, resistless forces of nature'" (180).

In this short allegory Norris presents many of the problems central to American naturalistic fiction. Is the universe governed by vague force, as the Queen's Bishop believes, and are humans subject to inexorable laws of cause and effect that determine action? Does one have free will within this system (however limited that will might be)? Or, as Japhet and the Doll argue, is there a God who governs the universe? But even if there is a God, does this rule out the possibility of determinism? Perhaps man is still subject to the determining effects of original sin, or perhaps God has allowed man to be formed in a flawed mold. Can one be held morally responsible for Falling-down when his or her standard is bent?

The epigraph to this story poses another interpretive problem. It reads: "There are more things in your philosophy than are dreamed of in Heaven and Earth." This possibly clever rephrasing of Shakespeare's famous line from *Hamlet* seems straightforward enough at first, but exactly who is Norris associating with "your philosophy"? The reason I say this epigraph is only "possibly" clever is that if the line were presented as it appears in *Hamlet* ("there are more things in heaven and earth, Horatio, / Than are dreamt of in your philosophy"), then it would seem an obvious barb at the limited theosophism of Annie Besant and her support of reincarnation. As rephrased by Norris, assuming now that the rephrasing was intentional, the epigraph can not be seen so easily as a satirical comment on Annie Besant, for her "philosophy" does not contain "more things" than dreamed of by the puppets, who represent a wide variety of metaphysical orientations. Arnold Goldsmith believes "more things" refers to the sudden appearance of Sobby, an event not "dreamed of" in the philosophies of the puppets. This interpretation is arguable, though it too is not without its problems. It seems unlikely, given the variety of positions adopted by the puppets, that Norris would be claiming there are "more things" than are represented by the continuum of orientations adopted by the puppets. The Lead Soldier's belief in "accident" as a major force in the universe would allow for the sudden, unpredictable appearance of the puppy. Still, given the ironic status of the "puppets" themselves as completely subject to, and dependent on, the manipulations of outside forces (and yet they debate among themselves questions of freedom and responsibility), the puppy might represent an outside agent not dependent upon, or subject to, determining forces. Or perhaps "your philosophy" is in reference to the philosophical positions taken by the various puppets en masse, which are clever but seem insubstantial in the face of the tangible flesh-and-blood experience of real life, as represented by the joyous destruction of the terrier.

For a century, virtually every study of naturalistic fiction in America has had something to say about determinism. These studies have often concluded that it is the presence of determinism in works by Norris, Crane, London, and Dreiser that makes them "naturalistic" and sets them apart from other "realistic" novels.[4] Many of these same studies often find fault with naturalistic narratives for failing to embody a strict determinism. They find naturalistic texts flawed for seeming to allow characters free will and for holding their characters morally responsible for their actions. Certain recent critics have attempted to explain these flaws by viewing naturalistic narratives as more philosophically and artistically complex than previous studies allowed. John Conder, for instance, argues that while nineteenth-century texts by Norris and Crane depict a more rigidly Hobbesian conception of man, there is a shift in the twentieth century toward a more Bergsonian orientation, in which man is both free and determined at the same time. Lee Clark Mitchell, on the other hand, has recently argued that determinism is woven into the verbal configurations of naturalistic narratives. Rather than approaching these texts through philosophy, as Conder does, Mitchell exposes the deterministic qualities of texts like *Vandover and the Brute* and "To Build a Fire" (1908) by looking at their style, their artistic complexity.

Understanding how determinism is embodied in American literary naturalism can be improved by both Conder's and Mitchell's methods. One needs a more philosophically sophisticated language in order to describe the role determinism plays in naturalistic fiction, and at the same time, one needs to pay greater attention to the ways determinism is artistically rendered in these same texts. Although I do not believe that determinism is the unifying and defining characteristic of American literary naturalism (maintaining that naturalistic narrative is not *necessarily* deterministic and that determinism does not form the ideological center of "literary naturalism") determinism is nevertheless a major theme in naturalistic fiction, and any study of American literary naturalism must deal with it in some fashion.[5]

In broad terms, philosophical and scientific naturalism in the nineteenth century opened the door for deterministic interpretations of nature, human nature, and experience. As the universe increasingly came to be understood as operating through force, law, and causal relationships, so too did humankind seem to be subject to these transcendent natural laws. Such a recognition readily pushed scientists, philosophers, and authors to a deterministic interpretation of the world and experience. And, indeed, Zola implies that causal materialistic determinism is central to the experimental novel. Still, for American literary naturalists in the late nineteenth century determinism was not a *statement,* but a *question.* Norris, Crane, and London did not so much create narratives that monologically incorporated a deterministic worldview as they created narratives that dialogically interacted with deterministic ideologies. They used their fiction not to preach determinism, but to engage in a struggle with determinism.

Sometimes these struggles grew remarkably complex. Consider the following: At his untimely passing in 1916 Jack London left behind a collection of notes and outlines for stories that he had considered writing. One of these outlines was for what he called his "Christ Novel."[6] Taking London's notes at face value, and piecing the strands of the story together, the basic plot of the "Christ Novel" seems to be as follows.[7] Set principally during Passion Week in Jerusalem, the story is either narrated by, or focalized through, a Goth in the service of Rome. This particular Goth is of enough rank and close enough to Pilate's court that he is able to witness firsthand many of the major events of Passion Week, including the several trials of Christ. The narrative begins by developing the relationship between the Goth and a Jewish heroine whose liberality distinguishes her from the crowd. Appealing to the Goth's love for her, the Jewish heroine pleads with him to attempt to rescue Christ. The Goth's self-discipline and Roman loyalty, however, prevent him from attempting such a rescue. Besides, argues the Goth, if Christ's crucifixion is a matter of prophecy, then who is he to inter- fere? Thus, Christ is tried before the Sanhedrin, Herod, and Pilate. Like the Goth, Pilate argues that if Christ's death by crucifixion has been prophesied, then who is he to make that prophecy void by releasing Christ? And so Christ is crucified. At his crucifixion, it is the Goth who orders the Roman soldier to pierce Christ's side with a spear, much in the same spirit as one might put an animal out of its misery. Following Christ's burial in the tomb of Jo- seph of Arimathea, Pilate sends the Goth to steal away his body. But the Goth discovers only an empty tomb. Did Christ rise from the dead, or did the Jews steal the body? The novel draws to a close with the "conversion" (did he really convert?) of the Goth. Following his ambiguous conversion the Goth struggles with the necessity of Christ's death. If Christ's death was prede- termined through prophecy, was Pilate to blame for sending him to the cross? Can Pilate be held morally responsible for his actions, or was he merely an instrument of higher laws?

Thus, London's novel ends in ambiguity. Did Pilate have free will, or was he subject to the "deterministic" pressure of prophecy? Could either the Goth or Pilate have rescued Christ? Given London's proposed framing epigraph for the novel, the suspended answers to these questions are dou- bly ambiguous. The epigraph states: "There is only one thing more won- derful than the reality of Christ, and that is, Christ never existing, that the imagination of man should have created him." Thus, the central ambiguity of Christ's divinity—was he son of God, or son of man? or both? did he rise from the dead? or was his body stolen?—is wrapped within the tale of Pilate and the Goth (who may or may not have been converted), both of whom may or may not have had the ability to rescue Christ, both of whom may or may not have been acting out of free will with their refusals to rescue Christ. Framing these questions within a perceived ambiguity regarding the historicity of Christ (as indicated in the epigraph), London's doubly ambiguous narrative is layered with a pervasive irony that casts over the story the possibility that the complexly ambiguous free will/determinism debate central to the narrative may have emanated solely from the subjective imagination of man.[8]

Paraphrasing Claude Bernard, Zola defines determinism in his essay "The Experimental Novel" as the "cause which determines the appearance of phenomena. This proximate cause . . . is nothing but the physical and material condition of the existence or manifestation of phenomena."[9] Zola elaborates on this definition in "A Letter to the Young People of France." Here he writes: "Bernard recognized what we call 'determinism' as the supreme law of the universe; that is to say, the inflexible connection of phenomena which prevents any supernatural agent from interfering to modify the result."[10] What Zola is suggesting is that for any event there are material conditions that inexorably give rise to that event. This definition of determinism used by Zola matches definitions accepted by contemporary scholars. Richard Taylor defines determinism as "the general philosophical thesis which states that for everything that ever happens there are conditions such that, given them, nothing else could happen."[11] Translating these sets of "conditions" into "causes," and "everything that ever happens" into "effects," one arrives at the definition of determinism given by Perry Westbrook in *Free Will and Determinism in American Literature* (1979): the "doctrine that all occurrences in the universe are governed by inexorable laws of cause and effect."[12]

Deterministic theories can be divided into two main types. The first, descending most directly from ancient concepts of fortune and fate, and later reformulated for the Christian world by Augustine, can be termed "providential determinism." Providential determinism is largely characterized by the positing of a transcendent and omniscient supernatural force that directs or predestines the course of events. The second type of determinism is the more secular or philosophically naturalistic orientation. This determinism removes God as an active agent in the universe and puts in God's place a set of natural laws that govern the universe and determine all action. This "scientific" determinism grew out of the Enlightenment and probably received its first major modern statement in the scientific world by Pierre-Simon Laplace, who in the late eighteenth and early nineteenth centuries generally confirmed and extended the work of Newton. Laplace contended that if one could determine the state of all particles in nature and the various forces acting upon those particles, then one could predict both past and future states of the universe.[13] One of the central differences between providential and scientific determinism is the absence in scientific determinism of an active transcendent agent playing a role in the unfolding of history. By positing a benign God directing history, providential determinists are able to balance their despair over the absence of human agency and will with the optimistic belief implicit in a Christian teleology in the utopian promise of the second coming of Christ and the establishment of a New Jerusalem. Some scientific determinists like Herbert Spencer compensated for the absence of this teleological hope by arguing that evolution is inherently progressive. In other cases nineteenth-century scientists and authors tried to reconcile providential and scientific determinism. Such is the case in *Looking Backward,* in which a teleologically driven post-Darwinian scientific determinism is joined with a renewed utopian millennialism. Thus, in Bellamy's text a belief in the ameliorative process of evolution is used as the basis for reconciling these two main types of determinism.

Although providential and scientific determinism may vary widely in their teleological perspectives, one important feature they have in common is that they both tend to incorporate a means of explaining—or at least classifying—the unexplainable. Providential determinism allows for "providence" or "fate" to help account for the more elusive and mysterious elements of a deterministic world. In scientific determinism "fate" or "providence" is often secularized as "chance." In either case, tychistic explanations function as methods of accounting for the mysteries of life that are not readily explainable through causal relationships.[14] These tychistic elements are of remarkable significance for American writers of naturalistic narrative. It is often these gaps in knowledge that form the basis for the epistemological themes prevalent in both American romanticism and American literary naturalism. It is the efforts of writers like Melville, Poe, Norris, and Crane to peer into the mysteries of nature, these gaps in knowledge, that characterize much of their art. Their ultimate inability to see clearly into these same mysteries, to view the whole of nature's design, is what forms the foundation for their "negative" romanticism. Sometimes they achieved Poe's brief glimpse of supernal beauty, or Melville's quick flashing forth of the axis of reality, but they just as often ran up against the inscrutable pasteboard mask of nature.

Throughout the nineteenth century both providential and scientific determinisms flourished, especially in Protestant America. During this period, as John Randall has documented, the impact Darwinian thinking had on religious belief was as pronounced as the impact it had on social belief.[15] Not only did the "social Darwinism" used by men like Carnegie to justify their aggressive capitalism have an effect on the Western intellect, but the impact on religion of Darwinian thinking significantly altered the Western world's perception of man and Nature. This tension between religion and science in the latter half of the nineteenth century resulted in numerous attempts to integrate and reconcile the two systems. For example, Herbert Spencer included in his synthetic philosophy the "Unknowable," a transcendent and mysterious force residing just beyond scientific cognition. Stanley Cooperman argues that in America scientific determinism did not "shatter the foundations of traditional faith, as it did in England, but rather was absorbed by it."[16] Thus, "Puritan determinism, a powerful force in America during the 1890s, found in scientific determinism a psychological ally, compounding the ancient dualism between nature and sin, on the one hand, and spirit and purity, on the other" (252).[17] The important point for understanding American literary naturalism is that it did not focus on scientific determinism alone, but on providential determinism as well. In fact, their struggle with determinism was often defined by the conflict between philosophical naturalism and traditional religious belief. In order to successfully juxtapose or reconcile these different deterministic orientations in their fiction, the American literary naturalists needed to create narratives with some degree of philosophical and aesthetic complexity. In order to discuss the complex role of determinism in some of these narratives, one needs to implement a critical terminology more sophisticated than simply the term *determinism*. William James provides us with such a vocabulary.

William James and the Dilemma of Determinism[18]

Much of the critical language needed to discuss the ways in which determinism is incorporated into naturalistic narratives was provided by William James in his 1884 lecture "The Dilemma of Determinism."[19] Determinism, writes James,

> professes that those parts of the universe already laid down absolutely appoint and decree what the other parts shall be. The future has no

ambiguous possibilities hidden in its womb: the part we call the present is compatible with only one totality. Any other future complement than the one fixed from eternity is impossible. . . . [Possibilities or choices] exist nowhere, and . . . necessity on the one hand and impossibility on the other are the sole categories of the real. Possibilities that fail to get realized are, for determinism, pure illusions; they never were possibilities at all. (150–51)

The opposite of determinism is "indeterminism," in which

the parts have a certain amount of loose play on one another, so that the laying down of one of them does not necessarily determine what the others shall be. It admits that possibilities may be in excess of actualities, and that things not yet revealed to our knowledge may really in themselves be ambiguous. Of two alternative futures which we conceive, both may now be really possible; and the one become impossible only at the very moment when the other excludes it by becoming real itself. Indeterminism thus denies the world to be one unbending unit of fact. It says there is a certain ultimate pluralism in it. (150–51)

Because there is more than one possible future, and because not all acts and events are necessitated, there is room for free will. Indeterminism does not deny the existence of natural law, or of God; it merely argues that the natural laws that govern the rotation of the earth around the sun do not also govern the will; it argues that the omniscience or omnipotence of God does not remove the ability of humans to choose whether or not to serve God. Indeterminism is the Arminian response to Calvinistic or providential determinism. It is the pragmatist response to scientific determinism.[20]

Opposed to indeterminacy, according to James, are not one, but two types of determinism: hard determinism and soft determinism. Hard, or "old-fashioned" determinism, James writes, did not "shrink from such words as fatality, bondage of the will, necessitation, and the like" (149). The hard determinist is the purely mechanical determinist for whom choice, free will, and agency evaporate. For the hard determinist, notions of personal responsibility, morality, and good and evil hold little or no value. Zola captured some of the essence of hard determinism when he wrote: "there is absolute determinism in the conditions of existence of natural phenomena both for living beings and for inert matter," and in time "science will discover the determinism of all the cerebral and sensory manifestations of man."[21] When it does, claims Zola, it will discover that the same determinism governs the "stone in the road and the brain of man." For Zola, these discoveries were positive things. Dreiser, on the other hand, expresses a pessimistic hard determinism in *Newspaper Days* (1931):[22] "With a gloomy eye I began to watch how the mechanical forces operated through man and outside him. . . . All I could think of was that since nature would not or could not do anything for man, he must, if he could, do something for himself. But of this I saw no prospect, he being a product of these self same accidental and so indifferent and hence bitterly cruel forces."[23] Mark Twain's exploration of hard determinism in *What Is Man?* (1906) is, at least on the surface, not so pessimistically expressed as Dreiser's, but is perhaps more entertaining. In a series of Socratic dialogues between two men—one young, one elderly—the elderly man systematically dismantles the younger man's beliefs in free will, altruism, and other idealistic conceptions of the human animal. In the views of the older man, humans are machines that operate as outside forces compel them to operate; they have no free will and are neither to be applauded for their good deeds nor to be condemned for their bad deeds, at least, any more than a well-built or poorly built machine is to be held responsible for its performance. Twain knew that he had written a potentially inflammatory book. Reflecting back upon *What Is Man?* a year after its publication, Twain noted that the controversial nature of the position he takes in the work held him back from early publication. That position can be summed up in a sentence: "According to my own gospel, as set forth in that small book, where there are two desires in a man's heart he has no choice between the two but must obey the strongest, there being no such thing as free will in the composition of any human being that ever lived." Because there is no free will, humans are not meritorious as individuals, for "man is merely a machine automatically functioning without any of his help or any occasion or necessity for his help, and that no machine is entitled to praise for any of its acts of a virtuous sort nor blamable for any of its acts of the opposite sort."[24]

If one desires to mix questions of personal responsibility and determinism, then hard determinism needs to be softened a bit. According to James, soft determinism "allows considerations of good and bad to mingle with those of cause and effect in deciding what sort of universe this may rationally be held to be" (166). Humans are still seen as confined to a universe governed by causal relationships, but the soft determinist allows for moral responsibility and, potentially, degrees of free will within this deterministic framework. Soft determinism, then, can lead to a situation in which humans are both free and determined at the same time, or a morally ambiguous situation in which determined humans are paradoxically held accountable for their actions.

Radical Indeterminacy and Fatalism

Building on James's provocative terminology, it might be beneficial to add two more relevant terms to the mix. To the left of indeterminacy one finds the realm of what I shall refer to as "radical indeterminacy." This is the realm of complete subjectivity. Emphasizing the ambiguity of perception to the extent that even sensory information seems an unreliable basis upon which to build an objective picture of reality, the indeterminacy of a system is heightened. Thus, in the nineteenth century, the belief in some type of objective reality—i.e., some form of epistemological realism that posits the existence of objects of perception independent from the knowing mind—that typically underlies indeterminate, transcendental, pragmatist, and libertarian worldviews evaporates under the pressure of what one might characterize as an extreme Humean skepticism; that is, a skepticism that emphasizes that all "natural laws" are merely human constructs subject to the vagaries of subjective perception, and do not necessarily reflect any objective reality. In the twentieth century radical indeterminacy can be found in theories of man and nature emerging out of scientific concepts like the uncertainty principle and in the extreme relativism of postmodernism.

Significantly, writers who find themselves on either end of this spectrum from radical indeterminacy to hard determinism often make some kind of theoretical or artistic move toward the center (that is, toward a more stable indeterminacy on the one hand, or a softer determinism on the other hand). For instance, consider T. S. Eliot's move to shore up the "fragments" of radical modernist subjectivity and indeterminacy through the use of myth and allusion—through the aesthetic. At the other end of the spectrum, consider Dreiser's discovery that there is indeed one value in the universe—aesthetic beauty—and it stands in hopeful opposition to the cruel, fearful, indifferent forces streaming through this mechanistic universe. Dreiser writes:

> What we plainly see is birth and death—the result of chemic and electrophysical processes of which at bottom we know exactly nothing. And beyond that—murder, the chase, life living on life, the individual sustaining himself at the expense of every other, and wishing not to die. And then beauty, beauty, beauty, which seems to derive as much and more from this internecine and wholly heartless struggle as from any other thing. And yet, beauty, beauty, beauty—the entire process, to the human eye at least, aesthetic in its results if by no means entirely so in its processes.[25]

This tendency for the hard determinist to make some gesture toward "softening" determinism can also be seen in Calvinism. In fact, the whole issue of free will was a particularly knotty problem for providential historiographers and philosophers who held to the hard providential determinism of Calvinist election and predestination (a problem that manifested itself, for instance, in the seventeenth-century debate over preparationism). The Calvinists tried to reconcile a completely predetermined history with the conversion process. They attempted this reconciliation by claiming that though each person's fate was predetermined and only the elect would receive salvation, the "elect" individual had to "will" to accept the saving grace of God—thus, an act of the will is rhetorically woven into Calvinist providential determinism.[26]

To the right of hard determinism is fatalism. Fatalism has in common with deterministic orientations the subjugation of the will to transcendent, controlling forces. The difference is that while the hard determinist argues for the rationality and uniformity and predictability of nature's control of man, fatalism allows for the intervention of the irrational and unpredictable in the general course of events. Zola makes a point of distinguishing his brand of hard determinism from fatalism by quoting Claude Bernard on the matter. Bernard writes: "We have given the name determinism to the proximate or determining cause of phenomena. We do not ever act on the essence of the phenomena of nature, but only on their determinism, and by the fact alone that we act on it determinism differs from fatalism, on which we could not act. Fatalism presupposes the necessary manifestation of a phenomenon independent of its conditions, whereas determinism is the necessary condition of a phenomenon, the manifestation of which is not forced."[27] The point here is that in a determined system every effect can be traced back to a cause that necessitated it, and insofar as man is able to manipulate causes in order to generate effects, so man is able to "act" in some fashion. In a fatalistic system, however, effects may be the result not of a recognizable system of causes, but of the directing "stick of destiny" (to use one of Zola's own phrases), upon which man has no power to act. William James also distinguished between fatalism and determinism in his *Principles of Psychology*. For James, to a certain extent the human will can remain free in a fatalistic system, although that *will* will be unable to act in such a way that the fated outcome of events will be altered.[28]

Whereas in the essay "The Experimental Novel" Zola explicitly distanced his brand of determinism from fatalism, this separation is less clear in American literary naturalism. Providential determinism relies heavily on fatalistic or "providential" interpretations of experience in order to explain nature's mysteries. The tychistic elements of scientific determinism are largely a secularization of fate and providence. Chance ultimately "softens" hard scientific determinism, for in a strict hard determinism with everything subject to causal relationships, chance can play no significant role. What seems like chance or coincidence will always have antecedent causes explainable through direct reference to the natural world. (James would not draw this conclusion, however. He conceived of "chance" ontologically—as a force with existence outside of individual human acts or decisions. Thus, for James, "chance" is a key component of an *indeterminate* system.[29]) Integrating an inscrutable, unexplainable element of chance into such a system is qualitatively no different from arguing that the hand of providence is intervening in the natural world. In either case, tychistic elements in a hard determinist system with no discoverable causal antecedents in the natural world frequently introduce into naturalistic narrative points of epistemological uncertainty that threaten to destabilize the unified deterministic orientation of the text.

Given some of the traditional definitions of literary naturalism over the past century, one might not imagine that a concept such as fate would play a significant role in naturalistic fiction. Yet, fatalism—both directly and indirectly addressed—plays an important role in many naturalistic texts. One of the best-known examples of this can be found in the refrain from "The Open Boat": "If I am going to be drowned . . . why in the name of the seven mad gods who rule the sea, was I allowed to come thus far and contemplate sand and trees? Was I brought here merely to have my nose dragged away as I was about to nibble the sacred cheese of life? It is preposterous. If this old ninny-woman, Fate, cannot do better than this, she should be deprived of the management of men's fortunes. She is an old hen who knows not her intention."[30] One finds some texts, like Norris's "The Jongleur of Taillebois" (1891), "The Riding of Felipe" (1901), and even, to an extent, "A Case for Lombroso" (1897) directly engaging "fate"—not to mention one of Howells's greatest achievements, *A Hazard of New Fortunes.* More often, however, as in *Sister Carrie* and *McTeague,* one finds something corresponding to fate occasionally intervening in the narrative. The closing of the safe as Hurstwood debates whether or not to take the money and the climactic meeting of McTeague and Marcus in Death Valley suggest the possibility of the directing hand of fate or destiny. In a more general sense, the frequent overlapping of providential and scientific determinism in American literary naturalism often results in a blending of causal determinism and fatalism such as one sees in Norris, London, and Dreiser. The result of this blending is what in part makes the comparison between Thomas Hardy's naturalistic fatalism and American naturalistic narratives a better one than the comparison between French and American literary naturalism.[31]

The Dilemma of Determinism

James argues that one of the problems with soft determinism is that it leads to a dilemma whose "left horn is pessimism and whose right horn is subjectivism" (166). Pessimism arises from the recognition that treachery and regret coexist in the world. In a deterministic universe, both treachery and regret are "foredoomed." This recognition leads to the realization that there must be something "fatally unreasonable, absurd, and wrong" with a world that foredooms one to feel regret for that which is inevitable (164). The universe is an absurd place when one regrets the evil in the world yet knows that this same evil is permanently woven into the deterministic fabric of the world. To escape the pessimistic implications of living in an absurd universe, determinism, James writes, "must leave off looking at the goods and ills of life in a simple objective way, and regard them as materials, indifferent in themselves, for the production of consciousness, scientific and ethical, in us" (166). This is subjectivism. Subjectivism escapes the pessimistic implications of determinism by retreating inward. It holds that the events that actually happen in the universe are morally neutral in themselves and that they gain their value through how they are perceived. Descriptions of perceived experience as good or evil become merely subjective designations with no direct correspondence with the natural world. From the subjectivist point of view, "not the doing either of good or of evil is what nature cares for, but the knowing of them" (165). Thus, "life is one long eating of the fruit of the tree of knowledge" (165; James's emphasis). For the subjectivist, the world "must not be regarded as a machine whose final purpose is the making real of any outward good, but rather as a contrivance for deepening the theoretic consciousness of what goodness and evil in their intrinsic natures are" (165). For James, subjectivism is not the view that values are merely subjective; it is, instead, the view that the value of a thing or event is measured by its being known.[32]

The fact that subjectivism leads to a knowledge of good and evil stems from the nature of human psychology. Humans are "born for the conflict" between good and evil, writes James, and they exalt in the "Rembrandtesque moral chiaroscuro, the shifting struggle of the sunbeam in the gloom" (168). A view of the world as pure goodness, with no evil counterpressure, soon grows tedious, like the vision of a harp-and-cloud heaven.[33] Perceived goodness must be occasionally threatened, or it will cease to hold its positive value. The ideal state, argues James, is "not the absence of vice, but vice there, and virtue holding her by the throat" (169).[34]

James argues that the subjectivist interpretation of nature based on the dramatic struggle between good and evil is a *romantic* interpretation of nature. To adopt the subjectivist point of view is to interpret nature as "a great unending romance which the spirit of the universe, striving to realize its own content, is eternally thinking out and representing to itself" (170). James notes that "in theology, subjectivism develops as its 'left wing' antinomianism. In literature, its left wing is romanticism" (171). To illustrate this link between soft determinism and romanticism, James briefly discusses "the last runnings of the romantic school" that can be seen in "that strange contemporary Parisian literature" (172). James writes: "the romantic school began with the worship of subjective sensibility and the revolt against legality of which Rousseau was the first great prophet: and through various fluxes and refluxes, right wings and left wings, it stands to-day with two men of genius, M. Renan and M. Zola, as its principal exponents" (172). Ernest Renan and Émile Zola, according to James, are subjectivists "of the most pronounced sort" (172). Both Zola and Renan, argues James, "are athirst for the facts of life, and both think the facts of human sensibility to be of all facts the most worthy of attention. Both agree, moreover, that sensibility seems to be there for no higher purpose" (172). Thus, neither Zola nor Renan "has a word of rescue from the hour of satiety . . . or from the hour of terror. . . . For terror and satiety are facts of sensibility like any others" (173). At the heart of their "romantic utterances . . . is this inward remedilessness, what Carlyle calls this far-off whimpering of wail and woe. And from this romantic state of mind there is absolutely no possible *theoretic* escape" (173; James's emphasis). In the end, therefore, both Renan's "romance of the spirit" and Zola's "roman expérimental" present a world that Carlyle would have called a "vast, gloomy, solitary Golgotha and mill of death" (173).

James concludes "The Dilemma of Determinism" with a discussion about the relative compatibility of free will with a providential teleology. James does not feel that a belief in free will is "in the least incompatible with the belief in Providence" (180). To illustrate, James writes: "An analogy will make the meaning of this clear. Suppose two men before a chessboard,—the one a novice, the other an expert player of the game. The expert intends to beat. But he cannot foresee exactly what any one actual move of his adversary may be. He knows, however, all the *possible* moves of the latter; and he knows in advance how to meet each of them by a move of his own which leads in the direction of victory. And the victory infallibly arrives, after no matter how devious a course, in the one predestined form of check-mate to the novice's king" (181). If the novice represents "finite free agents" (humankind) and the expert player represents "the infinite mind in which the universe lies" (Providence), James's chess analogy suggests that at various points in humankind's journey toward a predetermined end, ambiguous possibilities will be left open for free will to operate. These acts of the will, however, are constrained by a framing teleological determinism. (For clarity's sake, note that James is not attempting to reconcile free will and providential *determinism*, but free will and a *providence* in which possibilities really exist for human agents.[35])

James was not the only writer who used the chessboard as a metaphor for understanding determinism. As indicated at the beginning of this chapter, Norris used the chessboard metaphor in "The Puppets and the Puppy." Norris's Queen's Bishop notes that all chessmen believe there is a Force that moves them from time to time, but even this Force is subject to certain natural laws, for it "can move us only along certain lines." The Bishop still retains his individuality and will. The Bishop states: my "lines are not those of the knight, or the pawn, or the castle, and no power in the Room can make them so. I am a free agent—that's what is so terrible." The position taken here by the Queen's Bishop is similar to that taken by James. The Bishop is generally confined to the deterministic world of the chessboard, but he retains an element of free will in that it is not predetermined where on the board he will move next (provided that move does not violate the natural laws of the game). What sets Norris's story apart from James's is that Norris in this case is being ironic, while James is not. By shifting the focus from the novice to the chessman, and by drawing attention to the fact that the Bishop, like the other toys, is a mere "puppet," Norris subverts the Bishop's sense of freedom by noting that the Bishop's movements across the chessboard are determined by the whims of an external "force" that moves the pieces across the board.

The chessboard metaphor is a provocative one for interpreting the determinism found in American naturalistic narratives. The situation of James's chess novice is homologous to that of characters like Norris's McTeague, Dreiser's Hurstwood, Crane's Maggie, and London's protagonist in "To Build a Fire." Each of these characters is, like the chess novice, forced to play an intricate game of skill with an apparently unbeatable opponent. Furthermore, if one posits a third figure—an observer watching the game between the novice and the grand master—the metaphor becomes even more appropriate for naturalistic narratives. In a book like *McTeague,* Norris places the reader in the position of observer, watching the novice McTeague engage the expert deterministic laws of nature. What makes the chessboard metaphor so uncanny is that it represents a softer rather than harder determinism. Despite the heavy odds against the novice, an observer would have to allow that at the beginning of the game the ending is undetermined. It is conceivable—from one perspective—that the novice could beat the expert. Here lies some of the reason why one sympathizes with Martin Eden (even

London could not refrain from portraying his protagonist in a heroic light) despite the fact that London seemed to intend the book as a critique of the type of Nietzschean superhero Martin represents.

What one observes in these characters is both the struggle for victory against an opponent whose power eludes clear comprehension and the temerity of these characters in resisting checkmate as long as possible. Sydney Krause writes: "The characteristic mood of deterministic naturalism is mixed and paradoxical. Its key paradox centers on the brute refusal of the human to be sucked down into the vortex of natural law."[36] In a sense, the struggle of characters like McTeague and Martin Eden is akin to Prometheus's struggle against the gods, or Satan's struggle against God in *Paradise Lost*. It was the romantics in the nineteenth century who found in the tragic/hopeless efforts of Prometheus and Satan the elements of heroism and mythic analogues of the human condition. Dreiser formulates the problem this way in *Newspaper Days*:

> For plainly nature is dual. There are the exact facts of the mechanical laws of the universe, knowledge of which may be acquired via mathematics, chemistry, physics and those allied interpretations of fact which they permit: astronomy, geology, botany, physiology, et cetera— supposing life permits the development of a mind so to reason. But in addition to these facts, there is something,—an impulse and a power to betray them—which manifests itself in all forms of organized intelligence and which works apparently to undo or delay that which exact fact would achieve. (608–09)

Crane illustrated the struggle between the "fact" of nature and man's impulse to betray these facts in "The Fire" (1894).[37] In this story the narrator and a "stranger" are walking down a "shadowy" side street at midnight. While the stranger imparts to the narrator "some grim midnight reflections upon existence," a nearby bakery erupts in flame. Instantly, throngs of half-dressed people stream into the streets to stare "at the spectacle in a half-dazed fashion at times, as if they were contemplating the ravings of a red beast in a cage" (596). The force of the blaze is overwhelming. "The blaze had increased with a frightful vehemence and swiftness. Unconsciously, at times, the crowd dully moaned, their eyes fascinated by this exhibition of the strength of nature, their master after all, that ate them and their devices at will whenever it chose to fling down their little restrictions" (597). In fact, the power of the fire provokes one observer to utter "a half-coherent growling at conditions, men, fate, law." Soon, "as if apparitional," the firefighters with their fire patrol wagon arrive. Dwarfed by the conflagration, the firemen "became outlined like black beetles against the red and yellow expanses of the flames" (599). Despite the odds against them, with "the calm, unexcited vision of veterans," the firemen attack the "common enemy, the loosened flame." Crane's allegory illustrates the struggle of the novice against the grand master, of humankind against natural law and providence. The flame, humankind's "common enemy," is the "master" and flings down the "little restrictions" devised by humans to contain it. Still, humankind continues to struggle against deterministic forces with the determination of hardened veterans.

The terminology introduced by James has great potential for furthering our understanding of the ways in which the philosophical concept of determinism is integrated thematically into the texts of American literary naturalism. Aside from the astute observation by James that at some level there is a connection between romanticism in literature and certain forms of soft determinism in philosophy, in general we would not be far from the mark to claim that the romantic texts of Norris, Crane, London, and others are more often characterized by a soft rather than a hard determinism in that they frequently blend deterministic themes and motifs with questions of morality, value judgments based in metaphysical concepts of good and evil, and the potential efficacy of human agency. Nevertheless, one of the things that these writers did, collectively, is explore a variety of deterministic philosophies, at times seeming to accept determinism, at other times seeming to reject it, and often seeming to raise complex philosophical questions dialogically without advocating for one particular position.

The Forms of Determinism

From one perspective, then, we might be well served to take a closer look at some of the principal methods authors used to shape the deterministic themes within their works. If one may be allowed a momentary flirtation with taxonomy for the sake of illustration, I propose to briefly examine three of these methods in the next few pages. I engage in this exercise merely as an analytical aid rather than as a proposal that our difficulties understanding the complexities of certain texts will disappear if we begin to employ this terminology. Critics have spent long hours discussing the deterministic themes that arise in naturalistic narratives, but aside from a couple of notable exceptions mentioned earlier in the chapter, comparatively little time has been spent discussing the aesthetic strategies employed by the American literary naturalists as they strove to incorporate these themes into their texts. Such is the focus of this chapter as a whole and the next few pages in particular.

There were a number of attempts in the late nineteenth century to merge free will and determinism into a unified worldview. In a sense, these theories either veer toward indeterminism, or they "soften" hard determinism by leaving open some element(s) within nature that the human will may operate upon, even if the remaining components of nature are determined. In terms of the way such a theme is integrated into a particular novel, we might claim that such a novel possesses a *reconciled* soft determinism, meaning merely that the text incorporates a worldview, thematically, in which some elements of nature and human nature are determined, while others are subject to the manipulations of the human will. In other words, in these narratives the deterministic vision has been softened by reconciling it with some capacity for human agency, however limited. Often this *reconciled* soft determinism (or perhaps we could just as easily say this *limited* hard determinism) is achieved by appealing to some form of dualism in which the body is seen as subject to deterministic forces but the soul, mind, and/or spirit is seen as free. (In such a case, it might be just as valid to refer to the system as *indeterminate*, with the notation that this indeterminate worldview recognizes the deterministic pressures of certain physical laws that affect matter differently than mind.) Such is the case in Oliver Wendell Holmes's 1870 address "Mechanism in Thought and Morals."[38] The key to this essay is that Holmes posits two realms—one largely physical or instinctual and determined, the other principally mental, conscious, and undetermined. Holmes writes: "The moral universe [i.e., that part of nature and experience not independent of volition] includes nothing but the exercise of choice: all else is machinery. What we can help and what we cannot help are on two sides of a line which separates the sphere of human responsibility from that of the

Being who has arranged and controls the order of things" (301–02). Because there is an allowance in the moral universe for some free will, however limited, Holmes rejects "the mechanical doctrine which makes me the slave of outside influences, whether it work with the logic of Edwards, or the averages of Buckle; whether it come in the shape of the Greek's destiny, or the Mahometan's fatalism" (303). Thus, Holmes is a limited or "soft" determinist. Westbrook writes: Holmes "recognizes a certain amount of mechanism, or determinism, in human choice and action, but he also recognizes a large area where determinism does not operate" (74). Forty years later Henri Bergson would posit a similar reconciliationist stance.[39] In *Time and Free Will* (1910) Bergson argues that man has two selves: the physical self, which is subject to deterministic forces operating in linear time; and the mental self, which is free from deterministic influence because it operates outside of linear time.[40]

Reconciled soft determinism appears in naturalistic narratives that, like James, Holmes, and Bergson, posit a world in which freedom and determinism are merged into a unified cosmology. Perhaps the best example of reconciled soft determinism in American naturalistic fiction can be found in Jack London's *The Star Rover*. In fact, London may have been directly engaging Bergsonian soft determinism when he wrote this narrative. London had read Bergson around the time that he was composing *The Star Rover*. Although London, characterizing himself as a "hopeless materialist," dismissed Bergson in June 1914 as a "metaphysical" and "fly-by-night" philosopher,[41] a month earlier he had written: "You will note I have not made the story [of *The Star Rover*] nor the description of prison conditions grewsome [*sic*]. This is because of the fiction that is wrapped up in it, and the optimism of the story itself, which enables the victim to win to the largeness of the centuries by means of the jacket; which enables the victim to win to love, adventure, romance, and the life everlasting. Also note the tricks I have played with philosophy, expositing the power of mind over matter. . . . The key-note of the book is: THE SPIRIT TRIUMPHANT."[42] London expresses "the spirit triumphant" by turning to a "Bergsonian" soft determinism. The hero of the work, Darrell Standing, is comprised of two selves. His body, the physical self, existing solely in linear time, is subject to outside constraint and influence, held in the rigid, symbolically deterministic lock of the jacket. His mind, however, free from the deterministic forces of the material world and linear time, is able to course through time and space, visiting old incarnations of his self. This reconciliation of free will and determinism through a Bergsonian-style soft determinism results in a positive naturalistic romance that ends, paradoxically, with Darrell Standing facing the hangman's noose with relief, looking forward to his next incarnation.

Unlike *The Star Rover*, which illustrates in narrative form a world consistent with a reconciled soft determinism, in *The Sea-Wolf* London explores the clash of opposing determinate and indeterminate orientations. The story of *The Sea-Wolf* is built around a series of dialogues between Wolf Larson, Maud Brewster, and Humphrey Van Weyden. In these dialogues Larson's materialistic determinism contrasts with Brewster's sentimental idealism, and this contrast becomes evident as each of these characters interprets the events of the narrative through the lens of their respective ideologies. At one point in the narrative, for instance, the crew of the *Ghost* has taken heavily to the whiskey that Larson has made available to them. This prompts a discussion on the nature of temptation. Larson begins by suggesting that humans are driven completely by their desires. But what if one has two conflicting desires? Maud argues that it is in conflicts such as these that "the soul of the man is manifest. . . . If it is a good soul, it will desire and do the good action, and the contrary if it is a bad soul. It is the soul that decides."[43] Larson disagrees: "It is the desire that decides. Here is a man who wants to, say, get drunk. Also, he doesn't want to get drunk. What does he do? How does he do it? He is a puppet. He is the creature of his desires, and of the two desires he obeys the strongest one, that is all. His soul hasn't anything to do with it" (221–22). Van Weyden disagrees with both Larson and Maud, taking a more conciliatory stance. He claims that Larson lays "the stress upon the desire apart from the soul" and that Maud lays "the stress on the soul apart from the desire" (222). In fact, claims Van Weyden, "soul and desire are the same thing" (222). From here the conversation turns to the nature of love, and "as usual" Larson's "was the sheer materialistic side," while Maud's "was the idealistic" (222). "For myself," says Van Weyden, "beyond a word or so of suggestion or correction now and again, I took no part. [Larson] was brilliant, but so was Maud" (222–23). By favoring neither Maud's idealism nor Larson's materialism, but exploring both of these conflicting orientations, London structures his narrative around the juxtaposition of two widely different interpretations of nature and experience. What we are dealing with in this case is something we might refer to as *juxtaposed soft determinism,* although this label is probably less useful than the label *reconciled* soft determinism, because it is a purely formal label used to indicate a novel of ideas in which there is a conflict between two or more clearly divergent deterministic and indeterminate ideologies. In other words, the "softness" of the determinism is only a *formal* softness generated by the dialogical juxtaposition (in the case of *The Sea-Wolf*) of a materialistic hard determinism with an idealistic indeterminism. It is not necessarily a *thematic* softness, for no identifiable soft deterministic philosophy may be present in the narrative.

Although largely forgotten today, Oliver Wendell Holmes's *Elsie Venner* probably deserves considerable credit—along with Davis's "Life in the Iron Mills"—as one of the forebears of American literary naturalism. These two texts certainly represent the missing link—if there is one—between the metaphysical concerns of the American romantics and the metaphysical concerns of the American literary naturalists. Like *The Sea-Wolf, Elsie Venner* features a strong central narrative that incorporates a series of philosophical dialogues in which conflicting theories of determinism are juxtaposed. The story centers on Elsie Venner, a mysterious girl who is part human, part snake, her mother having been bitten by a rattlesnake while pregnant with Elsie. Holmes creates his dual-natured heroine in order to explore the feasibility of moral responsibility in a world in which hereditary and environmental influences impinge upon the human will. In his second preface Holmes writes: "The real aim of the story was to test the doctrine of 'original sin' and human responsibility for the disordered volition coming under that technical denomination. Was Elsie Venner, poisoned by the venom of a crotalus before she was born, morally responsible for the 'volitional' aberrations, which translated into acts become what is known as sin, and, it may be, what is punished as crime?" This question is addressed at length in several dialogues between some of the central characters of the romance. In one of these passages, Bernard Langdon, suspecting Elsie's dual nature, writes to the Professor (who is narrating the story). After asking if the Professor has read critically Keats's "Lamia" or Coleridge's "Christabel," Langdon writes: "Do you think there may be predispositions, inherited or ingrafted, but at any rate constitutional, which shall take out certain apparently voluntary determinations from the control of the will, and leave them as free from moral responsibility as the instincts of the lower animals?" (170). After noting that

Langdon's questions "belong to that middle region between science and poetry," the Professor, while not ruling out entirely the notion of moral responsibility, responds by suggesting that some aberrant behavior is provoked in people through determining forces. Regarding "automatic action in the moral world," the Professor urges some caution, however. The phrase itself, he argues, is oxymoronic, and such a belief is both dangerous and liable to abuse, for "people are always glad to get hold of anything which limits their responsibility" (176).

Not long after this exchange, the Reverend Doctor Honeywood, after Elsie's nanny, Sophy, tells him about Elsie's dual nature, speculates about what is to become of the "theory of ingrained moral obliquity" when challenged with a case such as Elsie's. Honeywood wonders if "by the visitation of God a person receives any injury which impairs the intellect of the moral perceptions, is it not monstrous to judge such a person by our common working standards of right and wrong?" (191).[44] This question carries over into a key debate that Honeywood engages in with Doctor Kittredge over the relative plausibility of religious and scientific interpretations of nature. Honeywood begins by pointing out to Kittredge that science tends to see "Nature" in place of the "God of Nature" (245). Kittredge replies that science does not separate God and Nature, as religion does, but sees God as operating through Nature. Science allows for the idiosyncrasies of human behavior, but religion does not. Beliefs, suggests Kittredge, are determined as much by "race and constitution" as they are by human choice (246). Honeywood counters that Kittredge's scientific determinism "would be considered a degrading and dangerous view of human beliefs and responsibility" by the religious community. For if one proves "to a man that his will is governed by something outside of himself," you will have "lost all hold on his moral and religious nature." Echoing the Professor's earlier comment, Honeywood notes that "there is nothing bad men want to believe so much as that they are governed by necessity" (247). Kittredge acknowledges that his scientific viewpoint does limit one's "estimate of the absolute freedom of the will," but adds that such a limitation is not necessarily dangerous or degrading, for it allows us to be more charitable to our fellow man, and one still has one's conscience to guide behavior (247).

In line with the scientific determinism of Kittredge, the text's direct and indirect references to Darwin's "struggle for existence" paradigm suggest that Elsie's struggle and eventual death may have been a product of the forces of natural selection.[45] The flaws in Elsie's constitution eventually get the better of her, and she falls victim to the principles of selection operating in Nature. Nature, when "left to her own freaks in the forest, is grotesque and fanciful to the verge of license, and beyond it" (207). Elsie Venner, an admirer of these "sculpture-like monstrosities" of nature, seems to have been subject to the creative whims of Nature herself, and she soon falls victim to Nature's filtering process.

There is also the rough framework of a Christian allegory in the text that offers an alternative interpretation of Elsie's downfall and death. Elsie is torn between the impulses of good and evil, and she struggles throughout the romance to exorcise her evil nature so that she can finally be free to love and be loved. The connection between Elsie and Eve is suggested by the Reverend Fairweather, who recalls that once, after tearing a frontispiece picturing the temptation of Eve out of a book, Elsie remarked that "Eve was a good woman,—and she'd have done just so, if she'd been there" (199). Her serpentine side symbolizes the taint of inherited sin, and her inner struggle throughout the text is characterized by her desire to live a righteous life and to bridge the gulf of original sin that keeps her separated from her Heavenly Father. Elsie finally seems to receive redemption at the end of the book when the snake within her dies and Elsie takes on the outward appearance of her departed mother (344–45). Then, in a moment that recalls Dimmesdale's embrace of Pearl upon the scaffold, Elsie's transformation is completed when her father, Dudley, kisses his daughter for the first time (symbolizing Elsie's acceptance by her Heavenly Father).

Holmes, therefore, not only explores the free will/determinism debate in *Elsie Venner,* but through these two different interpretations of Elsie's dual nature, the scientific and the religious, Holmes juxtaposes scientific and providential determinism. Did Elsie have free will? If she didn't, was it because of the deterministic forces operating in nature, or was it because of the determining effects of original sin?

Aside from *reconciled* and *juxtaposed* soft determinism, there is another label that might prove useful when discussing the role of determinism in the texts of American literary naturalism: *subversive* soft determinism. Rather than attempt to thematically present a philosophically reconciled soft determinism, or attempt to formally juxtapose conflicting determinate and indeterminate ideologies, the author of a *subversive* soft determinism undercuts a surface indeterminism through the skeptical or ironic revealing of deeper, hidden, deterministic forces that call into question human selfhood and agency. The reverse of this process—i.e., the complicating or subverting of a surface determinism with notions of moral responsibility, choice, or good and evil—produces a similar effect. In either case, rather than simply undercut a surface *appearance* through the revealing of an underlying *reality,* in many texts structured around a subversive soft determinism the question of which one of two or more interpretations of nature and experience remains open.

Frank Norris's *McTeague* illustrates a "subversive" form of soft determinism. The awakening of the brute within McTeague is described simultaneously in scientific and theological terms, and the path of his degeneration throughout the novel has both natural and supernatural implications.[46] On the surface McTeague's is a struggle against the atavistic impulses of hereditary determinism. But there is a deeper allegorical element to the work that represents McTeague's struggle as one against the spiritually corrupting influences of original sin.[47]

Some of the philosophical framework informing *McTeague* may have been derived from Joseph Le Conte. Donald Pizer has argued that the evolutionary theism of Joseph Le Conte played an important role in the development of Frank Norris's philosophy. According to Le Conte, humans have two natures: a higher and a lower. The key to progress lies in one's ability to keep the lower nature in subjugation to the higher. What distinguishes man from the brutes is the "human spirit—which for the first time directs evolution not by law from without but by choice from within through the conscious striving of man, guided by reason, toward a spiritual ideal" (Pizer, *Novels of Frank Norris* 15). For Le Conte it is through the exercise of reason that man elevates himself above manipulation by brute instinct. Norris uses Le Conte's concept of higher and lower natures in *McTeague* to help characterize his protagonist as one who lapses, or degenerates, into a lower state (or whose lower nature "rises" to usurp the proper place of the higher nature). It is the lower nature (the physical nature, the "flesh") that is more subject to deterministic forces. One's higher nature (the reason, the will, the "spirit") is less subject to deterministic forces, more responsive to the will. As McTeague's lower nature—the brute—gradually gains control, he becomes increasingly confined by natural law. That is, the more McTeague gives way to his lower nature, the "harder" the deterministic forces controlling his behavior become.

McTeague's downfall begins in the Dental Parlors. With the awakening of his sexual instincts comes the temptation to take advantage of the helpless Trina.[48] As she lies "absolutely without defense" in the chair, "suddenly the animal in the man stirred and woke; the evil instincts that in him were so close to the surface leaped to life, shouting and clamoring" (23). The brute within him leaps to life: "Blindly, and without knowing why, McTeague fought against it, moved by an unreasoned instinct of resistance. Within him, a certain second self, another better McTeague rose with the brute; both were strong, with the huge crude strength of the man himself. The two were at grapples. There in that cheap and shabby 'Dental Parlor' a dreaded struggle began. It was the old battle, old as the world, wide as the world" (23–24). Clenching his fists and muttering "No, by God!" McTeague realizes that "should he yield now he would never be able to care for Trina again. . . . Across her forehead . . . he would surely see the smudge of a foul ordure, the footprint of the monster. It would be a sacrilege, an abomination" (24). He yields to the temptation, kisses Trina, but then regains some semblance of control over himself. Still, despite his outer control, "the brute was there. Long dormant, it was now at last alive, awake. From now on he would feel its presence continually; would feel it tugging at its chain, watching its opportunity. Ah, the pity of it! Why could he not always love her purely, cleanly? What was this perverse, vicious thing that lived within him, knitted to his flesh?" (25). "Below the fine fabric of all that was good in him ran the foul stream of hereditary evil, like a sewer. The vices and sins of his father and of his father's father, to the third and fourth and five hundredth generation, tainted him. The evil of an entire race flowed in his veins. Why should it be? He did not desire it. Was he to blame?" (25). The "foul stream of hereditary evil" (symbolized by the brute) implies at the same time a scientific hereditary determinism and a providential original sin. In the context of scientific determinism, McTeague's struggle is between Le Conte's higher and lower natures; it is a conflict between reason and instinct—and McTeague gives way to his animal passion, and brute instinct overrides the control of reason. In the context of providential determinism, the foul stream of original sin influences McTeague to give in to temptation and lapse into a state of spiritual corruption. Seen in this light, *McTeague* is a psychomachia in which the struggle of McTeague is the spiritual battle between the forces of good and evil for the control of the soul of man.[49] At this level the characters in *McTeague* fall victim to two of the seven deadly sins: lust and avarice, or desire and greed. McTeague's kissing Trina marks his first major concession to illicit desire; and Trina hoards her bag of gold while McTeague and Marcus seek ways to possess it themselves. And so *McTeague* illustrates not a hard determinism, but a subversive soft determinism. While on the surface it is a tale of scientific determinism, it is also an ambiguous morality play in the tradition of the negative romance.

This allegorical reading of *McTeague* offers an explanation for the otherwise inexplicable passage late in the narrative when McTeague is approached by Big Jim. The remedy for the deadly sin of avarice, according to Chaucer's Parson, is one of the seven cardinal virtues: "mercy, and pity generously taken," that is, charity bestowed upon one who suffers. Performing acts of charity can "move a man to sympathy with Jesus Christ," who freed us from "our original sins."[50] Symbolically, as McTeague flees into the desert he is offered a chance to gain "sympathy with Jesus Christ" and escape the bonds of "original sin":

> an immense Indian buck, blanketed to the ground, approached McTeague as he stood on the roadbed stretching his legs, and without a word presented to him a filthy, crumpled letter. The letter was to the effect that the buck Big Jim was a good Indian and deserving of charity; the signature was illegible. The dentist stared at the letter, returned it to the buck, and regained the train just as it started. Neither had spoken; the buck did not move from his position, and fully five minutes afterward, when the slow-moving freight was miles away, the dentist looked back and saw him still standing motionless between the rails, a forlorn and solitary point of red, lost in the immensity of the surrounding white blur of the desert. (278)

Despite the fact that he has five thousand dollars in gold pieces wrapped up in his bundle, McTeague shows no charity to the Indian. In terms of the allegorical undercurrent in the text, McTeague symbolically relinquishes an opportunity to escape the deterministic bonds of "original sin"—or in other words, McTeague passes up the final opportunity he is given to feed his higher nature rather than the lower nature of the brute. McTeague soon finds himself staring at the burning sands of Death Valley—the Valley of Death.[51]

Subjectivism and *The Red Badge of Courage*

J. C. Levenson writes: "Crane believed that, despite man's readiness to project ideas of order—and even attitudes toward himself—upon external nature, the universe is only a neutral backdrop to human activity." Without the aid of firsthand knowledge of either William James or Chauncey Wright, Levenson argues, Crane "was reduced to showing how, reacting to his own changeable situation, a man might regard nature in various ways."[52] The indirect connection Levenson notices between James and Crane has recently been explored at length by Patrick Dooley, who examines the compatibilities of Jamesian thought with the philosophy of Stephen Crane. Dooley demonstrates that, like James, Crane was a philosophical pluralist who used conflicting observer/participant/reader perceptions to expose both the multiplicity of reality and the corollary fact that "truth" changes depending upon one's viewpoint. Crane is not "skeptical about humanity's ability to know the world," writes Dooley; however, "no single world exists. Accordingly, no single record of it can claim truth. On the contrary, because a multitude of worlds can be experienced, a plurality of true descriptions is both a realistic goal and a reasonable expectation." But the "search for relatively true accounts of the worlds of experience does not amount to a surrender to subjectivism because equal value is not attributed to every interpretative report."[53]

Dooley seems to use the term "subjectivism" in this passage to mean a relativism in which no one point of view can be judged better or worse than another. Indeed, Crane often points out in his fiction that certain subjective perceptions provide a false impression of reality. In chapter 6 of *Red Badge,* for example, Fleming's perception that the regiment is doomed is proven false when upon approaching the general he discovers that the regiment has won the battle after all. In this passage the general's perspective on the battle was superior to Henry Fleming's.

But James makes a related but special use of the term "subjectivism" in "The Dilemma of Determinism." As we have seen, the dilemma of determinism, in James's view, is that it leads either to pessimism or subjectivism.

Subjectivism, we recall, posits that one must stop viewing good and evil objectively and begin to view them as indifferent materials useful for the production of scientific and ethical consciousness in humankind. One of the better illustrations of James's concept of subjectivism can be found in Stephen Crane's *The Red Badge of Courage*. In order to avoid a pessimistic interpretation of nature based upon a conviction of the fundamental absurdity of war and human behavior, Henry Fleming retreats into subjectivism: his shifting perspectives on nature are grounded in a belief that the sensory data provided by nature are there to teach him how to interpret the meaning of his apparent cowardice. Thus, Fleming becomes a symbolist of sorts, seeking to interpret the signs presented to him by nature; yet, these attempts are veiled in what we might call a pervasive romantic irony, for the very signs Fleming attempts to decipher are, in part, products of the youth's subjective imagination.

The book begins by emphasizing Fleming's shifting perspectives on war. He had "dreamed of battles all his life—of vague and bloody conflicts that had thrilled him with their sweep and fire. In visions he had seen himself in many struggles. . . . But awake he had regarded battles as crimson blotches on the pages of the past. He had put them as things of the bygone with his thought-images of heavy crowns and high castles" (4–5).[54] With youthful eyes he "had long despaired of witnessing a Greeklike struggle" (5). His "busy mind had drawn for him large pictures extravagant in color, lurid with breathless deeds" (5). These great expectations are left unfulfilled. After enlisting he finds that his regiment does little but "sit still and try to keep warm" (7). He grows to regard himself merely "as part of a vast blue demonstration" (7).

The general inactivity of the regiment gives Fleming considerable time for self-analysis. He tries to "mathematically prove to himself that he would not run from a battle" (8). Such proofs do not present themselves to him, however, and he "was forced to admit that as far as war was concerned he knew nothing of himself" (8). In this crisis he finds "his laws of life were useless. Whatever he had learned of himself was here of no avail. He was an unknown quantity" (8). As a result, he concludes that he will have to perform an "experiment" and "accumulate information on himself" (8). The rest of the book concerns his "experiment." The problem for Fleming is that he has trouble interpreting the results.

Having set up the plot of the book and introduced its major theme in the first chapter, Crane uses the rest of the narrative to dramatize Fleming's experiment and to explore how he tries to integrate the information he collects into his perspectives on self, nature, and experience. The book, then, is built around shifting participant/observer perspectives. While conducting his "experiment," his perspective is that of a participant. When trying to interpret the results, his perspective is that of observer. Fleming thus shifts between an active and participatory "self in action" and a passive and observational "self in reflection." These two selves are mutually exclusive: he cannot both act and reflect at the same time. For instance, when early in the narrative the regiment, hearing gunfire, begins to run, he "was bewildered. As he ran with his comrades he strenuously tried to think, but all he knew was that if he fell down those coming behind would tread upon him. All his faculties seemed to be needed to guide him over and past obstructions" (17).

When Fleming does find time for self-analysis and reflection, he oscillates between deterministic and indeterministic interpretations of nature and experience. Fleming's shifting interpretations are linked to whether he perceives himself to have acted heroically or cowardly. In order to compensate for the guilt he feels for his cowardly acts, he turns toward determinism. But when he believes himself to have acted courageously, he shifts toward indeterminism. This pattern emerges shortly after the regiment's run in chapter 3. Here, realizing that his "experiment" is about to happen, and believing himself imprisoned in the mob of soldiers, he feels the first pangs of cowardice (17). In order to justify his apprehension, he formulates a deterministic interpretation of his position in the regiment.

> But he instantly saw that it would be impossible for him to escape from the regiment. It inclosed him. And there were iron laws of tradition and law on four sides. He was in a moving box.
>
> As he perceived this fact it occurred to him that he had never wished to come to the war. He had not enlisted of his free will. He had been dragged by the merciless government. And now they were taking him out to be slaughtered. (18)

Despite these apprehensions, "the ardor which the youth had acquired" during the march fades when the regiment lapses into inaction again (19). If an "intense scene had caught him with its wild swing as he came to the top of the bank, he might have gone roaring on" (19). But this "advance upon Nature was too calm" and it provided him with "opportunity to reflect" (19). In his reflections "absurd ideas" took hold of him: he "thought that he did not relish the landscape. It threatened him" (19). Soon he comes to the conclusion that the "generals did not know what they were about" and that the regiment was "going to be sacrificed" (19).

Although anxious over how he will react when the attack finally occurs, Fleming steadies himself by recalling that he "had been taught that a man became another thing in a battle. He saw his salvation in such a change" (20). When the first skirmish takes place, he does, in a sense, become "another thing," changing from observer/reflector to participant/actor.

> He got the one glance at the foe-swarming field in front of him, and instantly ceased to debate the question of his piece being loaded. Before he was ready to begin—before he had announced to himself that he was about to fight—he threw the obedient, well-balanced rifle into position and fired a first wild shot. Directly he was working at his weapon like an automatic affair.
>
> He suddenly lost concern for himself, and forgot to look at a menacing fate. He became not a man but a member. (26)

When the skirmish ended, he "awakened slowly" and "came gradually back to a position from which he could regard himself" (29). The initial experiment concluded, he regards himself as a hero whose "supreme trial had been passed. The red, formidable difficulties of war had been vanquished" (30). Believing himself courageous, he turns from his prior deterministic outlook to one that asserts individual agency. He sees his courage arising from the fact that he is a heroic man. Delighted with this estimation of himself, he "went into an ecstasy of self-satisfaction. . . . Standing as if apart from himself, he viewed the last scene. He perceived that the man who had fought thus was magnificent" (30).

Fleming's self-satisfaction is short-lived, for the gray army quickly renews their attack. Awed by the apparent "valor" of these "machines of steel," he turns and runs like the "proverbial chicken" (31). In order to justify his desertion, he interprets his flight as the deliberate act of a man with a superior sense of perception. Those who stayed to fight were "methodical idiots" and "machine-like fools," and he "pitied them as he ran" (32). Coming upon a general, whom he considers "unable to comprehend chaos," he contemplates telling him that the regiment was doomed (33). Before he does so, however, he overhears the general declare that the regiment has not been crushed, but has actually held the line (34).

His cowardice and misapprehension exposed, Fleming "cringed as if discovered in a crime" (34). Chapter 7 of *Red Badge* explores how he tries to reconcile himself with his guilt. He does so by turning back to a deterministic interpretation of Nature and experience. The chapter begins with his attempt to hold on to his sense of manhood and agency by arguing that, despite the fact that the line had held, he had run because of his "superior perceptions and knowledge," and he knew it could be proved that his comrades "had been fools" to stay and fight (35). This argument he knows is flawed, and he soon begins to "pity himself acutely," feeling himself "ill used" and "trodden beneath the feet of an iron injustice" (35). Then, "seeking dark and intricate places," he flees farther into the woods (35). Throwing a pinecone at a squirrel, he watches the frightened animal scurry up a tree. He uses this event to construct a deterministic interpretation of Nature that helps rationalize away his feelings of cowardice and guilt.

> The youth felt triumphant at this exhibition. There was the law, he said. Nature had given him a sign. The squirrel, immediately upon recognizing danger, had taken to his legs without ado. He did not stand stolidly baring his furry belly to the missile, and die with an upward glance at the sympathetic heavens. On the contrary, he had fled as fast as his legs could carry him; and he was but an ordinary squirrel, too— doubtless no philosopher of his race. The youth wended, feeling that Nature was of his mind. She reenforced his argument with proofs that lived where the sun shone. (35–36)

Fleming's deterministic reassurance does not last long, however. Wandering near a swamp, he sees "a small animal pounce in and emerge directly with a gleaming fish" (36). Then, passing from "obscurity into promises of a greater obscurity," he comes upon a place where the "high, arching boughs made a chapel" (36). Pushing open the "green doors" of the chapel and step-ping into the "religious half light," he finds himself staring at a dead man seated against a tree (36). The man's eyes had the dull hue of a "dead fish" and ants were crawling across the face (36). The detail of the dead-fish eyes connects the chapel scene with the preceding scene in which the animal catches a fish in the swamp. This connection suggests a different law of na-ture: life feeds or exists on death. This observation regarding the inherent violence in nature contrasts with the youth's earlier observation that nature itself—as exemplified in the squirrel's flight—abhors violence. A compari-son of these two different interpretations of the law of nature shows that the first privileges (and justifies) his flight; the other privileges the battle, and is another argument for Fleming's cowardice.[55]

The next several chapters of the book detail Fleming's further attempts to reconcile himself with his feelings of guilt and cowardice, and in so doing continue the process of interpreting the results of his earlier experiments with war. The difficulty of this interpretive process is compounded by the fact that Fleming's varying perspectives on nature and experience are driven by his subjectivism. What one observes repeatedly is that nature is described in a way that mirrors Fleming's own internal struggles. Nature acts as a back-drop upon which he projects his shifting perceptions. Fleeing from the chapel in the forest, for instance, he feels that the trees begin to "softly sing a hymn of twilight" and that the insects are bowing their beaks and "making a devotional pause" (37). When his legs get caught in some brambles as he walks toward the battlefield, he interprets this to mean that "Nature could not be quite ready to kill him" (38). As he gets within sight of the battle, he sees it as an "immense and terrible machine" and he wishes to get closer and "see it produce corpses" (38). Soon he comes across some wounded sol-diers. Here, the innocent probings of the tattered soldier remind him once again of his cowardice. He comes to believe that "his shame could be viewed. He was continually casting sidelong glances to see if the men were contem-plating the letters of guilt he felt burned into his brow" (40–41). Because of his shame Fleming wishes that "he, too, had a wound, a red badge of cour-age"; such a wound would give him an alibi to cover his guilt (41). He does have a wounded conscience, however, and the tattered soldier points out that internal wounds are sometimes the worst (46).

The "simple questions" of the tattered man were "knife thrusts" to Fleming, and he perceives them as evidence of a "society that probes pitilessly at secrets until all is apparent" (47). So powerful are these probing forces that he believes he will be unable to keep buried "those things which are willed to be forever hidden. He admitted that he could not defend himself against this agency" (47). As a result of this renewed fear that his guilt will eventually be exposed, he tries to construct yet another deterministic interpretation of nature to help assuage his conscience. Feeling that he will never join the ranks of the heroic and courageous, he "searched about in his mind for an adequate malediction for the indefinite cause, the thing upon which men turn the words of final blame. It—whatever it was—was responsible for him, he said. There lay the fault" (48).

Fleming's reflections shortly come to an end. In chapter 12 the "dragons" of the rebel army advance and the blue soldiers begin to retreat en masse (51–52). At the sight of soldiers running past him he becomes "horrorstricken" (52). Caught up in the midst of the activity, he shifts from observer to participant, from the reflective self to the active self. He "forgot that he was engaged in combating the universe. He threw aside his mental pamphlets on the philosophy of the retreated and rules for the guidance of the damned" (52). In the midst of this flurry of activity he is unable to formulate whole sentences and is reduced to asking fleeing soldiers "why—why—what—what's th' matter?" (52). It is here, in the middle of the book, that Fleming receives his red badge (52–53). With this wound and the help of the cheery soldier, he is able to return to his regiment, where he is nursed by Wilson and his "disordered mind" interprets the "hall of the forest as a charnel place" (60).

Enabled to rejoin the regiment without having his guilt exposed, Fleming is able to formulate a new theory of nature. This newest experience teaches him that "many obligations of a life were easily avoided. The lessons of yesterday had been that retribution was a laggard and blind" (65). He need not fear battles to come; instead he could "leave much to chance" (65). Besides, "a faith in himself had secretly blossomed. There was a little flower of confidence growing within him. He was now a man of experience" (65). The "dragons" of war were "not so hideous as he had imagined them," and they were "inaccurate; they did not sting with precision" (65). Furthermore, "how could they kill him who was the chosen of gods and doomed to greatness?"

(65). While others had fled the battlefield like "weak mortals," Fleming be-lieves himself to have "fled with discretion and dignity" (65). Thinking he has escaped detection from his peers, Fleming is thus able to reinterpret nature as governed by a "soft" determinism: "chance" is a law of nature, but it is "laggard" and therefore allows for those, like himself, with superior perceptions to act with "discretion."

When the time finally comes to prove himself in battle, Fleming's perspec-tive shifts back to that of participant. He fights without thinking, so uncon-scious of his surroundings that when a lull comes in the fighting he continues to fire his weapon for some time (71–72). When he does stop firing, he inter-prets his actions: "It was revealed to him that he had been a barbarian, a beast. He had fought like a pagan who defends his religion. Regarding it, he saw that it was fine, wild, and, in some ways, easy. He had been a tremendous figure, no doubt. . . . he was now what he called a hero. And he had not been aware of the process. He had slept and, awakening, found himself a knight" (72). Unfortunately, his high regard for himself is not corroborated by an officer who claims that the regiment not only fights like "a lot 'a mule driv-ers," but also is his most dispensable unit (75). These overheard remarks give him "new eyes," and he learns "suddenly that he was very insignificant" (75). The information that the 304th is to charge the rebels presents him with a new mystery. He had proven that he could maintain a line, but actually charg-ing the enemy was a different matter. As a result, he perceives "powers and horrors" in the foliage ahead of him (76). He is able to see his surroundings, but is unsure of their meaning, particularly as they relate to himself. His "mind took a mechanical but firm impression, so that afterward everything was pictured and explained to him, save why he himself was there" (77). The signs are there, but they elude interpretation.

The skirmish won, Fleming and other members of the 304th, feeling them-selves heroic again, return to an indeterminate theory of nature.

It had begun to seem to them that events were trying to prove that they were impotent. These little battles had evidently endeavored to demonstrate that the men could not fight well. When on the verge of submission to these opinions, the small duel had showed them that the proportions were not impossible, and by it they had revenged them-selves upon their misgivings and upon the foe.

. . . And they were men. (84)

As men they have the ability to stand up against "events" and prove themselves heroic (despite grand master/novice odds). They gain further evidence for this interpretation when the battle resumes and the 304th, with Fleming acting as color-bearer and Wilson capturing the enemy flag, wins yet another skirmish.

The book's final chapter is dedicated to self-analysis and reflection. This process of reflection begins when Fleming shifts back into the observational mode: "For a time the youth was obliged to reflect in a puzzled and uncertain way. His mind was undergoing a subtle change. It took moments for it to cast off its battleful ways and resume its accustomed course of thought. Gradually his brain emerged from the clogged clouds, and at last he was enabled to more closely comprehend himself and circumstance" (96). Having thus engaged his "machines of reflection" Fleming struggles to "marshall all his acts," but "at last they marched before him clearly. From this present view point he was enabled to look upon them in spectator fashion and to criticize them with some correctness, for his new condition had already defeated certain sympathies" (96). He sees "that he was good" (96), but in the midst of this goodness "the light of his soul flickered with shame" at the memory of deserting the tattered soldier in the field (97). As with his original desertion, he fears that "he might be detected in the thing" (97), and this fear darkens an otherwise "purple and gold" view of himself (97). One final time, then, he must adjust his interpretation of nature in order to accommodate "his vivid error":

> Yet gradually he mustered force to put the sin at a distance. And at last his eyes seemed to open to some new ways. He found that he could look back upon the brass and bombast of his earlier gospels and see them truly. He was gleeful when he discovered that he now despised them.
>
> With this conviction came a store of assurance. He felt a quiet manhood, nonassertive but of sturdy and strong blood. . . .
>
> So it came to pass that as he trudged from the place of blood and wrath his soul changed. He came from hot plowshares to prospects of clover tranquility. (97–98)

Fleming reconciles himself to his "sin," thus, by reading the events of the past two days as a redemption story. He may have "sinned," but that sin opened his eyes to the falseness of his "earlier gospels." This revelation changes his "soul." Now, having "rid himself of the red sickness of battle," he can look forward to "an existence of soft and eternal peace" (98). As a symbol of this newfound redemption, "over the river a golden ray of sun came through the hosts of leaden rain clouds" (98).

Fleming's deterministic interpretations of nature are at varying times natural and supernatural. On some occasions he interprets experiences by appealing to the scientific "laws" of nature, such as instinct, as in the case of the fleeing squirrel. On other occasions, combined with these scientific "laws" are supernatural and religious elements, some of which point toward a providential determinism. Fleming often turns toward religious imagery and language.[56] He is one of the "damned" and longs to prove himself one of the "chosen" or elect (see 48, 52, 64). He finally reconciles himself to his "sin" by turning to what amounts to a type of *felix culpa* argument: God allowed him to sin, for it ultimately led to the purification of his soul. That Fleming turns to this type of argument at the end of the book is made even more explicit in one of the uncancelled but unpublished passages in the manuscript version: "He was emerged from his struggles, with a large sympathy for the machinery of the universe. With his new eyes, he could see that the secret and open blows which were being dealt about the world with such heavenly lavishness were in truth blessings. It was a deity laying about him with the bludgeon of correction" (105).[57] Although Crane's irony does undercut attempts to read *Red Badge* as a positive redemption story, he does provide enough language within the text to at least legitimize *Fleming*'s various religious interpretations of nature. There is a "chapel" in the forest. The walk with the cheery soldier suggests the Emmaus road. Fleming divides the courageous and the cowardly into the "chosen" and the "damned." Fleming sees his desertions as "sins." When his "soul" changes at the end of the book, Fleming sets aside his "former gospels."

The irony of the ending does not arise so much from the reader's assumption (based presumably on a knowledge of the mind of Crane) that *Crane* believes there is no power in redemption, but rather it stems from the realization that Fleming's latest interpretation of nature is a product of his "machines of reflection." Once again he justifies his feelings of guilt by constructing a theory of nature that helps separate him from responsibility for his "sin." This irony was emphasized by Crane in another unpublished passage from the manuscript. After the line "Yet gradually he mustered force to put the sin at a distance," Crane had originally written:

> And then he regarded it with what he thought to be great calmness. At last, he concluded that he saw in it quaint uses. He exclaimed that its importance in the aftertime would be great to him if it even succeeded in hindering the workings of his egotism. It would make a sobering balance. It would become a good part of him. He would have upon him often the consciousness of a great mistake. . . .
>
> This plan for the utilization of a sin did not give him complete joy but it was the best sentiment he could formulate under the circumstances. (104–05)

Leaving out this and the "bludgeon of correction" passages takes the bluntness out of Crane's irony, but does not change the fact that Fleming's conviction of redemption is the product of subjective reflection.[58]

In the end, William James would reject the subjectivist approach to nature illustrated in the oscillating perspective on nature taken by Crane's Fleming. In "The Dilemma of Determinism" James quotes a passage from Carlyle, who wrote: "Hang your sensibilities! Stop your snivelling [*sic*] complaints, and your equally snivelling raptures! Leave off your general emotional tomfoolery, and get to WORK like men!" (174). Adopting such a position, argues James, requires a complete break with the subjectivist perspective, for it claims conduct, not perception, is the basis of value in the universe. And so James openly opposes his "romantic rival"—the subjectivism of soft determinism—by positing what he refers to as the "philosophy of objective conduct" (174). James describes his philosophy in this manner: "It is the recognition of limits, foreign and opaque to our understanding. It is the willingness, after bringing about some external good, to feel at peace; for our responsibility ends with the performance of that duty, and the burden of the rest we may lay on higher powers" (174–75). The distinction drawn here between a philosophy of objective conduct and the subjectivism of soft determinism is important for illustrating a key difference between realism and romanticism. Positing metaphysical and epistemological speculation so central to romanticism as subsidiary to the pragmatic action valorized by James goes far toward explaining the shift in the realistic novel away from the abstract speculation of the romance and toward an examination of social behavior and conduct.

Beyond illustrating this difference in realism and romanticism, James's discussion of the dilemma of determinism is remarkable for a number of reasons. First, predating Norris's "Zola as a Romantic Writer" by a dozen years, James adds his weight to Norris's claims by positioning Zola as a writer of romances, and of viewing the soft determinism so vital to American literary naturalism as a type of romanticism. Furthermore, James's observation that soft determinism often invites a fatalistic orientation generally confirms speculations raised earlier in this chapter about the intermingling of fatalism with scientific and providential determinism in American naturalist narratives.

But even more importantly, James makes some significant linkages among epistemology, perception, romanticism, and soft determinism that help open up the texts of American literary naturalism. Neither the antebellum romancers nor the later literary naturalists in America would have been satisfied with James's philosophy of objective conduct. They generally were not satisfied with the "recognition of limits, foreign and opaque to our understanding." On the contrary, writers like Brown, Poe, Melville, Hawthorne, Crane, Norris, and London attempted to push beyond these limits—and it is one of the chief characteristics of negative romanticism/naturalism that these attempts either failed, revealed further limits, or only served to open up more questions. Sometimes they achieved a brief glimpse of supernal beauty or a quick flashing forth of the axis of reality, but they just as often ran up against the inscrutable pasteboard mask of nature. They were left, like Crane's youth, walking around and around a dead soldier, trying "to read in dead eyes the answer to the Question."[59]

5

Reading American Literary Naturalism

What can we say with assurance about naturalistic texts? We can say that they all engage in the thematic exploration of naturalist theory—but, of course, that is how we defined the term "literary naturalism" in chapter 1, so there is no grand revelation to be realized in its restatement here. Beyond this bald definitional claim, there is little else we can claim about naturalistic texts with such sweeping assurance, and as it turns out, this is a good thing, for it emphasizes the fact that naturalism is a literary movement that benefits when it is taken for what it is rather than discussed as an afterthought at the end of studies of literary realism. More importantly, it reveals that our understanding of literary naturalism benefits most when we look at the evolution of this literary movement not solely within the context of literary realism, but within the context of the whole nineteenth century—socially, philosophically, culturally, and aesthetically. Fortunately, this is the direction some scholars have been taking in recent years. June Howard's study of the relationship between literary naturalism and the social and economic environment of the late nineteenth century in *Form and History in American Literary Naturalism;* Jennifer Fleissner's exploration of, among other things, the rise of the New Woman in the 1890s and the major figures of American literary naturalism in her essay "The Work of Womanhood in American Naturalism"; and Donna Campbell's remarkable study of the relationship between literary naturalism and American regionalism in *Resisting Regionalism,* all reach beyond earlier studies of literary naturalism in an attempt to demonstrate the vitality of the movement within the broad cultural context of the late nineteenth century.

One of the motifs in the current work is to join the efforts of these and other critics in their attempt to redefine how we read and discuss works by authors as diverse as Mark Twain, Stephen Crane, and Rebecca Harding Davis. In this examination we have noticed certain trends, such as the inclination on the part of many naturalistic authors to revitalize the tradition of the romance through the integration of scientific and philosophical themes in their works. We also note that scientific and philosophical naturalism—in its many shapes and guises—has played a much larger role in nineteenth-century American literature than we might have previously imagined. Although we still profit from focusing on the 1890s, works such as Holmes's *Elsie Venner* and Davis's "Life in the Iron Mills" from the early 1860s form a clear bridge between the first and second half of the nineteenth century and suggest that the literary roots of American literary naturalism (as opposed to merely the philosophical roots) stretch back further than the publication of *Maggie* in 1893. Surely these early texts, not to mention Mark Twain's exploration of certain deterministic themes in *A Connecticut Yankee in King Arthur's Court* in 1889, demonstrate that literary naturalism did not spring forth full-grown—like Athena from the head of Zeus—in the 1890s (although it's likely that the image of naturalism leaping forward in full battle dress from the cleft head of realism would have had some appeal for Norris). And what of the wave of utopian fiction in the late 1880s and 1890s? Surely a study of the relationship between utopian fiction and literary naturalism in the 1890s along lines similar to Campbell's *Resisting Regionalism* would broaden even further our understanding of naturalism as a literary movement in America. Equally rewarding for our understanding of literary naturalism and its prominent role in American literature are recent studies that examine how deterministic and evolutionary concepts play important roles in texts such as Chopin's *The Awakening* and Wharton's *The House of Mirth.*[1] Aside from broadening our appreciation of the impact of naturalism in American literature, these and studies like them underscore the fact that literary naturalism is certainly not a gender-specific movement, even though studies of the movement have tended to focus primarily on Norris, Crane, and Dreiser.

Even noting that the tradition of the romance in America had a dramatic impact upon literary naturalism only illustrates a trend, not a definitive characteristic, and when we read the texts of literary naturalism, we quickly become aware of their diversity, ranging from the out-and-out romance of *Elsie Venner* and *The Sea-Wolf,* to the more delicate Hawthorne-influenced romance of *The Damnation of Theron Ware*, to the utopian fantasies of Gilman and Bellamy, to the much more novelistic orientations of Dreiser's Cowperwood trilogy and Wharton's *The House of Mirth*. Therefore, it becomes a testament to the strength of literary naturalism as a movement in the second half of the nineteenth century that readings of these texts benefit from a variety of approaches—aesthetic, philosophical, historical, and otherwise. Thus, as with all literary movements, reading American literary naturalism can sometimes be a complicated enterprise. The possibilities for reading these works and gaining greater perspective on how they fit into our picture of late-nineteenth-century literature increase as scholars broaden the interpretative context into which these works are placed. This is, and has been, the work of scholars of American literary naturalism. Here, within the context of the present work, I offer one simple illustration of the possibilities for reading literary naturalism within the larger contexts discussed in chapters 1 through 4: the gothic fiction of Frank Norris.

Frank Norris and the Gothic Romance

Except for a few notable exceptions like Norris's "The Jongleur of Taillebois," in the 1890s the haunted castles and bleeding statues of Walpole, Radcliffe, and Lewis had largely disappeared. These trappings, however, were never really as central to American fiction as they were to European Gothic fiction. As Donald Ringe has noted in *American Gothic* (1982), the American brand of Gothic romance was characterized by a blending of the purely imaginary with a sense of reality more appropriate to early-nineteenth-century American life than by the wild improbabilities and high fantasy of much English and German Gothicism of the late eighteenth century.[2] That is, American Gothic was a mode of fiction that paralleled notions of the "modern romance" as defined by E. T. Channing, Nathaniel Hawthorne, and others in the early nineteenth century.

Although some of the conventions differ, the theory behind both English and American Gothic romance was similar. In 1765 Horace Walpole indicated that *The Castle of Otranto* "was an attempt to blend the two kinds of romance, the ancient and the modern."[3] That is, Walpole injected into the modern romance elements of the marvelous, fantastic, and supernatural characteristic of medieval romance, where "all was imagination and improb-

ability."[4] Clara Reeve modified Walpole's theory. In 1778 Reeve claimed that
The Old English Baron was the "literary offspring of *The Castle of Otranto*,
written upon the same plan."[5] Believing, however, that the heavy-handed
supernaturalism in *Otranto* diminished the overall impact of the narrative,
Reeve indicated that she had tried in *Baron* to keep "within the utmost *verge
of probability*" (299). She attempted to do this through a careful blending
of "a sufficient degree of the marvelous" and "enough of the manners of real
life" (299).[6] Thus, fairly early on the Gothic could be viewed as one of several modes of romance (along with historical romance, adventure romance,
and so forth), all of which emerged out of the creative alembic of the hybrid
romance-novel that blends the "actual" and the "imaginary."

Although some of the stock devices disappeared, many of the key elements
that characterize Gothic fiction remain in the "naturalistic" Gothic romances
in America.[7] The supernatural/spiritual environment of Gothic fiction typically features mysterious and isolated protagonists committing vile deeds and
then brooding upon themselves and their deeds. In a Gothic romance this
brooding hero/villain often struggles to overcome vague and malign forces
just beyond his or her control. There is often an ambiguity about the nature
of these mysterious forces: do they reside in nature or in the mind? Are they
natural or supernatural, rational or irrational?[8] In pursuit of answers to these
questions, Gothic heroes frequently set forth on a mythic, metaphysical, or
religious quest in search of knowledge or the absolute. These heroes are often
alienated from society in one or more of several different ways: socially, spiritually, and philosophically. They typically find themselves caught in a
psychomachiac struggle between good and evil, love and hate, faith and
skepticism. Often, this struggle is internalized in the conscious or uncon-
scious mind of the hero, causing the hero to become self-divided through
some form of split psyche. Whether internal or external, the psychomachiac
struggle of the hero often manifests itself in some variation of the
doppelgänger motif in which the self must engage in a battle with the mirror
image of the self. The strong interest in psychology in the Gothic often results in treatments of guilt, moral ambiguity, sin, death, the descent from
reason to madness, and metaphysical, spiritual, and social darkness. There
is also a strong interest in evoking powerful emotional responses in Gothic
fiction; hence the emphasis on terror, horror, dread, mystery, the sublime
(in which the self is engulfed by immensity), the grotesque, and the

numinous. This helps explain the propensity of Gothic fictions to make liberal use of ghosts, vampires, haunted castles, secret or missing manuscripts, burial vaults, and similar devices.

In "naturalistic" Gothic one can find many examples of alienated, divided selves caught in a struggle between contrary forces. The difference between antebellum Gothic romance and the Gothic romances of Norris, Crane, and London is that the latter often use the Gothic mode in order to explore naturalist theory. McTeague, Trina, and Marcus all to a greater or lesser extent feel a second self, a brute doppelgänger, rise up from their depths and engage their better, civilized selves in mortal combat. The Gothic hero's struggle with mysterious forces operating just beyond the realm of clear perception describes the struggles of characters such as McTeague, Vandover, Henry Fleming, Jimmie Johnson, Martin Eden, and even Hugh Wolfe from "Life in the Iron Mills" against the vague forces of providential and scientific determinism. As in antebellum Gothic romances, characters in naturalistic Gothic romances are often alienated and/or brooding (or simply struck dumb). They are frequently driven into madness and psychological and spiritual ruin. Just as antebellum Gothic romancers used the Gothic mode to explore epistemological themes, so too did naturalistic Gothic romancers. Norris, Crane, London, and Frederic frequently found the Gothic mode useful for exploring the mystery, inscrutability, and ambiguity of nature, as well as such themes as guilt, sin, and the nature of evil.

Occasionally, one can even find stock devices common to antebellum European and American Gothic romances in American naturalistic narratives. Wolf Larson's ship, upon which Van Weyden awakes after a symbolic death, is aptly named *The Ghost*. Norris's "A Memorandum of Sudden Death" is framed with an account of how the mysterious manuscript from which the story is pieced together came into the editor's hands. Madness abounds in stories by Crane, London, and Norris. Crane's Sullivan County Sketches are riddled with Gothic and grotesque elements. Norris wrote a comic Gothic tale, "The Ghost in the Crosstrees," about a mysterious ghost that appears in the crosstrees of a ship. "Death" himself makes an appearance in Norris's "The Guest of Honor." The Gothic "cathedral" passage in *The Red Badge of Courage* has been noted several times by critics, and Harold Frederic's *The Damnation of Theron Ware* bears a strong resemblance to the Gothic romances of Nathaniel Hawthorne. All this noted, perhaps the most renowned example of conventional Gothic devices appearing in a naturalistic romance is Vandover's bout with lycanthropy in *Vandover and the Brute*.

Norris's canon can be roughly grouped into four categories. The first consists of his adventure romances, many written in the manner of Kipling: texts such as *Moran of the Lady Letty, A Man's Woman* (especially the earlier chapters), and "Thoroughbred." One might also include in this category his Western humor stories like "A Bargain with Peg-Leg" and "The Passing of Cock-Eye Blacklock," as well as his "atelier" stories like "Buldy Jones, Chef de Claque" and his popular San Francisco stories like "Shorty Stack, Pugilist" and "The Heroism of Jonesee." A second group consists of the romance-novels *The Octopus, The Pit*, and stories like "A Deal in Wheat," "His Single Blessedness," and "The Salvation Boom in Matabeleland," which, while not written in the Gothic mode per se, often make use of the Gothic, the grotesque, symbolism, allegory, mysticism, and other romantic modalities. A third group consists of those stories that blend adventure romance and Gothic romance, as in "A Memorandum of Sudden Death," "Outside the Zenana," "The Wife of Chino," and "The Riding of Felipe." The fourth group contains Norris's more purely fantastic and Gothic romances. This group includes "The Guest of Honor," "Lauth," "The Jongleur of Taillebois," and his novels *Vandover and the Brute* and *McTeague*. In what follows I will offer readings of two of Norris's Gothic and Adventure-Gothic short stories and his novel *Vandover and the Brute* in an attempt to illustrate how the definitional, contextual, and aesthetic paradigms discussed in previous chapters can help one interpret naturalistic romances. In each of these works, Norris relies heavily upon the tradition of the Gothic romance in order to integrate naturalist theory into his narratives.

Lauth

One of Norris's earliest tales, "Lauth" is a blend of Gothic romance, chivalric romance, and naturalist theory. The tale is divided into four sections.[9] In the first, and longest, of these, Lauth dies after being struck by a crossbow bolt in the aftermath of a bloody conflict. During the battle Lauth loses "control of his more humane instincts" and becomes a mad, blood-lusty savage: "in the twinkling of an eye the pale, highly cultivated scholar . . . sank back to the level of his savage Celtic ancestors" (242–43). The bolt that strikes Lauth in the side does not kill him quickly. Norris takes several pages to describe in detail Lauth's protracted death. When first wounded, he refuses to believe that the wound is serious. When he finally accepts the severity of his injury, he tries to avoid death through sheer willpower. As death draws closer, he feels a "strange chilling and indefinable sensation, which, he knew not why, struck him with awe" (248). Delirious, Lauth realizes that he is going to die without confession or absolution; in fact, despite his "superior intelligence," he realizes that, like the horse outside, he is going to die like a soulless machine. The horse, having been felled with a crossbow bolt, has died while kicking out with his back legs "with the monotonous regularity of a machine" (242).[10] In his final moments Lauth thinks: "'This is death.' The great revolving cycle of life had flung him off its whirling circumference—out into the void. He was to die like the millions before him. He had to face it alone. And after?—O, the horrible blackness and vagueness of that region after death. He was to see for himself the solution of that tremendous mystery that for ages had baffled far greater intelligences than his. 'This is death'" (250).

The first section of the story is concerned with the mystery of death; the second section is concerned with the equally ambiguous mystery of life. Lauth's friend Chavannes, a doctor of medicine and chemistry professor who is intrigued with the inexplicable mysteries of life, decides to try to reanimate Lauth's corpse. He feels he can accomplish this because (1) "all forms of life were but the same," from the "spirited horse" to mankind to lower forms of life; (2) there is no "soul," only a pervasive life force; and (3) this life force cannot be destroyed, for science has shown that it is inexhaustible. Because life is inexhaustible, life must "exist in death itself." The problem of reanimation merely becomes a matter of figuring out how to restimulate the life that still exists in Lauth's corpse. God, Chavannes recalls, had himself reanimated the dead several times (as in the raising of Lazarus); might not man be able to do the same?

The third section opens with Chavannes discussing his proposed experiment with the suggestively named Anselm, who opposes the endeavor on religious grounds. "I must condemn the whole thing as altogether repulsive and wicked," Anselm says, but he admits a morbid curiosity in the experiment nonetheless. Unlike Chavannes, Anselm believes that it is not "life" per se but the soul that is the "motor of existence." Then, joined by two other scientists, Anselm and Chavannes attempt to bring Lauth back to life by stimulating his corpse with doses of nutritional elixirs and the blood of two sheep. After several long and tense hours, Lauth's corpse slowly begins to move, and Anselm rushes from the room "with a terrible cry: 'Horrible, horrible!'" (256).

The concluding section begins with Anselm trying to deal with the blow dealt his Christianity by the apparent success of the experiment. Was there no soul after all? Anselm thinks: "Everything had been a mistake, then,—civilization, beliefs, society, religion, heaven, and Christ Himself,—were all myths or founded upon falsity. Where could he turn for anything true?" (256). Lauth's complete restoration is not immediate, however. Over the course of many weeks he becomes increasingly aware of his surroundings. Eventually, "the bonds seemed to be loosed" and "Lauth began to speak" (257). Still, despite his ability to communicate, Chavannes and Anslem are unable to determine if Lauth has really been restored. Soon, however, Lauth begins to regress. "Then after this there came a peculiar relapse, a strange and unaccountable change. Lauth talked less, and an expression of daily deepening perplexity overcast his face. He seemed as one lost in mind, and grasping for some hidden clew" (258). Finally, at the "highest point of Lauth's second life," with "a glance of almost supreme intelligence," he stands to his full height and cries: "*This is not I; where am I? For God's sake, tell me where I am!*" (Norris's emphasis). After this he "fell upon the floor, foaming and wallowing" (258).

Lauth's grotesque degeneration happens quickly. He is soon reduced to growling and walking on all fours like a wolf. He then loses his motor ability and his senses. In the end he degenerates into a gelatinous blob no higher on the evolutionary chain than those "forms of existence wherein the line between vegetable and animal cannot be drawn" (259). Soon decomposition sets in and Lauth is "dead" a second time. The story closes with Anselm suggesting that both he and Chavannes were right: man is animated by the combination of the life force and the soul. Body, soul, and life join in mankind to form the animating trinity. Anselm says: "That which we call man is half animal, half God, a being on one hand capable of rising to the sublimest heights of intellectual grandeur, equal almost to his Maker; on the other hand, sinking at times to the last level of ignominy and moral degradation. Take life away from this being, and at once the soul mounts upward to the God that first gave it. Take from him his soul,—that part of him that is God,—and straight-way he sinks down to the level of the lowest animal" (260). The difference between the first Lauth and the second Lauth, suggests Anselm, is the absence in the second Lauth of the soul, and it is the presence of the soul that separates man from animal. Still, Anselm notes, there remains one mystery: "What that mystery in [Lauth] was which drove him to cry out that day, 'This is not *I*!' is beyond our power to say" (260).

The fact that Anselm offers no interpretation of Lauth's cry seems a mystery itself. After all, if one accepts Anselm's belief in the soul as the distinguishing characteristic of man, then Lauth's cry seems to stem from the fact that at the highest moment of his regeneration, at his epiphanic moment of introspective *self*-awareness, he fails to recognize himself, for his soul is absent. Taking this a bit further, his regeneration is a type of "ontogeny recapitulating phylogeny": his gradual regaining of movement, intelligence, and the ability to communicate all suggest the evolutionary cycle, the apex of which is humankind. When Lauth does reach this apex and the moment of self-awareness, he experiences an intense moment of epistemological uncertainty. His epiphanic moment—characterized as a flash of "supreme intelligence"—is one of dread and uncertainty and might be better called a "dark" or "negative" epiphany in the tradition of the negative romance. At the apex of the evolutionary cycle, when Lauth should have regained a positive sense of selfhood, he instead is confronted with a void.

Looking at the events of the story through Anselm's eyes, then, one views humans as a fusion of "God" and "animal," or the supernatural and the natural.[11] The natural half (the body and the "life force") is largely mechanical and controlled by force, law, and other elements of a largely mechanistic determinism. A human's supernatural half, the soul, is not subject to these same deterministic laws. At the moment of his first death Lauth's soul moved into the beyond. If he does experience a true "epiphany," it probably occurs when he dies at the end of the first section and presumably does "see for himself the solution of that tremendous mystery that for ages had baffled far greater intelligences than his" (250). Because the soul exists outside of the evolutionary chain, it does not regenerate with Lauth, resulting in his epistemological crisis and his subsequent degeneration and dissolution. In fact, the protracted nature of his "second" death may be explained by the fact that there was no departure of the soul to mark the event; without this turning point to mark the point of death, his life force is left to slowly evaporate as his body de-evolves. If Anselm's interpretation is correct, then "Lauth" is governed by a softer rather than a harder determinism. The dualistic interpretation of man offered by Anselm posits a reconciliation in man of the natural and the supernatural in such a way that humans are biologically determined but "spiritually" free.

Several elements in "Lauth" suggest comparisons with other stories. The comparison between Poe's "Facts in the Case of M. Valdemar" and Lauth's rapid postmortem degeneration at the end of the tale is readily apparent. In fact, a comparison of these two stories illustrates the difference between the antebellum negative romance and the "naturalistic" negative romance. In Poe's story, there is no significant difference established between the "soul" and the "life force." For Valdemar, the departure of the "soul" (for lack of a better term) results in the decay of the body. Valdemar's bodily decay is postponed because his soul is kept from departing through a mesmeric trance. When the mesmeric trance is finally lifted or "broken" and Valdemar is able to complete the death process, his body rapidly crumbles into a detestable mass. Norris essentially takes the story of Valdemar and revises it to accommodate naturalist theory. Norris divides the "soul" from the "life force" and has Lauth's reanimation and subsequent degeneration follow an evolutionary pattern.

Aside from "Valdemar," Lauth's descent into a wolfish state reappears in *Vandover and the Brute* in a different context, and Lauth's loss of his senses one by one is reworked by Jack London in *The Sea-Wolf* in the portrayal of Wolf Larson's deterioration at the end of the text. The metaphysical and spiritual obscurity emphasized in the Gothic also appears in "Lauth." Lauth's confrontation with an internal void at the moment of self-awareness is a supreme moment of psychological and spiritual darkness. Finally, the Gothic emphasis on the descent from reason into madness also plays a key role in "Lauth." In the heat of the battle Lauth moves by instinct and blood lust in a fog of madness. A leitmotif in Norris's fiction, degeneration into madness is one of the main subjects of *Vandover and the Brute,* and insanity is a major theme in the story "Outside the Zenana."

"Outside the Zenana"

"Outside the Zenana" is a mixture of adventure romance and Gothic romance.[12] Set in India, the story centers on an opera composer named Burr-Underwood, who, when the story opens, is "not right in his mind": "Inside of his head there was coiled a clock-spring, and during a great many days this would wind itself tighter and tighter, until it paused at its point of greatest tension. This would continue until he heard some sharp and sudden noise . . . and then the clock-spring would be suddenly loosed, and would uncoil almost in an instant, buzzing and whirling fiercely" (82). Whenever the figurative coil springs loose, Burr-Underwood bursts into song, stopping abruptly each time at the same place and grasping the back of his head (82). This song—an idyll upon the beauty and joy of memory—was one he was in the process of composing at the time of the accident that left him at the mercy of the "clock-spring" in his head. Although the details of the accident remain unclear—Burr-Underwood can remember very little himself—it appears that he was thrown from a horse into a ravine, where he struck the back of his head. At the time, he was humming the recently composed idyll. Some natives found him and brought him back to his traveling companions, but neither his horse nor the score of the song was found. All Burr-Underwood could remember, and this only vaguely, were the eyes of a European girl whom he saw bending over him while he lay in the bottom of the ravine, "on the shore-line between the ocean of the Void and the land of the Tangible; seeing but not knowing" (83). For about a year he was wracked with insanity, mumbling and muttering to himself in "the throes of brain fever" (84). During this year he often muttered something to the effect that the European girl had stolen the song out of his head and had replaced it with the clock-spring. Try as he might, he cannot remember the remainder of the song, only the first verse, which he sings each time the clock-spring uncoils.

One day, when the coil is wound tighter than ever before, Burr-Underwood leaves his friends and begins wandering around the streets and alleys of the village. He eventually comes to a cul-de-sac closed at one end by a great wall with a single window high up in the wall. The clock-spring in his head snaps and uncoils, and Burr-Underwood sings the first verse of the song, gasps, and claps his hand to the back of his head. In a moment he hears a woman singing the rest of the song from the window. As she sings, his "mind with the swiftness of light was throwing bridge after bridge across the great gulf that so long had separated him from his real self" (85). When the song is finished, the window grows dark, but his brain fever has broken.

When his friends find him, he is "a wild-eyed, disheveled man, with a voice hoarse from shouting without deaf walls, and with broken nails, and knuckles raw from battering on closed gates, reeling around corners and stumbling over street corners" (86). He tells them of his encounter and they set out to find the woman, but are never able to locate the cul-de-sac. The story ends with Burr-Underwood and his friend Sintram discussing possible explanations for these mysterious events. Burr-Underwood first suggests that the voice he has heard is the voice of the mysterious European girl he vaguely remembers seeing when the accident first occurred. She is the only one who could possibly have known the song (having taken the score from him while he lay half-unconscious from the accident). When she sang the song from the window, he regained his memory and his insanity departed. Sintram suggests a different possibility: The recovery of his memory and newfound sanity could be the result of a chance "coincidence of certain favorable conditions," such as the combination of the long walk, the cool night air, and so forth (86). Because Burr-Underwood cannot swear whether he regained his sanity before or after he heard the woman's voice, it could be, suggests Sintram, that the voice, the high wall, and the casement window were all simply a madman's delusions. The story ends with Burr-Underwood wishing he knew for certain what "mystery lies back of the whole affair" (86).

During his period of madness, Burr-Underwood's mind is seen as purely mechanical—a clock-spring. This mechanistic view is qualified by Norris's observation that, in the throes of his madness, Burr-Underwood was "separated from his real self." As in "Lauth," the implication in this story is that when one's "self" is severed from one's body or "life," one becomes a mere mechanism subject to deterministic forces. When Burr-Underwood is in this state, Norris notes, he is able to "see" but not "know." He can see the outward and visible signs but cannot penetrate these surface appearances to the mystery underneath. His inability to remember the rest of the song (which is about memory) represents his inability to bridge the gulf between mechanism and self. When he recovers the whole song, his madness departs and self is joined with self. What complicates this story is the ambiguity of the ending: if Sintram's theory is correct, Burr-Underwood's encounter with the woman and the recovery of his "self" are illusions prompted by an intricate network of causal relationships.

Vandover and the Brute

Perhaps the clearest example of "naturalist Gothic" is Norris's "werewolf" tale, *Vandover and the Brute,* in which lycanthropy serves as a forceful symbol of the influence of Vandover's lower, brute nature.[13] The question of how Vandover contracted lycanthropy has received considerable attention. Donald Pizer has argued that Vandover's lycanthropy might be an effect of syphilis contracted from Flossie or of his "general paralysis of the insane."[14] June Howard claims that Norris does not sacrifice plausibility, nor does he abandon a strict determinism when he gives Vandover lycanthropy. "Vandover is emphatically not a werewolf," Howard writes, "and the causes invoked to explain his transformation are natural and not supernatural."[15] Insofar as a potentially plausible explanation for Vandover's lycanthropy is offered, I agree with Pizer and Howard. In fact, the presence in *Vandover and the Brute* of a medical/biological explanation for Vandover's highly unusual condition continues a tradition in many Gothic romances of "explaining" the seemingly fantastic elements of texts. One sees this, for instance, in the way Charles Brockden Brown "explains" rationally (according to scientific presumption of the time) the mysterious self-combustion of the elder Wieland in *Wieland* (1798). Demonstrating that the text provides some (however scant) evidence for a rational explanation for Vandover's "nervous condition" still leaves unclear whether this condition is contracted by chance through natural causes, is some form of supernatural retribution for his many "sins," or is both naturally occurring and a supernatural retribution. The reason for the ambiguity lies, in part, in the text's soft determinism.

William James argued that soft determinism often led to illogical, ambiguous, and paradoxical interpretations of the world. One could, James claimed, successfully reconcile indeterminism with a providential teleology, but attempts to reconcile hard determinism with notions of good and evil and personal responsibility lead to a soft determinism of the worst sort. It is precisely this worst sort of soft determinism that Norris explores in *Vandover and the Brute.*[16]

Full of unresolved contradictions and ambiguities, *Vandover* is a difficult text to interpret. The foremost of its problems concerns the text's relative determinism and indeterminism. Simply, is Vandover responsible for his actions? The wide range of answers to this question can be represented by those of two critics. Charles Child Walcutt has argued that close examination of the text reveals that Vandover is morally responsible for his actions and that the forces that thrust him down are circumstantial rather than inevitable.[17] Lee Clark Mitchell, on the other hand, has argued that Vandover is not morally responsible for his actions, but is the victim of deterministic forces hidden behind an illusion of agency.[18] Rather than Walcutt's indeterminate *Vandover* or Mitchell's determined *Vandover,* the novel seems to be informed by a soft determinism. Paradoxically, Vandover appears to be both a pawn of deterministic forces and morally responsible for his actions. Rather than turning to an easier resolution of determinism and responsibility like that found in Holmes's "Mechanism in Thought and Morals," in *Vandover and the Brute* Norris concerns himself with a more ambiguous, uneasy resolution of determinism and human responsibility: Calvinism.

Stanley Cooperman has described *Vandover and the Brute* as Norris's "most complete statement" of the "Calvinist nightmare," the epic battle in the Calvinist anthropology between flesh and spirit.[19] This battle between the "good" spirit and the "evil" flesh is rendered in the "better" Vandover's conflict with his "brute" self. The "Calvinist nightmare" also involves a Providential determinism: because of the determining effects of original sin, humans are doomed to sin, yet, paradoxically, they know that they are being held responsible for their sins. The status of the "will" is implicated in this paradox. For the Calvinist, only a chosen few are among the elect. Only the elect will receive salvation and the rewards of heaven. Rather than completely abandoning the "will," however, Calvinistic providential determinism tries to escape a pure hard determinism by weaving an act of the will into the election process; the Calvinist initially receives the grace of God through an act of willed acceptance. Augustine claimed that only those who had been elected by God could in fact engage the will in such a manner: unregenerate man was powerless to will election. Perry Westbrook writes: to Augustine, "the unregenerate will is not really free, since it can will only evil. The regenerate will is free, despite God's foreknowledge of what it will do. But the will is unable to will its own regeneracy without the influx of God's grace, which no one controls except God."[20] Before eating the fruit of the Tree of the Knowledge of Good and Evil, Adam was free; once initiated into the knowledge of good and evil through an act of sin, Adam lapsed into a lower, unregenerate, determined state.

Notably, these are precisely the terms Norris uses to describe the beginning of Vandover's degeneration: he is at first tainted by being initiated into the knowledge of good and evil. His first stirrings of sexual temptation, prompted by the "vague and strange ideas" he finds written in the Bible, reveal to him the "knowledge of good and evil" (7). This knowledge shatters his "crude raw innocence" and awakens in him "something hidden, with the instinct of a young brute" (7). Then, the encyclopedia article on obstetrics that he reads marks the "end of all his childish ideals" and the "destruction of all his first illusions," prompting his "innate vice" to stir within him so that the "brute began to make itself felt" (8). The brute brings with it "the perverse craving for the knowledge of vice," and Vandover might have "been totally corrupted while in his earliest teens" had it not been for the saving power of his "artistic side" (8).

Norris's text is "naturalistic" in that he uses naturalist theory to help explain the mechanics of his "Calvinist nightmare."[21] Vandover's "innate vice" (his innate depravity) is represented by a lower, brute self ruled by animal instinct and subject to natural law. It is in this sense that Le Contean evolutionary theism shares some characteristics with Calvinist cosmology. Le Conte's attempt to reconcile traditional religion with evolution posits higher and lower states for mankind. Le Conte argues that the "whole mission and life-work of man is the progressive and finally the complete dominance, both in the individual and in the race, of the higher over the lower. The whole meaning of sin is in the humiliating bondage of the higher to the lower."[22] Vandover degenerates as his higher self becomes increasingly subject to his lower self. Through a prolonged participation in vice, Vandover allows his lower nature to dominate his higher nature; thus, Vandover becomes the brute—literalized in his bout with lycanthropy.

In order to explore these conflicts, Norris builds *Vandover and the Brute* around a series of interrelated oppositions. As in Gothic romances generally, the core conflict in Norris's Gothic romance is an "eternal struggle between good and evil" (188). Parallel to this central conflict are several related oppositions:

Good	*Evil*
Innocence	Guilt
Spirit	Flesh
Art	Decadence
Virtue	Vice
Higher Self	Lower Self
Free Will	Determinism
The "Better" Self	The Brute

Insofar as Vandover resists temptation he is able to keep the Brute at bay; giving in to temptation allows the Brute to grow, gain dominance, and subject Vandover's will to the manipulations of a "blind unreasoned instinct." Therefore, as Stanley Cooperman has pointed out, *Vandover and the Brute* is a type of naturalistic morality play, or psychomachia.[23]

In this morality play, however, Vandover seems to have little chance of acting morally. As presumably one of the damned, Vandover is plagued with a "pliable nature" that prevents him from successfully struggling against temptation. Rather than attributing Vandover's doom to the action of mere fate or providence, Norris explains the mechanism of his failure through naturalist theory. Vandover's fatal flaw, his "pliable nature," causes him to adapt to new environments and conditions rather than struggle against the temptations and failings that brought these new conditions upon him. His adaptable nature is introduced early in the text. At the beginning of chapter 2 Norris writes: "There was little of the stubborn or unyielding about Vandover, his personality was not strong, his nature pliable, and he rearranged himself to suit his new environment at Harvard very rapidly" (14). In fact, Vandover "found that he could be contented in almost any environment, the weakness, the certain pliability of his character easily fitting itself into new grooves" (23). As a side effect of this "weakness" he does not work hard at anything disagreeable, but seeks out the easy and the comfortable, even when this means not facing spiritual issues squarely. When he commits a "sacrilege" by attending communion service drunk, he knows that the time will come when he will be "called to account for it," but the horror of such a thought causes him to turn aside from these religious problems for fear that his "peace of mind" will be disturbed (55). After the death of Ida, Vandover is shocked at how quickly his "pliable character rearranged itself to suit the new environment" (104). The same is true after the death of his father (138). When his "career of dissipation" is well advanced and his ruin certain, Vandover announces to Dolly Haight, "*I can get used to almost anything*" (268; Norris's emphasis).

Having this weakness, however, does not release Vandover from personal responsibility. No matter how hard he tries to rationalize away his responsibility for Ida's suicide, "in that dreadful moment when he saw things in their true light, all the screens of conventionality and sophistry torn away," Vandover sees "his responsibility for her death and for the ruin of that something in her which was more than life" revealed to him "like the sudden unrolling of a great scroll" (90). The implication of Ida's suicide is, for someone "who hated responsibility of any kind," a heavy "weight of responsibility to carry" (90). Later, when his artistic ability has deteriorated, Vandover views his lycanthropy as a "punishment that he had brought upon himself, some fearful nervous disease, the result of his long indulgence of vice" (213). He sees himself as responsible for his condition, not merely as a victim of deterministic forces.

Throughout the narrative Vandover is given a series of "warnings" urging him to turn from his wicked ways. When he arrives at church drunk, the reverend's message is on earnest repentance (52). Dolly Haight warns Vandover on several occasions about the ill consequences of pursuing a path of vice (87). On board the sinking *Mazatlan* the "little Salvationist lassie" tells Vandover that it "isn't too late" for him now, if he will "only *believe;* that's all" (116). And when Turner Ravis breaks off her relationship with Vandover, she tells him that it "isn't too late to begin all over again. Just be your better self; live up to the best that's in you" (179). Accordingly, when Vandover is impressed with his depravity, he often tries to get back on the path of virtue, but his pliable nature and love of comfort and pleasure cause him to quickly fall victim to temptation again. The sense given through the first two-thirds of the text is that Vandover *might* be able to master the brute if he would only put forth the necessary effort. Yet, Vandover is never able to summon the necessary effort.

Justification for Vandover's moral responsibility seems to stem from this *possibility* that the brute might be defeated. This possibility is strongest at the beginning of the novel and becomes less likely as the narrative progresses and Vandover degenerates further and further. "He was sure that at the first the good had been the stronger. Little by little the brute had grown, and he, pleasure-loving, adapting himself to every change of environment, luxurious, self-indulgent, shrinking with the shrinking of a sensuous artist-nature from all that was irksome and disagreeable, had shut his ears to the voices that shouted warnings of the danger, and had allowed the brute to thrive and grow" (188). The process of shifting from the good to the evil, from the spirit to the flesh, is a process of isolation and alienation. The more Vandover feeds the brute, the more isolated he becomes; the more isolated, the less able to control the brute's cravings. This process of isolation takes place on five levels: social, economic, biological, spiritual, and psychological. Socially, Vandover alienates himself from his friends by impregnating Ida Wade, getting drunk, and associating with prostitutes. As the hold of vice grows upon him, Vandover's circle of friends shifts from Turner, Haight, Geary, and his other peers in Harvard and San Francisco "society" to Ellis and the Dummy. Eventually he is left in complete social isolation. Economic isolation comes from squandering his money, avoiding work, and heavy gambling. Biologically, as Vandover gradually transforms into the brute he becomes a grotesque distortion of humanity. Spiritual isolation begins when Vandover attends church drunk and continues with his repeated refusal to contend with "that strange other place where his crime would assume right proportions and receive right judgment, no matter how it was palliated or evaded here" (91). Psychologically he becomes afflicted with fear and dread, and his grip on reality becomes increasingly tenuous: at times "an immense unreasoning terror would come upon him all of a sudden, horrible, crushing, so that he rolled upon the bed groaning and sobbing, digging his nails into his scalp, shutting his teeth against a desire to scream out, writhing in the throes of terrible mental agony" (91–92).

While Vandover degenerates into a state of isolation, there remains the (ever evaporating) possibility of conquering the brute. The loss of his art, however, completes the victory for the brute, and all hope of recovery for his better self is lost. As an artist, he is attracted to images of isolation, specializing in "broad reaches of landscape, deserts, shores, and moors in which he placed solitary figures of men or animals" (54). His proposed masterpiece, "The Last Enemy," features a warrior dying in the desert as a crouching lion prepares to pounce. Symbolically these paintings are self-portraits. "The Last Enemy" portrays Vandover's dying "better" self lost in a moral desert, about to be destroyed by a fierce brute. Vandover's artistic ability is all that is left of him after years of dissipation: "In the wreckage of all that was good that had been going on in him his love for all art was yet intact. It was the strongest side of his nature and it would be the last to go" (182). The "great crisis" of Vandover's life comes when he decides to return to his art as a final attempt to revolt against the brute (187). In this crisis Vandover resolves to paint "The Last Battle."

When Vandover sketches the initial figures, he discovers that "the forms he made on the canvas were no adequate reflection of those in his brain; some third delicate and subtle faculty that coordinated the other two and that called forth a sure and instant response to the dictates of his mind was lacking" (196). Vandover makes several attempts to draw the figures, each time failing to transfer the images from his mind onto the canvas. "Still another time he dusted out what he had done and recommenced, concentrating all his attention with a tremendous effort of the will. Grotesque and meaningless shapes, the mocking caricatures of those he saw in his fancy, grew under his charcoal, while slowly, a queer, numb feeling came in his head, like a rising fog, and the touch of that unreasoning terror returned, this time stronger, more persistent, more tenacious than before" (197). After spending the day in a state of nervous agitation and unreasoned fear, Vandover returns at night to the canvas. Again, all he is able to produce are "changelings, grotesque abortions" of his imagination. It seemed to Vandover as though "the brute in him, like some malicious witch, had stolen away the true offspring of his mind, putting in their places these deformed dwarfs, its own hideous spawn" (201). At this point, Vandover realizes that "his art was gone, the one thing that could save him"; it died after years of being "dragged all fouled and polluted through the lowest mire of the great city's vice" (201).

With the loss of his artistic ability Vandover realizes that his higher nature has been completely subdued by his lower nature. When he subsequently learns that he is to be sued by Ida Wade's father, Vandover's depression and anxiety lead him into a Gothic dark night of the soul. His torment begins the night before with an attack of "unreasoning terror" that leaves him with a "loathing of life" (210). During the next day, he begins to "feel strange" (211): at first "the room looked unfamiliar to him, then his own daily life no longer seemed recognizable, and, finally, all of a sudden, it was the whole world, all the existing order of things, that appeared to draw off like a refluent tide, leaving him alone, abandoned, cast upon some fearful, mysterious shore" like a figure in one of his paintings (211–12). When night falls he goes "down into the pit" (212). Lying in bed he feels strange sensations creeping over his body and a numbness settling over the base of his spine (212–13). Terrified that he is going mad and feeling that he has descended into hell, Vandover, "moved by an impulse, a blind, resistless instinct," cries out to the universe for help (213). He gave no name to the "strange supernatural being" whom he addressed; it was "the cry of a soul in torment that does not stop to reason, the wild last hope that feels its own helplessness, that responds to an intuition of a force outside of itself—the force that can save it in its time of peril" (213–14). "Trembling" and waiting for a "miracle," Vandover seems to develop a "sixth sense" that tells him he will receive an answer from the beyond that night (214).

> Still he waited—there was nothing, nothing but the vast silence, the unbroken blackness of the night, a night that was to last forever. There was no answer, nothing but the deaf silence, the blind darkness. But in a moment he felt that the very silence, the very lack of answer, was answer in itself; there was nothing for him. Even that vast mysterious power to which he had cried could not help him now, could not help him, could not stay the inexorable law of nature, could not reverse that vast terrible engine with its myriad spinning wheels that was riding him down relentlessly, grinding him into the dust. And afterward? After the engine had done its work, when that strange other time should come, that other life, what then? No, not even then, nothing but outer darkness then and the gnashing of teeth. (214; Norris's emphasis)

Here Vandover feels confirmed as one of the damned. His isolation is complete. He is mad. He is completely alienated from God and enveloped in spiritual darkness. Unable to tolerate the overwhelming existential isolation he feels, he places the muzzle of a gun in his mouth and pulls the trigger (216). He does not die, but faints, for the gun is not loaded. When he comes to, he realizes that "his whole life had been one long suicide" (218). From this point to the end of the book Norris simply maps out the rest of Vandover's career of "ruin and pollution" (55).

Although the paradoxical soft determinism of Vandover's "Calvinist nightmare" provides an apt metaphor for describing his plight, it is difficult to apply the same model to other elements in the text. Aside from Vandover's "eternal struggle" between good and evil, there is a second major theme in the narrative, that of the "engine of life" that powers the ongoing struggle for survival. In a Gothic romance, the alienated protagonist often struggles to overcome vague and malign forces just beyond his or her control. This trope was useful for naturalistic authors; after all, what are "laws of nature" but ambiguous forces that manipulate and/or control behavior? In a naturalistic Gothic romance, this device is useful for exploring the ambiguous possibilities of soft determinism and the controlling, malign characteristics of hard determinism. Norris makes use of this Gothic trope through the "engine of life" theme.

After discovering that he has lost his artistic ability, Vandover, overcome with a sense of claustrophobia and the sensation that he is losing his mind, opens the window upon the sleeping city. With the noises of the day gone, Vandover becomes aware of the "prolonged and sullen diapason" of the city:[24] "It was Life, the murmur of the great, mysterious force that spun the wheels of Nature and that sent it onward like some enormous engine, resistless, relentless . . . crushing out inexorably all those who lagged behind the herd and who fell from exhaustion . . . driving it recklessly, blindly on and on toward some far-distant goal, some vague unknown end, some mysterious, fearful bourne forever hidden in thick darkness" (202). This vision of the engine of life helps Vandover explain his "punishment" for his "long indulgence of vice": "It was Nature inexorably exacting. It was the vast fearful engine riding him down beneath its myriad spinning wheels, remorselessly, irresistibly" (213). Notably, Vandover is not the only character to have a vision of the "engine of life"; Charlie Geary does too:

> Every man for himself—that was his maxim. It might be damned selfish, but it was human nature: the weakest to the wall, the strongest to the front. Why should not he be in the front? Why not in the very front rank? Why not be even before the front rank itself—the leader? Vast, vague ideas passed slowly across the vision of his mind, ideas that could hardly be formulated into thought ideas of the infinite herd of humanity, driven on as if by some enormous, relentless engine, driven on toward some fearful distant bourne, driven on recklessly at headlong speed. All life was but a struggle to keep from under those myriad spinning wheels that dashed so close behind. Those were happiest who were farthest to the front. (288)

What these parallel visions accomplish first and foremost is to emphasize the contrast between Vandover and Geary.[25] Vandover falls, while Geary rises. Vandover is weak, while Geary is strong. The problem arises when one tries to reconcile the "engine of life" with a Calvinistic cosmology.

There are three ways to account for the "engine of life" theme. First, Norris could be working out some of the mechanics of Vandover's "Calvinist night-mare" by using a "survival of the fittest" paradigm as a metaphor for describing the separation of the elect and the damned. The "engine of life" is God's tool for enacting the separation. Damned through his innate vice, Vandover is "weak" and is crushed by the wheels of life. If the metaphor holds, however, it means that Geary is being portrayed by Norris as one of the elect. This being the case, the final message of the book is unremittingly pessimistic, a complete subversion of the Calvinistic hope of salvation and election by painting one of the "elect" as a scheming, back-stabbing social Darwinist.

One of the benefits of this reading is that it helps account for other elements in the text, such as the *Mazatlan* passage. As the *Mazatlan* sinks, Vandover meets a "Salvation Army lassie" who is *positive* that Christ will save her from death (115–16). She is not saved, however; a loosened boom strikes her lifeless to the deck. "She dropped in a heap upon the deck. . . . Vandover ran forward and lifted her up, but her back was broken; she was already dead. He rose to his feet exclaiming to himself, 'But she was so sure— she *knew* she was going to be saved,' then suddenly fell silent again, gazing wonderingly at the body, disturbed, very thoughtful" (118). Her death is understandable if one interprets the text as Norris's ironic undercutting of conventional religious belief. The virtuous Haight's contraction of syphilis can be explained in the same manner.

Reading the text as subverting spiritual belief forces us to take a new look at Vandover's "Calvinistic" cosmology. If the final message is that conventional religion is a sham, that wickedness flourishes, and that only the ruthless survive, then the "eternal struggle" between "good" and "evil" that defines Vandover's life is shown to be a mere fiction.[26] Although this reading of the text fits well with "traditional" accounts of "literary naturalism," it does not really match what we know of Norris.[27] Throughout his corpus Norris often turns toward religious/Christian themes as positive and redemptive elements of an otherwise harsh, violent world. Of course, just because some of Norris's personal sympathies and ideals do not match the apparent "message" revealed in this reading of *Vandover and the Brute* does not mean that this reading is inaccurate. Nevertheless, the discrepancy suggests that there may be other more viable interpretations.

A second method of dealing with the "engine of life" material rests in the thesis that, although Norris clearly sets up Vandover and Geary as polar opposites (Vandover all weakness, Geary all strength),[28] he never intended to conflate the Calvinist theme in the text with the struggle-for-survival theme. That is, he never intended the engine-of-life passage to be read as a metaphor of election and damnation. The "struggle for existence" element in the text might be introduced to give a sense of the powerful, transcendent natural laws forming the backdrop for the drama of the text. This background helps explain Geary's character and gives us some insight into the forces that lie behind Vandover's degeneration, but it has little or nothing to do with the moral and spiritual issues confronting Vandover and Geary. The strengths of this interpretation are that it helps alleviate some of the pessimism of the book and allows the book to fit more comfortably into Norris's corpus of work. Its weaknesses are that it does not provide any insight into how to interpret the death of the "Salvationist lassie" or Haight's sufferings.

A third solution to this interpretive dilemma might lie in the concept of Jamesian "subjectivism." Perhaps the parallel visions of Vandover and Geary are intended to contrast their two different subjective interpretations of the "engine of life." Interpreting the "engine of life" as enacting a "punishment" for his sins, Vandover reads his vision as embodying a distinctly spiritual and moral component. It is a sublime and numinous moment, in which Vandover is swallowed up in the fearful and awe-inspiring perception of immensity. Geary interprets the vision more "naturalistically" through the lens of a social Darwinism. Through the juxtaposition of these interpretations, certain weaknesses are highlighted: Vandover's pliability and moral weakness is revealed; Geary's ethical weakness and scheming nature are revealed. Vandover does not have the moral strength to prevent his mingling in the world of vice; Geary does not have the ethical character to temper his exploitation of others on his way to the top.[29] Both characters, therefore, are wicked: Geary's behavior results in an ethical wickedness; Vandover's behavior results in a moral wickedness. Reading the "engine of life" passages in this manner allows for a reasonable reconciliation of the Calvinistic and struggle-for-survival themes in the text. It still offers little insight into the character of Haight or the death of the woman on the *Mazatlan*.

Although the first solution to the dilemma does more to unify the text than the other two, critical intuition resists it, for its dark and subversive pessimism regarding spiritual issues runs counter to the rest of Norris's work. The second and third solutions seem more likely candidates, even though they leave several issues unresolved. The difficulty of arriving at a single, intellectually satisfying answer to the problem probably stems from the fact that *Vandover and the Brute* is a first novel by a young novelist. Still, despite its shortcomings, *Vandover* is a compelling work written in the tradition of the Gothic romance. As in other negative Gothic romances like Brown's *Wieland* and Hawthorne's *The Scarlet Letter,* Norris's novel is an intense psychological study of a character struggling with questions of guilt, sin, madness, and spiritual darkness.

Finally, perhaps it is Norris himself who can best tell us how to read the story of Vandover's fall. In the middle of the novel Norris makes several allusions that hint at three different ways to read the text. When, for economic reasons, Vandover is forced to move out of his late father's house and into an apartment, he purchases a "tiled stove" over which he fawns. The tiles of the stove are covered with little ornamental pictures of "the Punishment of Caliban and His Associates, Romeo and Juliet, the Fall of Phaeton" (159). Indeed, the story of Vandover is the romance of Caliban, a pliable, self-indulgent brute punished by a higher power; it is the romance of Romeo and Juliet, a tale of forbidden love leading to tragic consequence; it is the romance of Phaeton, a foolish youth whose weak and cavalier attitude toward the forces of nature sends him spiraling downward, out of control, struck down by Zeus.

Afterword

The American literary naturalists were reformist not only in a social sense, but also in the sense that they revealed new dimensions of the human experience. They brought late-nineteenth-century fiction out of the drawing room and into the open air. They took their characters into wheat fields and Death Valley, battlefields and frontiers, slums and the open ocean. These borderlands and sweeping settings gave the literary naturalists the space they needed to create vast, extraordinary dramas. Their need to stage dramas and to explore heightened experience stemmed, at least in part, from their investigations of naturalist theory. The implications of philosophical and scientific naturalism, particularly as they clashed with religious belief, loomed large enough in the minds of the American literary naturalists to require the creation of expansive, symbolic, extraordinary narratives.

When the American literary naturalists succeed, they do so by integrating the scientific and philosophical concepts they are working with seamlessly into a narrative structure that can support them. When they fail, they fail through an inability to match their narrative structure with the ideas it contains, resulting in a disjointed narrative or an unappealing melodrama. Fortunately, their successes are many. But because the literary naturalists are often misunderstood, they are often undervalued. To be sure, few would claim that the coterie of Crane, Norris, London, and Dreiser produced what Hawthorne, Melville, Whitman, and Thoreau created in the 1850s or what Faulkner, Lewis, Hemingway, and Fitzgerald created in the 1920s. Even in their own time—the twenty years between 1890 and 1910—one would be hard-pressed to claim they were the leaders per se in American literature; after all, these are also the years of James, Howells, Twain, Jewett, Freeman, Wharton, and Stein. And what was the reading public consuming? Kipling?

Well-thumbed copies of *Ben Hur? Trilby?* Sheldon's *In His Steps?* Certainly some London as well, of course.

Even still, there is a distinct sense that late-nineteenth-century American literature would be a much-diminished spectacle for want of Crane, Norris, and London, not to mention Frederic and Dreiser. They provide something no others provided: a body of writing that grasps without flinching at the most provocative scientific and philosophical theories of their day. Perhaps the core group of literary naturalists is difficult to come to terms with because their productions are so unique in comparison to their own peers. It is hard to imagine Crane in the same category as London, who is in the same category as Norris and Dreiser. One can say that James is *like* Wharton, who is *like* Howells, or that Sarah Orne Jewett is like Mary Wilkins Freeman, who is like Charles Chesnutt and George Washington Cable. But is it equally plausible to suggest that the works of London are like Dreiser, or that the works of Norris are like Crane? Somehow the analogy doesn't seem to work.

Within the larger context of American literary history, however, there is a more reasonable comparison, and this is the comparison of the core American romantics and the American literary naturalists. Although Charles Brockden Brown is indeed *like* Hawthorne and one doesn't balk at lumping Melville together with Poe, still, Crane, London, and Norris share with these authors (as well as Emerson and Whitman) an artistic orientation different from that of James, Howells, or other major nineteenth-century figures associated with the "rise of the novel" and the "rise of realism." Namely, these authors use their texts to grapple with things *beyond us,* while the realists grappled intensely with *ourselves.* The realists asked—directly or indirectly, as the individual case may be—what can we know about nature and human nature by studying, directly and with careful regard for honest, nonembellished documentation, human behavior, culture, and psychology themselves? The romantics and the literary naturalists asked a slightly different question—what can we know about nature and human nature by studying the relationship between facets of human behavior and human psychology and the environment of forces influencing these facets of behavior and affecting our interpretation of them? This "environment of forces" takes a wide variety of shapes, from Hawthorne's "truth of the human heart," to Poe's glimpse of "supernal beauty," to Melville's threatening visage behind the "pasteboard mask" of nature, to the natural laws of Dreiser, the brute within *McTeague,* and the blend of scientific and providential determinisms in Crane. Of course, it would be naïve to think that James and Howells did not bring to bear upon their texts their own theories of nature and human nature, but there is clearly a shift in focus when one reads texts such as *Pierre* and *The Sea-Wolf.* These are, in a sense, *novels of ideas* in ways that *The Portrait of a Lady* and *The Rise of Silas Lapham* are not.

Do we understand our world better by turning toward the everyday, the details of life, the subtle and complex behaviors of people not unlike ourselves? Or do we better understand our world by judging human behavior against the backdrop of various cosmologies and theories of human nature? Perhaps this very question is pointless: both methods have been valuable, and will likely continue to be so. For the literary artist, of course, these questions are tied to conceptions of narrative form and strategy. The medium the artist uses to create his or her vision is a direct result of the themes and ideas the artist wishes to explore. For Howells, James, Jewett, Chesnutt, Cable, and others, the economic, political, psychological, and interpersonal themes they explored called for a realistic treatment of the material, and the end products tended to veer toward the novel of social realism. Norris, equally fascinated with the raw material of daily life perhaps, nevertheless took his tale of psychological and social degeneration another direction in *Vandover and the Brute,* creating a work that confronts scientific, pseudo-scientific, and philosophical issues in something approaching allegory.

What does the future hold for studies of American literary naturalism? The field seems to remain wide open. Great work has already been done, but much remains for critical investigation. As I have suggested earlier in this study, perhaps the first thing that needs to be done is to revise the standard definitions of American literary naturalism and revisit some of the axioms of past scholarship. The mere fact that many of the best known utopian novels of the late nineteenth century seem to be drawing upon the same, or similar, scientific and philosophical precepts as the literary naturalists suggests that our portrait of the late-nineteenth-century American literary landscape may need some slight adjusting. Clearly, however, a century after the careers of Crane, Norris, Frederic, London, Wharton, Twain, Dreiser, and Chopin, current trends in scholarship suggest that the place of the American literary naturalists within the pantheon of American literary history is secure.

Notes

Preface

1. "The Passing of Naturalism," *Outlook* 64 (10 March 1900): 570–71.
2. Sidney Gendin, "Was Stephen Crane (or Anybody Else) a Naturalist?" *Cambridge Quarterly* 24.2 (1995): 89–101.

Chapter 1

1. Frederic Taber Cooper, "Frank Norris, Realist." *Bookman* 10 (November 1899): 234–38.
2. This is one of the central points in John A. Garraty's *The New Commonwealth: 1877–1890* (New York: Harper & Row, 1968).
3. These are all actual titles from articles appearing in the *North American Review* and the *Forum* in the last third of the nineteenth century.
4. An English translation of Alas's preface is reprinted in George Becker, ed., *Documents of Modern Literary Realism* (Princeton, N.J.: Princeton UP, 1963) 266–73. All page references will be to this edition.
5. These statements by Valdes can be found in his prologue to *La hermana San Sulpicio* (1899). An authorized English translation of this work by Nathan Haskell Dole, *Sister Saint Sulpice* (New York: Thomas Y. Crowell & Co.), appeared in 1890. In the Dole translation, see pages 17–18 for Valdes's definition of "the so-called French Naturalism."
6. See Lilian R. Furst and Peter N. Skrine, *Naturalism*, 33–36. Donald Pizer also notes that the traditional linkage of French and American naturalism is problematic. See his *Theory and Practice of American Literary Naturalism*, 39.
7. Edwin H. Cady, *Light of Common Day*, 8. For further discussion of

the difference between the romantic and the realistic use of symbols, see chapter 2 of the present study.

8. Or as Furst and Skrine note: "Fortunately, with rare exceptions, the adherents of Naturalism did not quite practice what they preached" (70).

9. For a discussion of Zola's reception in America, see Herbert Edwards, "Zola and the American Critics," 114–29; and William C. Frierson and Herbert Edwards, "The Impact of French Naturalism on American Critical Opinion 1877–1892," 1007–16. For a comparative treatment of Zola's reception in England, see Clarence R. Decker, "Zola's Literary Reputation in England," 1140–53.

10. See *Theodore Dreiser: A Selection of Uncollected Prose,* ed. Donald Pizer (Detroit: Wayne State UP, 1977), 186. Regarding Zola, Crane wrote in a letter in early 1897: "Zola is a sincere writer but—is he much good? He hangs one thing to another and his story goes along but I find him pretty tiresome" (Stanley Wertheim and Paul Sorrentino, eds., *The Correspondence of Stephen Crane* [New York: Columbia UP, 1988], 2:673). For a collection of Jack London's writings on the craft of fiction, including many essays on the business of writing, see Jack London, *No Mentor But Myself,* ed. Dale Walker (Port Washington, N.Y.: Kennikat, 1979).

11. Donald Pizer holds a comparable view. See *Theory and Practice,* 39. There are occasional individual texts that show a distinct influence from some of Zola's work. As a whole, however, the American strain of literary naturalism developed largely independent of direct influence by the French school. Also see Philip Rahv's treatment of this issue in his 1942 essay "Notes on the Decline of Naturalism," reprinted in Becker, 579–90. See also Anthony Savile, "Naturalism and the Aesthetic," 46–63. Among other points, Savile remarks in some detail on the theory/praxis discrepancy in Zola's aesthetic concept of the "experimental" novel.

12. Both of these essays are easily accessible in English translation in Becker, 162–229. All page references will be to this edition.

13. "Zola's Essays," *Atlantic Monthly* 41 (January 1881): 116–19; quotation, 118.

14. Thomas Hardy, "The Science of Fiction" (1891); reprinted in *Thomas Hardy's Personal Writings: Prefaces, Literary Opinions, Reminiscences,* ed. Harold Orel (Lawrence: U of Kansas P, 1966), 134–38.

15. "Naturalism," *Westminster Review* 132.2 (1889): 185–89.

16. Émile Zola, *Germinal* (New York: Penguin, 1954), 28.

17. Paul Alexis, "Naturalism Is Not Dead," reprinted in Becker, 407–11; quotation, 410.

18. Some selections from the journals of Edmond and Jules de Goncourt relevant to naturalism are reprinted in *The Modern Tradition: Backgrounds of Modern Literature,* Richard Ellmann and Charles Feidelson Jr., eds. (New York: Oxford UP, 1965), 297–99; quotation, 298.

19. Although *L'Assommoir* may have been the first translated into English, the first book in the series was Zola's *La Fortune des Rougon* (1871).

20. Of course, by 1894 Norris had published only a few items, the most significant of which may be his short story "Lauth."

21. For a list of English translations of Zola's fiction appearing in the United States, see Gwendolyn Jones, "Zola's Publications in English in the United States, 1876–1902," *Frank Norris Studies* 14 (autumn 1992): 8–11. In my research I have uncovered no concrete evidence to suggest that Norris ever read Zola's *Le roman expérimental.* Perhaps the most thorough research into the particular question of whether Norris ever read *Le roman expérimental* has been conducted by Christine Harvey (see, for instance, her article "Dating Frank Norris's Reading of Zola" in *Resources for American Literary Study* 24.2 [1998]: 187–206). In her research, Harvey, backed by a provocative circumstantial argument, concludes that Norris did read *Le roman expérimental* and, moreover, that it had a direct, leading influence upon his novels.

   In my view, the central issue breaks down into four key questions: (1) did Norris read *Le roman expérimental?* (2) if he did, did it influence (and to what extent) his own fiction? (3) to what extent can we interpret Norris's aesthetic theories through comparison with the principles established in *Le roman expérimental?* and (4) to what extent can we define the aesthetic practices of the American literary naturalists—the "naturalist aesthetic," as it were—through reference and/or comparison to Zola's aesthetic program? These four questions are of course closely related, and an answer to one has a necessary influence upon the answers to the others.

   Focusing on the first two of these four questions, Harvey concludes that *Le roman expérimental* was the "decisive influence" on Norris's developing aesthetic theories and, on his own aesthetic practice. Accepting this claim, however, requires that the critic explain away certain seemingly incongruous claims made by Norris himself in essays such as "Zola as a Romantic Writer" and "A Plea for Romantic Fiction." Reading these essays against a broader nineteenth-century critical context has the effect of minimizing the influence of Zola's critical writings.

22. For several examples, see: Anthony Zielonka, "Huysmans and Grunewald: The Discovery of 'Spiritual Naturalism,'" *Nineteenth-Century French Studies,* 18.1–2 (fall/winter 1989–1990): 212–30; Christopher Lloyd, "French Naturalism and the Monstrous: J. K. Huysmans and *A Rebours,*" *Durham University Journal* 81.1 (December 1988): 111–21; Mary E. Stewart, "Naturalism and the Supernatural," *Journal of European Studies* 12.4 (December 1982): 249–59; and David Goldin, "The Metaphor of Original Sin," *Philological Quarterly* 64.1 (winter 1985): 37–49.

23. The *Oxford English Dictionary* (OED) definition of *philosophical naturalism* reads: "A view of the world, and of man's relations to it, in which only the operation of natural (as opposed to supernatural or spiritual) laws and forces is admitted or assumed. Also, the view that moral concepts can be analyzed in terms of concepts applicable to natural phenomena" (*OED,* 2nd ed., 10:245 [Oxford: Clarendon, 1989]).

24. James T. Farrell, "Some Observations on Naturalism, So Called, in Fiction," 142–55; quotation, 150. Cf. David Baguley, *Naturalist Fiction: The Entropic Vision,* 44.

25. After the success of *L'Assommoir* (1877), Zola purchased some property in Médan. On Thursday evenings the core figures of the French school of literary naturalism—Paul Alexis, Henri Ceard, J. K. Huysmans, Leon Hennique, and Guy de Maupassant—would gather with Zola at his villa in Médan.

26. Paul Alexis, "Naturalism Is Not Dead," reprinted in Becker, 407–11; quotation, 408.

27. Lars Åhnebrink, *The Beginnings of Naturalism in American Fiction,* vi; Åhnebrink's emphasis.

28. See Zola's "Naturalism in the Theatre," in Becker, 199. See also Zola's "The Experimental Novel," in Becker, 189 and 191.

29. Zola, "Experimental Novel," 167.

30. Becker, 207.

31. *Letters of Henry James,* I: 104. Quoted in Frierson and Edwards, 1014.

32. William R. Thayer, "The New Story-Tellers and the Doom of Realism," *Forum* 18 (December 1894): 470–80; quotation, 475.

33. H. B. Marriott Watson, "The Old Controversy," *Living Age* 239 (14 November 1903): 430–39; quotation, 430.

34. Edmund Gosse, "The Limits of Realism in Fiction," *Forum* 9 (June 1890): 391–400.

35. Clarence S. Darrow, "Realism in Literature and Art," *Arena* 9 (December 1893): 98–113; quotations, 101, 107 (my emphasis).

36. James Herbert Morse, "The Native Element in American Fiction: Since the War," *Century Magazine* 26.3 (July 1883): 362–75; quotation, 372. Part 1 of this article, titled "The Native Element in American Fiction: Before the War," appeared in *Century Magazine* 26.2 (June 1883): 288–98.

37. Hamlin Garland, *Crumbling Idols: Twelve Essays on Art and Literature* (Gainesville, Fla.: Scholars' Facsimiles and Reprints, 1952), 6 and 10.

38. F. W. J. Hemmings, "The Origin of the Terms *Naturalisme, Naturaliste,*" *French Studies* 8.2 (April 1954): 109–21.

39. Pierre Loti, "The Literature of the Future," *Forum* 14 (October 1892): 178–88.

40. Frank Norris, "Zola as a Romantic Writer" (1896), reprinted in Donald Pizer, ed., *Novels and Essays/Frank Norris* (New York: Library of America, 1986) 1106–08; quotation, 1107–08. Frank Norris's theory of literary naturalism is given extensive treatment in chapter 2 of the present study.

41. For a contrary position, see the work of Christine Harvey.

42. American critic Eugene Benson could have predicted this discrepancy as early as 1866, when he noted that "the literary spirit is flexible; the scientific spirit is not flexible" ("About the Literary Spirit," *Galaxy* 1 [15 July 1866]: 487–92, quotation, 488). The point Benson makes is that the process of writing literature requires a creative latitude that is not allowed in the sciences.

43. The theories of these thinkers have all been summarized and their works extracted many times. For a few examples, see Willard O. Eddy, "The Scientific Bases of Naturalism in Literature," *Western Humanities Re-*

view 13.3 (summer 1954): 219–30; Bert James Loewenberg, "Darwinism Comes to America, 1859–1900," *Mississippi Valley Historical Review* 28.3 (December 1941): 339–68; Richard Hofstadter, *Social Darwinism in American Thought;* Edward Stone, ed. *What Was Naturalism?* and Roland N. Stromberg, ed. *Realism, Naturalism, and Symbolism.* Also of use is Paul Edwards, ed., *The Encyclopedia of Philosophy,* vol. 1 (New York: Macmillan and Free Press, 1967).

44. Charles R. Lepetit, "The Decline and Fall of the Naturalistic Novel in France," *Living Age* 224 (1900): 57–58, 584–85, 837–39; quotation, 56. Lepetit attributes the fall of naturalism to, among other things, the fact that Zola's theory as set forth in *Le roman expérimental* was inadequate for explaining naturalist narrative.

45. Zola, "Experimental Novel," in Becker, 176.

46. "Zola's Essays," *Atlantic Monthly* 47 (January 1881): 116–19.

47. Zola, "Experimental Novel," 176. With this phrase Zola seems to mean contemporaneous narrative in a quasi-inclusive sense, with special emphasis on the products of literary realism.

48. See Zola, "Naturalism in the Theatre," in Becker, 203.

49. Charles Child Walcutt, *American Literary Naturalism: A Divided Stream,* vii.

Chapter 2

1. Merrell R. Davis and William H. Gilman, eds., *Letters of Herman Melville* (New Haven, Conn.: Yale UP, 1960), 71.

2. Simms's "Advertisement" to *The Yemassee* is reprinted in *American Romanticism: A Shape for Fiction,* ed. Stanley Bank (New York: Capricorn Books, 1969), 208–10.

3. *The Works of Nathaniel Hawthorne,* ed. George Parsons Lathrop (Boston: Houghton Mifflin, 1882–1893), 3:13.

4. I am not the only critic to complain of this tendency in Norris, London, Dreiser, and Crane criticism. Donald Pizer, June Howard, and Lee Clark Mitchell have all called for a treatment of American naturalist narrative that explores the thematic and structural possibilities for tensions and contradictions in naturalist fiction (see Pizer, *Theory and Practice,* 86; June Howard, *Form and History in American Literary Natu-*

ralism, 36–69; and Lee Clark Mitchell's *Determined Fictions: American Literary Naturalism*).

5. For a much more detailed discussion of these issues in nineteenth century American letters, see G. R. Thompson and Eric Carl Link, *Neutral Ground: New Traditionalism and the American Romance Controversy.*

6. Richard Burton, "The Persistence of the Romance," *Dial* 15 (16 December 1893): 380–81; quotation, 381.

7. For further discussion of determinism in *Elsie Venner,* see chapter 4.

8. The following discussion of the novel/romance distinction and its transgeneric features is largely a brief overview of an issue given extensive treatment in Thompson and Link, *Neutral Ground.*

9. *The Works of Nathaniel Hawthorne,* ed. George Parsons Lathrop (Boston: Houghton Mifflin, 1882–1893), 3:13.

10. The critical writings by those just mentioned and many others have been collected in *Novel and Romance, 1700–1800: A Documentary Record,* ed. Ioan Williams (New York: Barnes and Noble, 1970). For further discussion of the novel/romance distinction in English criticism, see chapter 2 of Thompson and Link, *Neutral Ground.*

11. *Encyclopaedia Britannica,* supplement (1824), 6:435.

12. For example, in an 1818 review of Maria Edgeworth's *Harrington, a Tale, and Ormond, a Tale* (1817), American reviewer Willard Phillips identifies Edgeworth as a writer not of romances, but of novels. As such, Edgeworth "carries us into the throng of living, suffering, and enjoying men and women, animated by the passions with which real life is glowing, and busy with pursuits in which we ourselves are interested." Romance writers, on the other hand, "imagine situations that never can be realized and elaborate personages that come into the world upon absurd errands." (Willard Phillips, review of *Harrington, a Tale, and Ormond, a Tale,* by Maria Edgeworth, *North American Review* 6 [January 1818]: 153–78.)

In another instance, in an 1819 review of William Dunlap's *The Life of Charles Brockden Brown* (1815), the reviewer suggests that the writer who "frames a story to call forth extraordinary and violent interest, and lays the scene amongst ourselves" must "encounter the difficulty of creating an illusion, where his events and characters are broad exceptions to all we witness or should expect, and where our imaginations are kept from wandering, and from deceiving us into a faint conviction of reality, by the mention of some place or circumstance which is too stubbornly familiar and unpoetical for any thing but common incidents and feelings. We are speaking of that kind of tale-writing in which Brown delights, the romantic." In the novel, on the other hand, "the object is to present what exists, to appeal to men's observation and daily experience." Instead of presenting an "imaginary world," the novel provides a "sketch of ordinary society." ([Gulian C. Verplanck?], Review of *The Life of Charles Brockden Brown* by William Dunlap, *North American Review* 9 [June 1819]: 58–77.)

13. In Bank's *American Romanticism,* 208–10.

14. For more on this topic, see Eric Carl Link, "Romance as Epic in Simms's 1835 Advertisement," *Simms Review* 3.2 (winter 1995): 9–13.

15. *American Monthly Magazine* 5.1 (March 1835): 171–81.

16. In the years following Hawthorne's *House of the Seven Gables,* it is no surprise to find American critics discussing the novel/romance distinction in terms that were quite familiar to their readers. For instance, in an 1853 review of several novels for the *North American Review,* Caroline M. Kirkland writes, "The romance proper dealt only with an ideal world; which, though it borrowed terrors and motives from this lower, every-day sphere, yet made them all its own by a judicious mixture of elegance and absurdity. One returned from its illusions to humdrum, common-sense life and duty, as we come out of a panorama exhibited by gas-light, to the sunny street and jostling crowd,—uncertain at first which is the false and which the true" (*North American Review* 76 [January 1853]: 104–13; quotation, 105).

   In the same review Kirkland reprises some of the history of the novel/romance distinction, noting that the illusions of the "romance proper" were set aside by novelists such as Fanny Burney and Maria Edgeworth, who "held the mirror up to nature" and confined themselves to the natural world. But in Scott, she writes, the illusions of the "old romance were, for a time, revived." Following Scott's "period of enchantment," novelists like Susan Ferrier and Jane Austen "tried the power of everyday character to interest the general heart. The sensible and amusing novels of these ladies are the product of much knowledge of society, and sharp, though not ill-natured, observations of its motives and pretences" (108).

17. In two parts: part 1 appeared in *Century Magazine* 26.2 (June 1883): 288–98; part 2 appeared in *Century Magazine* 26.3 (July 1883): 362–75.

18. Hjalmar Hjorth Boyesen, "The Hero in Fiction," *North American Review* 148 (May 1889): 594–601.

19. The shift advocated by Boyesen in the later nineteenth century from the romantic to the realistic, and from the romance to the novel, was analyzed repeatedly by critics in the 1880s and 1890s. In an article on the fiction of H. Rider Haggard in *The Dial*, Samuel M. Clark remarks that the British novelist "has shown the old distinction between the novel and the romance. In the former the imagination pictures what is: in the latter it invents what is not" ("Mr. Haggard's Romances," Dial 8 [May 1887]: 5–7; quotation, 5). Like Boyesen, Clark associates the novel form with literary realism: "The novel dealing with the actual but slightly transposed has come in these latter days to an almost unmixed realism." But despite the fact that "the present generation of readers do not take readily to romance," Mr. Haggard "surprises us with romances as fantastic as those that Cervantes caricatured to immortal death." Haggard, writes Clark, "has shown that the alternative of the vapid commonplace of realism is not what Mr. Ruskin calls foul fiction—a morbid introspection of evil passions on their way from the slums to the morgue—but that romanticism, using a clean imagination, appealing to the faculty of wonder, is for most men and women the supreme and perpetually attractive form and matter of story-telling" (7).

20. William Dean Howells, "James's Hawthorne," *Atlantic Monthly* 45 (February 1880): 282–85; quotation, 283.

21. Henry James, "The Art of Fiction," in *Essays on Literature, American Writers, English Writers,* ed. Leon Edel (New York: Library of America, 1984), 54–55.

22. For a discussion of James's use of the romance in his fiction that is framed within a discussion of the novel/romance distinction, see Elsa Nettels, *James and Conrad* (Athens: U of Georgia P, 1977), chapters 4 and 5.

23. See the Norton Critical Edition of *The American: An Authoritative*

Text, Backgrounds and Sources, Criticism, ed. James W. Tuttleton (New York: W. W. Norton, 1978), 10–11.

24. Reprinted in William Dean Howells, *Selected Literary Criticism,* vol. 3: 1898–1920 (Bloomington: Indiana UP, 1993), 3:215–31; quotation, 218.

25. William Dean Howells, *Heroines of Fiction* (New York: Harper and Brothers, 1901), 1:162. Compare Howells's statements with similar reflections in Brander Matthews, "Romance against Romanticism" (1900), reprinted in Matthews's *The Historical Novel and Other Essays* (New York: Charles Scribner's Sons, 1901), 31–46. For further comparison, note Frank Norris's distinction between romanticism and sentimentalism discussed later in this chapter.

26. William Dean Howells, "The New Historical Romances," *North American Review* 171 (December 1900): 935–48.

27. Here are two more examples: in 1894 Amelia E. Barr finds in Fielding, Richardson, and Burney "the real indicators of the province of the novelist: laughing at the follies of society, ridiculing its petty vices, and making picture of the every-day life of the period," while the romances of Stevenson are filled, as the realists would say, with "improbabilities" ("The Modern Novel," *North American Review* 159 [November 1894]: 592–600). In another instance, Margaret Steele Anderson in 1897 associates the realistic novel with a concern for "the analysis of character, sometimes the delicate and subtle setting forth of episode, and sometimes the portrayal of life as it appears on the surface"; she associates the romance with "the revival of wonder at the mystery and the greatness of life" ("A New Ideal in American Fiction," *Dial* 23 [16 November 1897]: 269–70).

28. See William Gilmore Simms, *Views and Reviews in American Literature, History, and Fiction,* reprint ed. (Cambridge, Mass.: Belknap Press, 1962), 56; and Henry James, Preface to *The American* (New York: W. W. Norton, 1978), 10–11.

29. E. T. Channing, review of *Rob Roy, North American Review* 7.2 (July 1818): 149–84.

30. The transgeneric nature of the modern romance is also indicated in a lengthy review of *York Town, A Historical Romance* that appeared in the *American Quarterly Review.* Romances in America, writes the re-

viewer, are "the offspring of distance and obscurity; cradled in the mists of unsubstantial fiction, or woven in the web of distorted truth." The "region of romance and improbability is beyond the reach of the naked eye" and pursues things "supernatural, or out of the ordinary course of nature." "Modern romance," continues the reviewer, "is the combined offspring of history, tradition, and fancy," and as the romance writer "recedes from the present time, or the domestic sphere of action, he may indulge a greater latitude of improbability" (*American Quarterly Review* 2.3 [September 1827]: 19–46).

31. *American Monthly Magazine* 1.3 (June 1829): 187–94.

32. *Knickerbocker* 2 (December 1833): 479.

33. *North American Magazine* 4.22 (August 1834): 287–88. For one more example, in an essay titled "American Literature" published in the *Knickerbocker* in 1835, the critic talks of the intermingling of the "unnatural" and "extravagant" with "characters and events, some of them, at least, not altogether imaginary" in Scott's historical romances. Furthermore, the reviewer notes that Scott's historical romances are not quite as extravagant as the "early romances of chivalry." Then, using a metaphor that sounds rather Jamesian, the reviewer notes that some of the more unrestrained modern romances "launch forth without rudder or compass into the boundless ocean of extravagance." Opposed to the historical romance of Scott, concludes the reviewer, is the novel, which concerns itself with "a state of society" and "domestic and social affections, and with the habits of life" (*Knickerbocker* 5 [April 1835]: 317–26).

34. For more on the realism/idealism debate, see chapter 3. Also, see Eric Carl Link, "The War of 1893; or, Realism and Idealism in the Late Nineteenth Century," *American Transcendental Quarterly* 11.4 (December 1997): 309–21.

35. Julian Hawthorne, "The American Element in Fiction," *North American Review* 139 (August 1884): 164–78; quotation, 176.

36. Henry A. Beers, *Initial Studies in American Letters* (Meadville, Pa.: New York, Flood, and Vincent, 1895), 142.

37. John Burroughs, "The Real and the Ideal. A Hint from Nature," *Dial* 19 (1 November 1895): 239–40; quotation, 239.

38. George Pellew, "The New Battle of the Books," *Forum* 5 (July 1888): 564–73; quotation, 566.

39. James Sully, "The Future of Fiction," *Forum* 9 (August 1890): 644–57.

40. "The Revival of Romance," *Dial* 25 (1 December 1898): 387–89.

41. Katharine Pearson Woods, "Edward Bellamy: Author and Economist," *American Fabian* 4.7 (July 1898): 7–9; quotation, 9.

42. William Dean Howells, "The Romantic Imagination" (1898), reprinted in *Criticism and Fiction and Other Essays,* ed. Clara Marburg Kirk and Rudolf Kirk (New York: New York UP, 1959), 250–55; quotation, 251.

43. Jack London's "impassioned realism" took its basic shape from this sentiment. See the discussion of London later in the present chapter.

44. *Letters of Sarah Orne Jewett,* ed. Carl J. Weber (Waterville, Maine: Colby College Press, 1947), 37.

45. Edmund Gosse, "The Limits of Realism in Fiction," *Forum* 9 (June 1890): 391–400; quotation, 400.

46. Lewis E. Gates, *Studies and Appreciations* (New York: Macmillan, 1900). The phrase "renovating imaginative realism" is used on page 65, but the transgeneric features of the romance are also discussed in chapter 2, "The Return to Conventional Life." See also *A Novelist in the Making: A Collection of Student Themes and the Novels* Blix *and* Vandover and the Brute, ed. James D. Hart (Cambridge, Mass.: Belknap, 1970), 13.

47. Richard Chase, *The American Novel and Its Tradition* (Baltimore: Johns Hopkins UP, 1957), 12.

48. Donald Pizer approaches a similar conclusion regarding the "transgeneric" potential of American literary naturalism. Pizer finds that a "naturalistic novel" is an "extension of realism" in its dealings with the "local and contemporary." In this material, however, the naturalist finds "the extraordinary and excessive in human nature" (*Theory and Practice,* 86–87). Like Pizer, in his essay "American Naturalism and the Problem of Sincerity," Christopher P. Wilson also recognizes the blending of romance and realism in naturalist narrative (*American Literature* 54.4 [December 1982]: 511–27). Looking at London's *Martin Eden,* Norris's *Responsibilities of the Novelist,* and Sinclair's "What Life Means to Me" (1906), Wilson argues that by blending realism and romance literary naturalists were able to "write of the material life without losing light of man's 'divine' spirit" (517). For the naturalists, realism enhanced their claims to "expertise and

experience," while romance "lifted their writing above mere journalism" (517).

49. James O. Pierce, "New Phases of the Romance," *Dial* 26 (1 February 1899): 69–72.

50. John Herman Randall Jr., "The Changing Impact of Darwin on Philosophy," *Journal of the History of Ideas* 22.4 (October–December 1961): 435–62; quotation, 441.

51. Oscar W. Firkins, "The Commonplace in Fiction," *New Englander and Yale Review* 50 (May 1889): 333–47; quotation, 335–36.

52. Hall Caine, "The New Watchwords of Fiction," *Contemporary Review* 57 (April 1890): 479–88; quotation, 488.

53. For information on the break between Thompson and Howells, see Gary F. Scharnhorst's two articles on the subject: "Maurice Thompson's Regional Critique of William Dean Howells" (*American Literary Realism* 9 [1976]: 57–63); and "William Dean Howells and Maurice Thompson: At War Over Realism?" (*Old Northwest* 5 [1979]: 291–302). In these two articles Scharnhorst demonstrates that the rift between Howells and Thompson in the late 1880s cannot be understood as a mere separation between two artists with competing literary creeds; rather, their rift may have as much, if not more, to do with Thompson's ties to the promotion of the Midwest and Midwestern literature.

54. Maurice Thompson, "The Domain of Romance," *Forum* 8 (November 1889): 326–36.

55. This and the other essays by Frank Norris discussed in this chapter can be found in *The Literary Criticism of Frank Norris,* ed. Donald Pizer (Austin: U of Texas P, 1964). All page references are to this volume.

56. William Dean Howells, "Mr. Howells on Some Modern Novelists," *Critic* 11 (16 July 1887): 32.

57. William Morton Payne, "Recent Fiction," *Dial* 31 (1 September 1901): 135–40; quotation, 140.

58. Wilbur Larremore, "Realists in Prose Fiction," *Overland Monthly* 13 (May 1889): 510–22.

59. George Merriam Hyde, "The Allotropy of Realism," *Dial* 18 (16 April 1895): 231–32; quotation, 232.

60. W. H. Mallock, "The Relation of Art to Truth," *Forum* 9 (March 1890): 36–46; see especially 44–45. For another example, in Andrew Lang's essay "Realism and Romance" (1887), after noting the intense debate in American periodicals over the relative merits of realism and romanticism, Lang makes the claim that Zola is "as little a Realist as the king was a royalist." (Andrew Lang, "Realism and Romance," *Contemporary Review* 52 [1887]: 683–93; quotation, 687).

61. "The Passing of Naturalism," *Outlook* 64 (10 March 1900): 570–71; quotation, 571.

62. Charles R. Lepetit, "The Decline and Fall of the Naturalistic Novel in France," *Living Age* 224 (1900): 57–58, 584–85, 837–39.

63. For a contrary position, see the work of Christine Harvey.

64. Frank Norris, "A Problem in Fiction: Truth versus Accuracy," reprinted in Pizer, *Literary Criticism of Frank Norris,* 55–58.

65. A similar view is taken by William Siward Edmonds in "Realism and the Real.—A Suggestion, Not a Reply," *Dial* 14 (16 March 1893): 173–74. Edmonds writes: "By all means be realistic in your method, but remember that truth is something infinitely above details." Edmonds also warns critics about the pitfalls of confusing a realistic philosophy with a realistic technique. Like Daudet, argues Edmonds, one can use realistic techniques and yet still be a "romanticist at heart." Relating Edmonds's point to American literary naturalism, one notes with Norris that a person can write romances and yet still implement the techniques of literary realism.

66. As a side note, one can occasionally see critics in the late nineteenth century try to describe, without adequate terminology, the naturalistic romance-novel. For example, in an essay titled "The New Realism" (*Fortnightly Review* 61 [1897]: 63–73), H. D. Traill, without the aid of Norris's terminology, tries to describe the transgeneric naturalistic romance-novel. This "New Realism," argues Traill, is "unreal with the falsity of the half truth, and as old as the habit of exaggeration." One of the professors of the "New Realism," argues Traill, is Stephen Crane.

67. These comments by Norris should not be taken to mean that Norris was against the historical romance, but rather that he was opposed to the sentimental extravagances taken by popular chivalric romances of the day. At the time of his death, Norris himself was planning to write a

trilogy of historical romances focusing on the Battle of Gettysburg. As Norris's friend and reviewer Isaac Marcosson writes in *Adventures in Interviewing* (New York: John Lane, 1919): "'The Epic of the Wheat' only represented one big Norris vision. The really great work that he yearned to do was a Civil War series. He regarded the Battle of Gettysburg as the supreme event in American history. . . . His idea was to divide his novel into three books, each dealing with one day of the struggle that marked the turning point of the war" (241).

Not only was Norris planning this trilogy of historical romances, in his essay "The True Reward of the Novelist" (1901; reprinted in Pizer, *Literary Criticism of Frank Norris*, 84–87), Norris laments that the artless popular historical narratives of the 1890s (written by the "copyists") are being associated with the term "romance." The "lamentable result" of this flood of historical romances, writes Norris, "will be that these copyists will in the end so prejudice the people against an admirable school of fiction—the school of Scott—that for years to come the tale of historic times will be discredited."

68. Norris's theory of naturalism has been discussed several times, and on occasion critics from Norris's initial reviewers forward have pointed out the "romantic" elements found in his fiction. Regarding Norris's theory of naturalism, two essays stand out. Donald Pizer's essay "Frank Norris's Definition of Naturalism" (1962–63; reprinted in *Theory and Practice*, 120–23) discusses "Zola as a Romantic Writer" as well as "A Plea for Romantic Fiction" and his "Weekly Letter" of August 3, 1901. George W. Johnson's "Frank Norris and Romance" (*American Literature* 33.1 [March 1961]: 52–63) works toward placing Norris's theory within a broader late-nineteenth-century literary context and contains some insightful readings of Norris's major novels.

69. Arnold Bennett, "The Future of the American Novel" (1903, published 1912); reprinted in *A Storied Land: Theories of American Literature from Whitman to Edmund Wilson,* ed. Richard Ruland (New York: E. P. Dutton, 1976), 193–99; quotation, 199.

70. Hamlin Garland, "The Work of Frank Norris," *Critic* 42 (March 1903): 216–18; quotation, 216.

71. William Dean Howells, "Frank Norris," *North American Review* 175 (December 1902): 769–78.

72. Howells expressed comparable sentiments in his 1899 essay on Norris called "A Case in Point." He writes that Norris "reminds you of Zola also in the epical conception of life. He reminds you of Zola also in the lingering love of the romantic, which indulges itself at the end in an anticlimax worthy of Dickens." This essay is reprinted in Kirk and Kirk, eds., *Criticism and Fiction,* 279–82.

73. Frederick Taber Cooper, "Frank Norris, Realist," *Bookman* 10 (November 1899): 234–38; quotation, 236.

74. Ernest Peixotto, "Romanticist Under the Skin," *Saturday Review of Literature* (27 May 1933): 613–15.

75. "Notes of a Novel Reader," *Critic* 36 (April 1900): 352.

76. Marcosson, 233.

77. Reprinted in Williams, ed., *Novel and Romance,* 298–99.

78. See the discussions of Melville and Poe in Thompson and Link, *Neutral Ground.*

79. Pierce, "New Phases of the Romance," 71–72. Also focusing on Hawthorne, E. P. Peabody writes: "Nathaniel Hawthorne made a discovery, which was that we might be taken out of the prose of life into the region of the 'perfect good and fair,'—and into the mysteries of the Inferno as well,—without transcending the common boundaries of daily life" (as quoted in Julian Hawthorne, "The Salem of Hawthorne," *Century Magazine* 28.1 [May 1884]: 3–17; quotation, 16).

80. Frank Norris, *Blix,* 114, reprinted in *A Novelist in the Making,* ed. James D. Hart (Cambridge, Mass.: Belknap, 1970). All page references to *Blix* are to this volume.

81. See, for example, Blix, 227 and 272.

82. George E. Fortenberry, Stanton Garner, and Robert H. Woodward, eds. *The Correspondence of Harold Frederic* (Fort Worth: Texas Christian UP, 1977), 394.

83. Other letters also hint that Frederic may have considered himself a writer in the romance tradition. See Fortenberry, Garner, and Woodward, *Correspondence,* 17, 100, and 230. For more context on Frederic and the relationship between Hawthorne and the romance tradition, see Samuel Coale, "Frederic and Hawthorne: The Romantic Roots of Naturalism," *American Literature* 48 (1976): 29–45.

84. Jack London, *Novels and Social Writings* (New York: Library of America, 1982), 194, 199.

85. London's review of *The Octopus* appeared in *Impressions* in June 1901. It is reprinted in London, *No Mentor But Myself,* 33–36; quotation, 35.

86. Jack London, *The Letters of Jack London,* ed. Earle Labor, Robert C. Leitz, III, and I. Milo Shepard (Stanford, Calif.: Stanford UP, 1988) 1:328–29. For another discussion of Jack London's "impassioned realism," see Charles N. Watson Jr., *The Novels of Jack London: A Reappraisal* (Madison: U of Wisconsin P, 1983), chapter 1. For a very general discussion of the romantic elements in London's early Klondike fiction, see Alfred S. Shivers, "The Romantic in Jack London," *Alaska Review* 1 (winter 1963): 38–47. For a more involved interpretation of London as a romantic writer, see Earle Labor, *Jack London* (New York: Twayne, 1974). Labor notes that "for all London's insistence of Realism, he was a blatant Romantic" (60). In his best fiction, writes Labor, London "reaches the level of other great American symbolists like Poe, Hawthorne, and Melville; and his primitive sensitivity to archetypes gives him a special affinity to Melville" (59).

87. Quoted in Watson, 14.

88. London, *Letters of Jack London,* 1:103.

89. London, *Novels and Social Writings,* 764–65.

90. Cf. Watson, 15. He writes: In his theory of fiction, London "aligned himself with those who sought a middle ground between the more extreme claims of realism and romance."

91. Henry Wadsworth Longfellow, review of Nathaniel Hawthorne's *Twice-Told Tales, North American Review* (April 1842).

92. London, *Letters of Jack London,* 18.

93. Ibid., 313.

94. These essays are reprinted in *Prose and Poetry/Stephen Crane,* ed. J. C. Levenson (New York: Library of America, 1984), 457, 615–18.

95. All page references to Crane's letters are to *The Correspondence of Stephen Crane,* 2 vols., eds. Stanley Wertheim and Paul Sorrentino (New York: Columbia UP, 1988).

96. See, for example, Oscar Wilde, "The Decay of Lying: A Dialogue," *Nine teenth Century* 25 (1889), 35–56.

97. Robert Wooster Stallman, introduction, *The Red Badge of Courage* (New York: Modern Library, 1951), vii–viii.

98. Howells, "Frank Norris," *North American Review* 175 (December 1902): 770.

99. Larzer Ziff, *The American 1890s,* 191–93.

100. Edwin H. Cady, *Stephen Crane,* rev. ed. (Boston: Twayne, 1980), 119–32.

101. Quoted in Becker, 156.

102. R. N. Mookerjee, "Dreiser's Views on Art and Fiction," *American Literary Realism* 12 (1979): 338–42; Donald Pizer, "'True Art Speaks Plainly': Theodore Dreiser and the Late-Nineteenth-Century American Debate over Realism and Naturalism," *Nineteenth-Century Prose* 23.2 (fall 1996): 76–89. Of these two articles, Pizer's is perhaps the more significant, though both are of interest.

    Mookerjee culls together an assortment of brief statements on art and fiction made by Dreiser in a handful of essays and letters over the course of a thirty-year period and concludes, essentially, that Dreiser was a realist, although one who accepted the label reluctantly, who did not use his fiction as propaganda, and who took full license to explore all aspects of life—both the tasteful and the distasteful. Pizer, on the other hand, takes a close look at Dreiser's brief essay "True Art Speaks Plainly" and successfully places it within the context of a late-nineteenth-century critical debate over realism and naturalism, particularly as it related to an author's freedom to represent the less seemly side of life.

103. Dreiser, quoted in Malcolm Cowley, "'Not Men': A Natural History of American Naturalism," *Kenyon Review* 9 (summer 1947): 414–35; quotation, 421–22. Cowley does not cite this quote in his article, but the first part of the Dreiser quote comes from *Dawn* (New York: Horace Liveright, 1931), 198; the second part of the quote comes from *A Book About Myself* (New York: Boni and Liveright, 1922), 9. My thanks to members of the Dreiser Society for helping me locate these references.

104. See Cady, 8, 43.

105. Cf. Pizer, *Theory and Practice,* 105–08.

106. Theodore Dreiser, *The Financier* (New York: Boni and Liveright, 1925), 11.

107. Ibid., 779.

108. Perhaps even more so than *The Financier, Sister Carrie* is another interesting case study in the merging of literary history, aesthetic theory,

philosophy, and narrative, and it has, understandably, received its fair share of critical attention. Within the current context, two treatments of this novel are worth particular mention. In his essay "The Problem of American Literary Naturalism and Theodore Dreiser's *Sister Carrie*," Donald Pizer addresses the problems inherent in some of the more limiting definitions of literary naturalism, and he uses *Sister Carrie* to illustrate that the term "naturalism" can still be of use, so long as we allow an author to drift toward naturalism without having the burden of having to fully articulate a particular philosophy within his or her narrative. In this manner, Pizer seems to take a position congenial with the one I set forth in chapter 1, arguing that literary naturalism is best understood as a thematic use of naturalist theory, not the embodiment of a particular scientific methodology or a particular philosophical position.

A second essay of note concerning *Sister Carrie* is Yoshinobu Hakutani's "Dreiser's Romantic Tendencies" (*Dreiser Studies* 21.2 [fall 1990] 40–47); a slightly revised version of this essay was published as the first chapter of *Theodore Dreiser and American Culture: New Readings,* ed. Yoshinobu Hakutani (Newark: U of Delaware P, 2000). Hakutani argues that *Sister Carrie* is born out of both romantic and realist tendencies, and that it emerges as a hybrid product of both the novel and the romance.

109. Theodore Dreiser, "What I Believe," reprinted in *Theodore Dreiser: A Selection of Uncollected Prose,* ed. Donald Pizer (Detroit: Wayne State UP, 1977), 245–58; quotation, 245. In her article "Theodore Dreiser, Beyond Naturalism" (*Mark Twain Quarterly* 9 [winter 1951]: 5–9), Florence Leaver, though she does not quote the essay by Dreiser cited above, makes use of Dreiser's pursuit of the *Why* of things. For some of Dreiser's thoughts on romanticism, see his brief essay "Man and Romance," *Reedy's Mirror* (28 August 1919): 585.

110. Richard Lehan, *Theodore Dreiser: His World and His Novels* (Carbondale: Southern Illinois UP, 1969), 47. Cf. Richard P. Adams, "Permutations of American Romanticism" (*Studies in Romanticism* 9.4 [fall 1970]: 249–68), who also briefly discusses Dreiser as working broadly within a tradition of American romanticism.

111. William Dean Howells, "Mr. Howells's Paper" (1912); reprinted in Kirk and Kirk, eds., *Criticism and Fiction,* 377–84; quotation, 381.

112. Along these lines, toward the end of the nineteenth century one can find some critics reacting against Howellsian realism, particularly in its more staid and sanitized manifestations, and, like Norris, making a plea for romantic fiction. For example, Samuel M. Clark calls Howellsian realism "babbling folly" and "sheer and unmixed nonsense," and Howells's dedication to his realistic art is an "apostleship of inanity" ("Mr. Haggard's Romances," *Dial* 8 [May 1887]: 6). See also James Lane Allen, "Caterpillar Critics," *Forum* 4 (November 1887): 332–41.

113. Jack London, "The Terrible and Tragic in Fiction," *Critic* 42 (June 1903): 539–43.

114. London, *Letters of Jack London*, 2:901.

115. See chapter 1 of Chase, *American Novel and Its Tradition*.

116. Ibid., 2.

Chapter 3

1. Cf. Richard Lehan, "American Literary Naturalism: The French Connection," *Nineteenth-Century Fiction* 38.4 (March 1984): 553–54.

2. See Rod W. Horton and Herbert W. Edwards, *Backgrounds of American Literary Thought* (Englewood Cliffs, N.J.: Prentice-Hall, 1974), 166.

3. See Hofstadter, 85.

4. This is one of the central ideas in Morse Peckham's essay "Darwinism and Darwinisticism" (*Victorian Studies* 3.1 [September 1959]: 19–40). A detailed treatment of optimistic evolutionary orientations is given in Frederick William Conner, *Cosmic Optimism: A Study of the Interpretation of Evolution by American Poets from Emerson to Robinson* (Gainesville: U of Florida P, 1949), 3–36.

5. Henry C. Payne, "The Reality of the Ideal," *Dial* 28 (16 March 1900): 191–92; quotation, 192.

6. See the introduction to Donald H. Meyer, *The Democratic Enlightenment* (New York: Capricorn Books, 1976).

7. Horton and Edwards, 73. For a brief and succinct treatment of the Enlightenment and theories of progress, see Horton and Edwards, 54–79; especially 73–75.

8. Norman S. Grabo, "Crevecoeur's American: Beginning the World Anew," *William and Mary Quarterly* 48 (1991): 159–72; quotation, 160.

A sentiment similar to Grabo's can be found in Mary E. Rucker, "Crevecoeur's *Letters* and Enlightenment Doctrine," *Early American Literature* 13 (1978): 193–212; and Thomas Philbrick, *St. John de Crevecoeur* (New York: Twayne, 1970). Rucker takes up the argument that Crevecoeur's *Letters* are an expression of Enlightenment doctrine. While acknowledging that they are "predicated" on Enlightenment concepts, Rucker suggests that the *Letters* function as a dialogue between the naïve optimism of the Enlightenment (expressed through the voice of the farmer, James) and a pessimistic critique of the Enlightenment (through the intrusions of the author, Crevecoeur). Thus, the text involves a "simultaneous affirmation and denial" of the dominant doctrine, involving "two opposing consciousnesses that espouse two opposing views."

9. J. Hector St. John de Crevecoeur, *Letters from an American Farmer* (New York: Penguin, 1986), 51.

10. This work was reprinted as the initial essay in Morse Peckham, *The Triumph of Romanticism: Collected Essays* (Columbia: U of South Carolina P, 1970), 3–26. All page references will be to this volume.

11. For further treatment of positive and negative romanticism, see Michael J. Hoffman, *The Subversive Vision: American Romanticism in Literature* (Port Washington, N.Y.: Kennikat, 1972). Hoffman applies Peckham's dialectic, tracing romanticism through several recognizable stages (analogism, transcendentalism, realism, and stylism) as it progresses in linear fashion toward the twentieth century.

12. Upton Sinclair, "What Life Means to Me," *Cosmopolitan* 41.6 (October 1906): 591–95.

13. René Wellek, *A History of Modern Criticism: 1750–1950* (New Haven, Conn.: Yale UP, 1955), 3:163–64.

14. Ibid., 164.

15. For a discussion of the term "negative closure" see G. R. Thompson, *The Art of Authorial Presence: Hawthorne's Provincial Tales* (Durham, N.C.: Duke UP, 1993), 13. Michael J. Hoffman's chapter on negative romanticism in *The Subversive Vision* focuses on a reading of "The Fall of the House of Usher." Of particular note is his belief that the house itself is a symbol of the Enlightenment. Thus, with the fall of the house, Poe is narratizing the rejection of progressive Enlightenment doctrine, and the black tarn represents the resulting void of negative romanticism.

16. Peckham would not necessarily have disagreed with this. In fact, in "Toward a Theory of Romanticism," he writes: "Although Negative and then Positive Romanticism developed by reaction out of the static-mechanistic-uniformitarian complex, with its cosmic Toryism, its sentimentalism, and its Deism, they were also superimposed upon it. At any point in nineteenth- or twentieth-century culture it is possible to take a cross section and find all three actively at work. The past 150 years or so must be conceived as a dramatic struggle, sometimes directly between Positive Romanticism and static, mechanistic thought, sometimes three-cornered" (25).

17. Cady, 6. For Cady, negative realism is the antithesis to romanticism and takes the shape of attacks on the excesses of romanticism, as in Mark Twain's *Life on the Mississippi* and "Fenimore Cooper's Literary Offenses." Positive realism is the more developed state of the genre, found in Howells and James, in which the genre has come to fruition with its own set of values, conventions, and forms.

18. For further discussion of the realism/idealism debate in the 1890s, see Eric Carl Link, "The War of 1893; or, Realism and Idealism in the Late Nineteenth Century," *American Transcendental Quarterly* 11.4 (December 1997): 309–21.

19. For a topically analyzed survey of late-nineteenth-century English and American critics writing on the nature of realism, the realism/idealism debate, and the revival of romance in the 1890s, see Houghton W. Taylor, "Some Nineteenth-Century Critics of Realism," *Studies in English* 8 (1928): 110–28.

20. W. H. Mallock, "The Relation of Art to Truth," *Forum* 9 (March 1890): 36–46; quotation, 36–38.

21. F. Marion Crawford, *The Novel: What It Is,* reprint ed., (Westport, Conn.: Greenwood, 1970), 76. An earlier version of this monograph, under the title "What Is a Novel?" appeared in *Forum* 14 (January 1893): 591–99.

22. See page 59 of the *Forum* article by Crawford, for example.

23. Reprinted in William Dean Howells, *Criticism and Fiction and Other Essays,* eds. Kirk and Kirk.

24. William Dean Howells, *A Hazard of New Fortunes* (New York: Penguin, 2001), 126.

25. Paul Bourget, "The Limits of Realism in Fiction," *Littell's Living Age* 196 (18 March 1893): 739–41; quotation, 739.

26. Hjalmar Hjorth Boyesen, "The Great Realists and the Empty Story-Tellers," *Forum* 18 (February 1895): 724–31. This article by Boyesen is in part a response to an earlier article by William R. Thayer titled "The New Story-Tellers and the Doom of Realism," *Forum* 18 (December 1894): 470–80. Thayer argues that realism has failed in its efforts to reign as the supreme genre for fiction and that the new wave of romances, by the likes of Kipling and Stevenson, mark the reassertion of the romantic or idealistic school of fiction in Anglo-American letters.

27. For several more examples of critics who associate the novel with realism and the romance with idealism, see the following: Henry James, "Lothair," *Atlantic Monthly* 26 (August 1870): 249–51; Albert S. Cook, "Fine Art in Romantic Literature," *Overland Monthly* 6 (July 1885): 52–66; Joseph Kirkland, "Tolstoi, and the Russian Invasion of the Realm of Fiction," *Dial* 8 (August 1886): 79–81; Samuel M. Clark, "Mr. Haggard's Romances," *Dial* 8 (May 1887): 5–7; Charles Dudley Warner, "The Novel and the Common School," *Atlantic Monthly* 65 (June 1890): 721–31; and Henry A. Beers, *Initial Studies in American Letters* (New York: Flood and Vincent, 1895), 213–14.

28. Burton, "Persistence of the Romance," 380–81; quotation, 381.

29. Charles Child Walcutt's landmark study of American literary naturalism titled *American Literary Naturalism: A Divided Stream* develops at length the connections between transcendentalism and both literary idealism and literary naturalism.

30. Henry Steele Commager, as quoted in Jay Martin, *Harvests of Change: American Literature, 1865–1914* (Englewood Cliffs, N.J.: Prentice-Hall, 1967), 204.

31. J. Martin, 209.

32. Cf. Lehan, "American Literary Naturalism," 529–57. Lehan sees utopian fiction, like *Looking Backward,* as developing out of an "obsession with the theme of force" (553–54).

33. Edward Bellamy, *Looking Backward* (New York: Magnum, 1968), 348.

34. Herbert Spencer, as quoted in Hofstadter, 40. The ellipsis is Hofstadter's. In this passage Spencer uses a dynamic and organic meta-

phor to describe the process of evolution; this helps corroborate Norris's claim that naturalism is really a type of romanticism. See chapter 2 of the present study.

35. Katharine Pearson Woods, "Edward Bellamy: Author and Economist," *American Fabian* 4.7 (July 1898): 7–9.

36. Quoted in Woods, 8. Again, note the dynamic and organic metaphors employed to describe the process of evolution.

37. Chapter 19 of *Looking Backward* deals with the problem of crime.

38. See Hofstadter, chapter 3.

39. Jack London, "Goliah," in *The Science Fiction Stories of Jack London,* ed. James Bankes (New York: Citadel, 1993), 100.

40. Ibid., 101.

41. See Edward Bellamy, *Equality* (New York: Appleton, 1898), 150–51.

42. The "Declaration of Principles" of Bellamy's Nationalist movement was printed in the first issue of the *Nationalist* (1889) and is reprinted in Hofstadter, 113.

43. A brief description by Bellamy of the aims of Nationalism appeared under the title "The Programme of the Nationalists," *Forum* 17 (March 1894): 81–91.

44. For a fine discussion of the relationship between *Herland* and the tradition of utopian fiction, see Chris Ferns, "Rewriting Male Myths: Herland and the Utopian Tradition," in *A Very Different Story: Studies on the Fiction of Charlotte Perkins Gilman,* eds. Val Gough and Jill Rudd (Liverpool UP, 1998), 24–32.

45. For some exploration of these connections, see Lois N. Magner, "Darwinism and the Woman Question: The Evolving Views of Charlotte Perkins Gilman," in *Critical Essays on Charlotte Perkins Gilman,* ed. Joanne B. Karpinski (New York: G. K. Hall, 1992), 115–28, and Minna Doskow's introduction to *Charlotte Perkins Gilman's Utopian Novels* (Madison, N.J.: Fairleigh Dickinson UP, 1999), 9–29.

46. For additional discussion of these connections, see Gary Scharnhorst, *Charlotte Perkins Gilman* (Boston: Twayne, 1985), 90–95.

47. From *Herland,* 200, as reprinted in Doskow, ed., *Gilman's Utopian Novels.* All page references to *Herland* will be to this edition.

48. Howells, "The Romantic Imagination," 250–55; quotation, 251.

49. William Dean Howells, *A Traveler from Altruria,* reprinted in *The Altrurian Romances* (Bloomington: Indiana UP, 1968), 1–179; quotation, 145.

50. Note that at age seventeen, Thomas Granger was publicly executed for multiple acts of bestiality, an episode much lamented by Bradford.

51. Henry Childs Merwin, "On Being Civilized Too Much," *Atlantic Monthly* 79 (June 1897): 838–46; quotation, 839.

52. C. T. Hopkins, "Evil as a Factor in Evolution," *Overland Monthly* 1 (February 1883): 150–57.

53. Mary Parmele, "Relation the Ultimate Truth," *Forum* 3 (July 1887): 483–91.

54. Hofstadter, 98.

55. Horton and Edwards, 254.

56. Richard Burton, "The Dark in Literature," *Forum* 30 (February 1901): 752–60; quotation, 756.

57. James Herbert Morse, "The Native Element in American Fiction: Before the War," *Century Magazine* 26.2 (June 1883): 288–98; quotation, 289, my emphasis.

58. Thomas Carlyle, *Sartor Resartus: Lectures on Heroes* (London: Chapman and Hall, 1894), 1:132–33.

59. Frank Norris, *Vandover and the Brute* (Garden City, N.J.: Doubleday, Doran, 1928), 202.

60. Stephen Crane, *Poetry and Prose/Stephen Crane* (New York: Library of America, 1984), 1335.

61. Cf. chapter 1.

62. Zola, "Experimental Novel," in Becker, 184–85.

63. Burton, "Persistence of the Romance," 380–81; quotation, 381.

64. Bellamy, *Looking Backward,* 7.

65. Don Graham, "Naturalism in American Fiction: A Status Report," *Studies in American Fiction* 10.1 (spring 1982): 1–16.

66. Pizer, *Theory and Practice,* 104.

67. Cf. Lehan, "American Literary Naturalism," 554.

68. See Furst and Skrine, *Romanticism,* 2.

69. John Addington Symonds, "Realism and Idealism," *Fortnightly Review* 42 (1887): 418–29.

70. Charles Child Walcutt, "Harold Frederic and American Naturalism," *American Literature* 11 (March 1939): 11–22.

71. Coale, "Frederic and Hawthorne," 29–45.
72. Roy R. Male as quoted in Darrel Abel, "The Loom of Fiction," *The Moral Picturesque: Studies in Hawthorne's Fiction* (West Lafayette, Ind.: Purdue UP, 1988), quotation, 93.
73. Norris, "Zola as a Romantic Writer," 72.

Chapter 4

1. All page references to this story will be to *Frank Norris of "The Wave"* (San Francisco: Westgate, 1931), 175–80. The story originally appeared in *The Wave* 16 (22 May 1897). When the story was originally published, it was "Disrespectfully Dedicated to Annie Besant." This dedication was omitted when it was subsequently reprinted in *Frank Norris of "The Wave."*

    For a reading of the story that treats it as a direct response to the theosophism of Besant, see Joseph R. McElrath, "Frank Norris's 'The Puppets and the Puppy': LeContean Idealism or Naturalistic Skepticism," *American Literary Realism* 26.1 (fall 1993): 50–59. McElrath reads the allegory as a repudiation of Besant's mystical and evolutionary theosophism and Le Conte's theistic evolutionary idealism. Arnold L. Goldsmith, in "The Development of Frank Norris's Philosophy" (*Studies in Honor of John Wilcox,* ed. A. Dayle Wallace and Woodburn O. Ross [Detroit: Wayne State UP, 1958], 175–94), though unconcerned with the Besant connection, comes to a similar conclusion as McElrath. He argues that the story is central to an understanding of Norris's philosophy, particularly during the period from 1895 to 1899. According to Goldsmith, during these years Norris was his most pessimistic, mechanistic, and deterministic. Goldsmith finds the dialogue between the puppets, and the climactic entrance of the fox terrier puppy, to be a thinly veiled expression of Norris's own beliefs at the time.

2. The "chessboard" metaphor used to describe mankind's relative indeterminism/determinism was also used by William James in "The Dilemma of Determinism." James's use of the metaphor, discussed at length later in this chapter, is similar in some ways to the Queen's Bishop.

3. Goldsmith interprets "Falling-down" as either (a) committing suicide or (b) failing to "live realistically in a world marked by a fierce struggle

for existence" (see pages 181–82 of his article). Reading "Falling-down" as a moral lapse of some sort seems to fit the text better, however.

4. For example, Lars Åhnebrink writes: "*Realism* is a manner and method of composition by which the author describes *normal, average life* in an accurate and truthful way (exemplified in Howells' *The Rise of Silas Lapham*). *Naturalism,* on the other hand, is a manner and method of composition by which the author portrays *life as it is in accordance with the philosophic theory of determinism* (exemplified in Zola's *L'Assommoir*)" (*Beginnings of Naturalism,* vi). See chapter 1 of the present work for further examples and related discussion.

5. Cf. Pizer, *Theory and Practice,* 39.

6. Some of London's notes have been reprinted in *Critical Essays on Jack London,* ed. Jacqueline Tavernier-Courbin (Boston: G. K. Hall, 1983), 253–72. References to London's proposed "Christ Novel" are to this collection, pages 259–62.

7. London would rework these notes into the story of Ragnar Lodbrog in chapter 17 of *The Star Rover.* Lodbrog's story follows fairly closely the notes for the "Christ Novel." The few discrepancies between the notes and the episode in *The Star Rover* can be accounted for in two ways: (1) as London wrote the episode for *The Star Rover,* he changed his mind about several of the details in the notes, and (2) the limited scope of the *Star Rover* chapter compelled London to leave out some of the material he might have used in a longer, full-length treatment.

8. Cf. William James's definition of subjectivism, discussed later in this chapter.

9. Zola, "Experimental Novel," in Becker, 163.

10. Émile Zola, *The Experimental Novel and Other Essays,* trans. Belle M. Sherman (New York: Haskell House, 1964), 83.

11. As qtd. in Conder, *Naturalism in American Fiction,* 9.

12. Westbrook, *Free Will and Determinism,* ix.

13. Berofsky, ed., *Determinism,* 3.

14. Here I am borrowing a philosophical term. "Tychism" is a word derived from the Greek word *tyche,* which means fortune or chance. Charles Sanders Pierce used the term to express any theory that regards chance as an objective reality operating in the universe. Tychism also refers to the hypothesis that evolution occurs due to fortuitous varia-

tions. See Dagobert D. Runes, ed., *Dictionary of Philosophy* (Totowa, N.J.: Littlefield, Adams, 1966), 324.

15. John Randall, "The Changing Impact of Darwin on Philosophy," *Journal of the History of Ideas* 22.4 (October–December 1961): 435–62.

16. Stanley Cooperman, "Frank Norris and the Werewolf of Guilt," *Modern Language Quarterly* 20.3 (September 1959): 252–58; quotation, 252.

17. An example of an American philosopher who attempted to join providential and scientific determinism is Joseph Le Conte (one of Frank Norris's professors at Berkeley). He sought to reconcile religion and evolution in his *Evolution: Its Nature, Its Evidences, and Its Relation to Religious Thought* (1888). Donald Pizer discusses at some length the influence of Joseph Le Conte on Frank Norris in *The Novels of Frank Norris* (Bloomington: Indiana UP, 1966).

18. For an excellent and concise treatment of William James's positions regarding free will and determinism, see Donald Viney, "William James on Free Will and Determinism," *Journal of Mind and Behavior* 7.4 (autumn 1986): 555–56.

19. Reprinted in William James, *Essays on Faith and Morals* (New York: Longmans, Green and Co., 1949), 145–83. All page references will be to this volume. This essay by James has been almost completely neglected by scholars of American literary naturalism. Although one can find discussions of this essay in James scholarship and in philosophical criticism dealing with the free will/determinism debate, there are very few discussions of this remarkable essay in literary scholarship. Perry Westbrook briefly highlights some of James's main points in *Free Will and Determinism in American Literature,* 215–19. Gay Wilson Allen has a few summary remarks on the essay in his "William James's Determined Free Will," *Essays on Determinism in American Literature,* ed. Sidney J. Krause, 67–76. To date, the most significant use of James's essay in scholarship on American literary naturalism is in John Conder, *Naturalism in American Fiction.* Conder borrows from James's essay the terms "soft" and "hard" determinism and uses these terms to aid in classifying the fiction of Crane, Norris, and Dreiser. Conder finds that the tensions arising out of the dilemma of soft determinism most often lie outside of the primary texts themselves (see pages 12–13 of Conder's text). On the contrary, I believe one of the chief char-

acteristics of American literary naturalism is that the epistemological themes welling up out of the dilemma of determinism are formally woven—through the aesthetic possibilities available to the romance writer—into the texts of Norris, Crane, and London. Like James E. Caron, who responded to Conder in his article "Grotesque Naturalism: The Significance of the Comic in *McTeague*" (*Texas Studies in Literature and Language* 31.2 [summer 1989]: 288–317; see especially page 310), I believe *McTeague* tends more toward a softer than a harder determinism.

20. Richard Hofstadter discusses pragmatism's response to determinism in *Social Darwinism in American Thought,* 125–35.

21. Zola, "Experimental Novel," in Becker, 163 and 172.

22. *Newspaper Days* is the title of Dreiser's republished version of *A Book about Myself.*

23. Theodore Dreiser, *Newspaper Days* (Philadelphia: U of Pennsylvania P, 1991), 611–12.

24. Twain on *What Is Man?* as reprinted in Bernard DeVoto, ed., *Mark Twain in Eruption* (New York: Grosset and Dunlap, 1922), 239–43.

25. Theodore Dreiser, "What I Believe" (1929), reprinted in *Theodore Dreiser: A Selection of Uncollected Prose,* ed. Donald Pizer, 247.

26. For a more detailed discussion of this reconciliation, see Westbrook, *Free Will and Determinism,* 4–8.

27. Quoted in Zola's "Experimental Novel," in Becker, 180.

28. See Viney, "William James on Free Will and Determinism," 557.

29. My thanks to Donald Viney for pointing this out to me.

30. Levenson, ed., *Prose and Poetry/Stephen Crane,* 894.

31. Hardy's fiction was seen as fatalistic in the late nineteenth century. See Burton, "Dark in Literature," 759.

32. Again, my thanks to Donald Viney for his insights here. In my correspondence with him (January 2001), Viney clarified the matter in this way: "The subjectivists that James was criticizing were philosophers who actually believed in objective values. However, the value they elevated above all else—and this is what bothered James—was the value of knowing. It is not that James objected to knowledge or that he viewed it as a bad or insignificant thing. Rather, doing—the making of some outward good, as he says—not knowing, is the point of existence."

33. Melville makes a similar point in chapter 11 of *Moby-Dick.*

34. James's image of good holding evil by the throat bears a notable resemblance to Joseph Le Conte's evolutionary ethical dualism. For Le Conte, people have "two natures," the higher and the lower. One's higher nature is the realm of the spirit or soul; the lower nature is more physical, governed by animal instinct. The key to "true virtue" rests not in the elimination of the lower nature, but in the subjugation of the lower to the higher. See Pizer, *Novels of Frank Norris*, 17.

35. Again, the author thanks Donald Viney for help with this clarification.

36. Krause, *Essays on Determinism*, 9.

37. This story is reprinted in Levenson, ed., *Prose and Poetry/Stephen Crane*, 594–99.

38. This address was collected in Oliver Wendell Holmes, *Pages from an Old Volume of Life* (Boston: Houghton Mifflin, 1892), 260–314. For two brief accounts of this essay, see Westbrook, *Free Will and Determinism*, 71–75; and Miriam Rossiter Small, *Oliver Wendell Holmes* (New York: Twayne, 1962), 116–19.

39. For brief discussions of Bergson's philosophy see Conder, *Naturalism in American Fiction*, 14–16, and the article on Bergson in Paul Edwards, ed., *The Encyclopedia of Philosophy*, vol. 1 (New York: Macmillan and Free Press, 1967), 287–95.

40. Conder, 14–15.

41. London, *Letters of Jack London*, 3:1339.

42. Ibid., 3:1314–15.

43. Jack London, *The Sea-Wolf* (New York: Oxford UP, 1992), 221.

44. This is the same question posed by the puppets in Norris's "The Puppets and the Puppy" when they wonder if they are held responsible for "Falling-down" when the "Boy" has bent their standard.

45. Darwin's "struggle for life" theory is specifically mentioned on page 72.

46. My reading of *McTeague* owes much to work done by the following critics: Stanley Cooperman, "Frank Norris and the Werewolf of Guilt," *Modern Language Quarterly* 20.3 (September 1959): 252–58; Nan Morelli-White, "The Damnation of *McTeague*: Frank Norris's Morality Play," *Frank Norris Studies* 13 (spring 1992): 5–10; Winifred Farrant Bevilacqua, "From the Ideal to its Reverse: Key Sociocultural Concepts in McTeague," *Centennial Review* 33.1 (winter 1989): 75–88; and Pizer, *Novels of Frank Norris*.

47. Cf. Bevilacqua, 78.

48. All page references are to Frank Norris, *McTeague* (New York: Vintage/Library of America, 1990).

49. For a treatment of *McTeague* as a psychomachia, see Morelli-White.

50. Chaucer, *The Canterbury Tales* (Norwalk, Conn.: Heritage Press, 1974), 531.

51. As a side note, just as Norris may have been playing off the "love of money is the root of all evil" passage in I Timothy 6:10, so too he may have been working with Matthew 25:31–46 in the Big Jim passage. This section of Matthew details the final judgment when Christ shall divide the sheep from the goats. What is notable about this passage is that Jesus emphasizes that individual acts of human charity have a direct impact on the given individual's sympathetic relationship with Christ. The goats are banished to hell in large part because they failed to offer charity to their fellow humans. As Christ says: "Inasmuch as ye did *it* not to one of the least of these, ye did *it* not to me" (Matt. 25:45). In America in the 1890s a solitary, barely literate Indian wrapped in a blanket and begging for charity in a western train station would be perceived as one of the "least of these." Insofar as McTeague does not offer charity to Big Jim, he did not offer it to Christ.

52. J. C. Levenson, introduction, *The Works of Stephen Crane*, vol. 2. *The Red Badge of Courage*, ed. Fredson Bowers (Charlottesville: UP of Virginia, 1975), lvi–lvii.

53. Patrick K. Dooley, *The Pluralistic Philosophy of Stephen Crane* (Urbana: U of Illinois P, 1993), 29–30.

54. All page references are to *The Red Badge of Courage*, ed. Donald Pizer (New York: W. W. Norton, 1994).

55. In one of the manuscript versions of *Red Badge*, Crane was more explicit about the juxtaposition of these two conflicting laws of nature. In a passage that originally followed Fleming's confrontation with death in the chapel, Crane wrote: Fleming "thought as he remembered the small animal capturing the fish and the greedy ants feeding upon the flesh of the dead soldier, that there was given another law which far-over-topped it—all life existing upon death, eating ravenously, stuffing itself with the hopes of the dead" (qtd. in Levenson, lviii). The effect of removing this passage from the final draft is to leave the question open as to which law of nature was the greater.

56. There have been many attempts to interpret the religious imagery and language in *Red Badge*. Ever since Stallman in 1951 suggested that *Red Badge* could be interpreted as a positive redemption story, critics have argued about whether Fleming's "redemption" at the end is ironic or not. Some have even argued that there is no substantial religious component to *Red Badge* at all. One of the main questions stems from asking if the author of *The Black Riders* would also write a narrative that concludes with a positive redemptive vision. It seems to me that the answer lies in the realization that it is not *Crane* who turns to the hope of redemption at the end of *Red Badge,* but Henry Fleming. The answer, therefore, lies in Fleming's subjectivism. Regardless, virtually every study concerned with the religious imagery in the novel includes a discussion of the symbolism (or lack thereof) in the novel.

For a sample of some of the more important essays that tackle this problem see the following: R. W. Stallman, "Notes Toward an Analysis of *The Red Badge of Courage,*" in *Stephen Crane: A Collection of Critical Essays,* ed. Maurice Bassan (Englewood Cliffs, N.J.: Prentice-Hall, 1967), 128–40; the articles by Isaac Rosenfeld, John E. Hart, Edward Stone, and James B. Colvert reprinted in *Stephen Crane's* The Red Badge of Courage: *Text and Criticism,* eds. Richard Lettis, Robert F. McDonnell, and William E. Morris (New York: Harcourt, Brace, 1959); Scott C. Osborne, "Stephen Crane's Imagery: 'Pasted Like a Wafer,'" in *The Red Badge of Courage,* eds. Sculley Bradley, Richmond Croom Beatty, E. Hudson Long (New York: W. W. Norton, 1962), 163–64; R. W. Stallman, "The Scholar's Net: Literary Sources," *College English* 17 (1955): 20–27; James Trammell Cox, "The Imagery of 'The Red Badge of Courage,'" *Modern Fiction Studies* 5 (1959): 209–19; James W. Tuttleton, "The Imagery of *The Red Badge of Courage,*" *Modern Fiction Studies* 8 (1963): 410–15; Marston LaFrance, "Stephen Crane's Private Fleming: His Various Battles," in *Patterns of Commitment in American Literature,* ed. Marston LaFrance (Toronto: U of Toronto P, 1967), 113–33; and Ben Satterfield, "From Romance to Reality: The Accomplishment of Private Fleming," *CLA Journal* 24 (1980–1981): 451–64.

Curiously, in his introduction to *The Red Badge of Courage and Other Writings* (Boston: Houghton Mifflin, 1960), Richard Chase claims that Crane is not a symbolist and that *Red Badge* does not have a "symbolic center," but if it did, the chapel scene in chapter 7 would certainly be it (see xi and xvi).

57. The uncancelled but unpublished passages from the manuscript version of *Red Badge* are printed in an appendix to the Norton Critical Edition.

58. There is a further irony to be found in the ending of *Red Badge*. As John E. Curran Jr. points out, Fleming's feelings of glory are incongruous with the fact that the battle of Chancellorsville was one of the single worst defeats of the Union Army during the entire Civil War. See Curran's article "'Nobody seems to know where we go': Uncertainty, History, and Irony in *The Red Badge of Courage*," *American Literary Realism* 26.1 (fall 1993): 1–12.

59. Stephen Crane, *The Red Badge of Courage* (New York: Signet, 1980), 31.

Chapter 5

1. See, for example, two articles by Donald Pizer: "A Note on Kate Chopin's *The Awakening* as Naturalistic Fiction" (*Southern Literary Journal* 33.2 [spring 2001]: 5–13); and "The Naturalism of Edith Wharton's *The House of Mirth*" (*Twentieth Century Literature* 41.2. [summer 1995]: 241–48).

2. Donald A. Ringe, *American Gothic: Imagination and Reason in Nineteenth-Century Fiction* (Lexington: UP of Kentucky, 1982), 1–12; see especially 8–9.

3. Horace Walpole as quoted in Arthur L. Cooke, "Some Side Lights on the Theory of the Gothic Romance," *Modern Language Quarterly* 12 (1951): 429–36; quotation, 429.

4. Qtd. in Ringe, 18.

5. This preface is reprinted in Williams, ed., *Novel and Romance*, 298–300.

6. Cf. Cooke, 429; Ringe, 8–9.

7. The brief discussion of the Gothic romance that follows is derived primarily from the following two sources: Robert D. Hume, "Gothic versus Romantic: A Revaluation of the Gothic Novel," *PMLA* 84 (1969): 282–90; and G. R. Thompson, "Introduction: Gothic Fiction of the Romantic Age: Context and Mode," in G. R. Thompson, ed. *Roman-*

tic Gothic Tales (New York: Harper and Row, 1979), 1–43. Collateral sources include Donald Ringe, *American Gothic;* G. R. Thompson, ed., *The Gothic Imagination: Essays in Dark Romanticism* (Pullman: Washington State UP, 1974); Arthur L. Cooke, "Some Side Lights on the Theory of the Gothic Romance"; Robert L. Platzner and Robert D. Hume, "'Gothic versus Romantic': A Rejoinder," *PMLA* 86 (1971): 266–74; and Frederick Garber, "Meaning and Mode in Gothic Fiction," in Harold E. Pagliaro, ed., *Racism in the Eighteenth Century* (Cleveland: Case Western Reserve UP, 1973), 155–69.

8. This is G. R. Thompson's "dark romantic" thesis. While not universally accepted, Thompson's thesis does accurately describe the central conflict in many Gothic romances in Europe and America.

9. All page references are to Frank Norris, "Lauth," *Overland Monthly* 21 (March 1893): 241–60.

10. Norris describes Trina's death in *McTeague* using a similar metaphor: Trina "died with a rapid series of hiccoughs that sounded like a piece of clockwork running down" (266).

11. Donald Pizer suggests that the dualistic interpretation of humankind offered here can be traced to the influence of Le Conte's evolutionary ethical dualism (see Pizer, *Novels of Frank Norris,* 18). Because Norris wrote this story while at Berkeley and studying under Le Conte, this does seem likely.

12. "Outside the Zenana," *Overland Monthly* 24 (July 1894): 82–86. This story is the third part of Norris's five-part story cycle "Outward and Visible Signs."

13. Warren French calls Vandover's lycanthropy a "hangover from the Gothicism of *Yvernelle* and 'Lauth'" (*Frank Norris* [New York: Twayne, 1962], 56). Use of this device, claims French, is evidence of the "artist's immaturity" (56). It is precisely this type of judgment that arises from viewing the works of Frank Norris (and other American naturalistic authors) as realistic novels rather than romances. Lycanthropy certainly doesn't fit in a text geared toward representing social reality. Symbolic fantastic transformations have a long tradition in romantic literature, however, and can hardly be seen as evidence in and of itself of an artist's immaturity. Artistic immaturity might be evidenced through the author's relative success at handling such a device.

14. Pizer, *Novels of Frank Norris*, 37.

15. Howard, *Form and History*, 67.

16. Frank Norris, *Vandover and the Brute* (Garden City, N.J.: Doubleday, Doran, 1928). All page references to *Vandover and the Brute* will be to this edition.

17. Charles Child Walcutt, "The Naturalism of Vandover and the Brute" (1948); reprinted in Don Graham, ed., *Critical Essays on Frank Norris* (Boston: G. K. Hall, 1980), 169–76.

18. Lee Clark Mitchell, "'Little Pictures on the Lacquered Surface': The Determining Vocabularies of Norris's *Vandover and the Brute*," *Papers on Language and Literature* 22.4 (fall 1986): 386–405.

19. Stanley Cooperman, "Frank Norris and the Werewolf of Guilt," *Modern Language Quarterly* 20.3 (September 1959): 252–58; quotation, 255.

20. Westbrook, *Free Will and Determinism*, 3–4.

21. Cf. Pizer, *Novels of Frank Norris*, 39.

22. As quoted in Pizer, *Novels of Frank Norris*, 15.

23. Cooperman, 253. See also George W. Johnson, "Frank Norris and Romance," *American Literature* 33.1 (March 1961): 52–63.

24. A "diapason" is a rich and deep harmonic burst of sound akin to a chord played on an organ.

25. Cf. Pizer's discussion of the Vandover/Geary doubling in *Novels of Frank Norris*, 39–43.

26. This is essentially the thesis of Joseph R. McElrath Jr., "Frank Norris's *Vandover and the Brute:* Narrative Technique and the Socio-Critical Viewpoint," in Graham, ed., *Critical Essays on Frank Norris*, 177–93. McElrath writes: "*Vandover* is a Naturalistic tale of degeneration in which Norris uses the basic degeneration-tale structure to psychologically explore the root causes of Van's self-destructive life-vision. As such it is a critical attack upon nineteenth-century popular morality and the archaic life-vision of a world of fixed certainties which informed it" (192). It is my belief that Norris is not so much rejecting religion or spirituality in the text as he is lambasting Vandover's lackadaisical responses to his religious convictions. Vandover acknowledges the reality of a spiritual afterlife, but he takes a weak, shallow attitude toward it (see pages 91 and 191). He takes this attitude because, as Father Mapple would say, "if we obey God, we must disobey ourselves," and

Vandover's comfort-loving nature will not allow him to "disobey" himself.

27. Cf. Pizer, *Novels of Frank Norris,* 42.
28. Ibid., 42–43.
29. Ibid., 42.

Selected Bibliography
of American Literary Naturalism

Represented in this bibliography are major statements on the school of American literary naturalism, as well as a few of the major sources related to American literary realism. Not represented here are primary texts, nineteenth-century critical essays on aesthetic theory, and other random sources used throughout this study; when used these sources are fully documented in the endnotes. For a comprehensive bibliography of works dealing with the American Romance Tradition and the Novel/Romance distinction, see G. R. Thompson and Eric Carl Link, *Neutral Ground: New Traditionalism and the American Romance Controversy* (Louisiana State UP, 1999).

Åhnebrink, Lars. *The Beginnings of Naturalism in American Fiction.* Cambridge, Mass.: Harvard UP, 1950.
———. *The Influence of Émile Zola on Frank Norris.* Cambridge, Mass.: Harvard UP, 1947.
Baguley, David. "The 'Lure' of the Naturalist Text." *Canadian Review of Comparative Literature* 19.1–2(March/June 1992): 273–80.
———. *Naturalist Fiction: The Entropic Vision.* New York: Cambridge UP, 1990.
Becker, George J., ed. *Documents of Modern Literary Realism.* Princeton, N.J.: Princeton UP, 1963.
Bell, Michael Davitt. *The Problem of American Realism: Studies in the Cultural History of a Literary Idea.* Chicago: U of Chicago P, 1993.
Berofsky, Bernard. *Determinism.* Princeton, N.J.: Princeton UP, 1971.
Berthoff, Warner. *The Ferment of Realism: American Literature, 1884–1919.* New York: Collier-MacMillan, 1965.
Bowron, Bernard R., Jr. "Realism in America." *Comparative Literature* 3.3 (summer 1951): 268–85.

Cady, Edwin H. *The Light of Common Day: Realism in American Fiction.* Bloomington: Indiana UP, 1971.

Campbell, Donna M. *Resisting Regionalism: Gender and Naturalism in American Fiction: 1885–1915.* Athens: Ohio UP, 1997.

Cargill, Oscar. *Intellectual America: Ideas on the March.* New York: Macmillan, 1941.

Carter, Everett. *Howells and the Age of Realism.* Philadelphia: Lippincott, 1954.

———. "The Meaning of, and in, Realism." *Antioch Review* 12.1 (spring 1952): 78–94.

Chase, Richard. *The American Novel and Its Tradition.* Baltimore: Johns Hopkins UP, 1957.

Chevrel, Yves. *Le naturalisme.* Paris: Presses universitaires de France, 1982.

Civello, Paul. *American Literary Naturalism and its Twentieth-Century Transformations: Frank Norris, Ernest Hemingway, Don DeLillo.* Athens: U of Georgia P, 1994.

Clark, Harry H. "The Influence of Science on American Literary Criticism, 1860–1910." *Transactions of the Wisconsin Academy of Sciences, Arts, and Letters* 44 (1955): 109–64.

Conder, John J. *Naturalism in American Fiction: The Classic Phase.* Lexington: UP of Kentucky, 1984.

Conner, Frederick William. *Cosmic Optimism: A Study of the Interpretation of Evolution by American Poets from Emerson to Robinson.* Gainesville: U of Florida P, 1949.

Cowley, Malcolm. "Naturalism in American Literature." *Evolutionary Thought in America,* ed. Stow Persons. New Haven, Conn.: Yale UP, 1950.

———. "'Not Men': A Natural History of American Naturalism." *Kenyon Review* 9 (summer 1947): 414–35.

Decker, Clarence R. "Zola's Literary Reputation in England." *PMLA* 49 (1934): 1140–53.

Den Tandt, Christophe. *The Urban Sublime in American Literary Naturalism.* Urbana: U of Illinois P, 1998.

Dudley, John. "Inside and Outside the Ring: Manhood, Race, and Art in American Literary Naturalism." *College Literature* 29.1 (winter 2002): 53–82.

Eddy, Willard O. "The Scientific Bases of Naturalism in Literature." *Western Humanities Review* 13.3 (summer 1954): 219–30.

Edwards, Herbert. "Howells and the Controversy Over Realism in American Fiction." *American Literature* 3 (1931): 237–48.

———. "Zola and the American Critics." *American Literature* 4 (May 1932): 114–29.

Falk, Robert P. "The Rise of Realism, 1871–91." *Transitions in American Literary History,* ed. Harry H. Clark. Durham, N.C.: Duke UP, 1953.

Farrell, James T. "Some Observations on Naturalism, So Called, in Fiction." *Reflections at Fifty and Other Essays.* New York: Vanguard, 1954.

Figg, Robert M., III. "Naturalism as a Literary Form." *Georgia Review* 18.3 (fall 1964): 308–16.

Fisher, Philip. *Hard Facts: Setting and Form in the American Novel.* New York: Oxford UP, 1985.

Fleissner, Jennifer. "The Work of Womanhood in American Naturalism." *Differences* 8.1 (spring 1996): 57–93.

Frierson, William C., and Herbert Edwards. "The Impact of French Naturalism on American Critical Opinion 1877–1892." PMLA 63 (1948): 1007–16.

Furst, Lilian R., and Peter N. Skrine. *Naturalism.* London: Methuen, 1971.

Geismar, Maxwell. *Rebels and Ancestors: The American Novel, 1890–1915: Frank Norris, Stephen Crane, Jack London, Ellen Glasgow [and] Theodore Dreiser.* Boston: Houghton Mifflin, 1953.

Gendin, Sidney. "Was Stephen Crane (or Anybody Else) a Naturalist?" *Cambridge Quarterly* 24.2 (1995): 89–101.

Giles, James R. *The Naturalistic Inner-City Novel in America: Encounters with the Fat Man.* Columbia: U of South Carolina P, 1995.

Graham, Don. "Naturalism in American Fiction: A Status Report." *Studies in American Fiction* 10.1 (spring 1982): 1.16.

Hakutani, Yoshinobu, and Lewis Fried, eds. *American Literary Naturalism: A Reassessment.* Heidelberg: C. Winter, 1975.

Hemmings, F. W. J. "The Origin of the Terms *Naturalisme, Naturaliste.*" *French Studies* 8 (1954): 109–21.

Hoffman, Frederick J. "From Document to Symbol: Zola and American Naturalism." *Revue des Langues Vivantes* (1976): 203–12.

Hoffman, Michael J. *The Subversive Vision: American Romanticism in Literature.* Port Washington, N.Y.: Kennikat Press, 1972.

Hofstadter, Richard. *Social Darwinism in American Thought, 1860–1915.* Philadelphia: U of Pennsylvania P, 1945.

Holman, C. Hugh. "Of Everything the Unexplained and Irresponsible Specimen: Notes on How to Read American Realism." *Georgia Review* 18.3 (fall 1964): 316–24.

Hook, Sidney, ed. *Determinism and Freedom in the Age of Modern Science: A Philosophical Symposium.* New York: Collier Books, 1961.

Howard, June. *Form and History in American Literary Naturalism.* Chapel Hill: U of North Carolina P, 1985.

James, William. "The Dilemma of Determinism." *Essays on Faith and Morals.* New York: Longmans, Green and Co., 1949. 145–83.

Jones, Gwendolyn. "Zola's Publications in English in the United States." *Frank Norris Studies* 14 (autumn 1992): 8–11.

Jones, Howard M. *The Age of Energy: Varieties of American Experience, 1865–1915.* New York: Viking, 1971.

Kaplan, Harold. *Power and Order: Henry Adams and the Naturalist Tradition in American Fiction.* Chicago: U of Chicago P, 1981.

Kazin, Alfred. *On Native Grounds: An Interpretation of Modern American Prose Literature.* New York: Reynal and Hitchcock, 1942.

————. "American Naturalism: Reflections from Another Era." *The American Writer and the European Tradition,* ed. Margaret Denny and William H. Gilman. Minneapolis: U of Minnesota P, 1950.

Kolb, Harold H., Jr. *The Illusion of Life: American Realism as a Literary Form.* Charlottesville: UP of Virginia, 1969.

Krause, Sydney J., ed. *Essays on Determinism in American Literature.* Kent, Ohio: Kent State UP, 1964.

Lawlor, Mary. *Recalling the Wild: Naturalism and the Closing of the American West.* New Brunswick, N.J.: Rutgers UP, 2000.

Lehan, Richard. "American Literary Naturalism: The French Connection." *Nineteenth-Century Fiction* 38.4 (March 1984): 529–57.

Levy, Leo B. "Naturalism in the Making: De Forest's *Honest John Vane.*" *New England Quarterly* 37.1 (March 1964): 89–98.

Levin, Harry. "What Is Realism?" *Comparative Literature* 3.3 (summer 1951): 193–99.

Link, Eric Carl. "The War of 1893; or, Realism and Idealism in the Late Nineteenth Century." *American Transcendental Quarterly* 11.4 (December 1997): 309–21.

Loewenberg, Bert James. "Darwinism Comes to America, 1859–1900." *Mississippi Valley Historical Review* 28.3 (December 1941): 339–68.

Martin, Jay. *Harvests of Change: American Literature, 1865–1914.* Englewood Cliffs, N.J.: Prentice-Hall, 1967.

Martin, Ronald E. *American Literature and the Universe of Force.* Durham, N.C.: Duke UP, 1981.

Meyer, George Wilbur. "The Original Social Purpose of the Naturalistic Novel." *Sewanee Review* 50 (October 1942): 563–70.

Michaels, Walter Benn. *The Gold Standard and the Logic of Naturalism: American Literature at the Turn of the Century.* Berkeley and Los Angeles: U of California P, 1987.

Miller, Perry. "Novel and Romance." *Nature's Nation.* Cambridge, Mass.: Belknap, 1967.

Mitchell, Lee Clark. *Determined Fictions: American Literary Naturalism.* New York: Columbia UP, 1989.

Nelson, Brian, ed. *Naturalism in the European Novel: New Critical Perspectives.* New York: Berg, 1992.

Norris, Frank. *The Responsibilities of the Novelists, and Other Literary Essays.* New York: Doubleday, Page & Co., 1903.

Parrington, Vernon Louis. *Main Currents in American Thought.* Vol. 3. New York: Harcourt, 1930.

Peckham, Morse. "Darwinism and Darwinisticism." *Victorian Studies* 3.1 (September 1959): 19–40.

————. "Toward a Theory of Romanticism." *The Triumph of Romanticism: Collected Essays.* Columbia: U of South Carolina P, 1970.

Persons, Stow, ed. *Evolutionary Thought in America.* New York: George Braziller, 1956.

Pizer, Donald, ed. *The Cambridge Companion to American Realism and Naturalism.* New York: Cambridge UP, 1995.

————, ed. *Documents of American Realism and Naturalism.* Carbondale: Southern Illinois UP, 1998.

————. "The Problem of American Literary Naturalism and Theodore Dreiser's *Sister Carrie.*" *American Literary Realism* 32.1 (fall 1999): 1–11.

————. *Realism and Naturalism in Nineteenth-Century American Literature.* Rev. ed. Carbondale: Southern Illinois UP, 1984.

————. "Recent Studies of Nineteenth-Century American Realism and Naturalism." *ESQ* 30.3 (1984): 193–99.

————. *The Theory and Practice of American Literary Naturalism.* Carbondale: Southern Illinois UP, 1993.

Powers, Lyall H. *Henry James and the Naturalist Movement.* Michigan State UP, 1971.

Rahv, Philip. "Notes on the Decline of Naturalism." *Image and Idea: Fourteen Essays on Literary Themes.* Norfolk, Va.: New Directions, 1949.

Randall, John H. "The Changing Impact of Darwin on Philosophy." *Journal of the History of Ideas* 22 (October/December 1961): 435–62.

Savile, Anthony. "Naturalism and the Aesthetic." *British Journal of Aesthetics* 40.1 (January 2000): 46–63.

Schutze, Martin. "The Services of Naturalism to Life and Literature." *Sewanee Review* 11 (October 1903): 425–43.

Seamon, Roger. "Naturalist Narratives and Their Ideational Context: A Theory of American Naturalist Fiction." *Canadian Review of American Studies* 19.1 (spring 1988): 47–64.

Seltzer, Mark. *Bodies and Machines.* New York: Routledge, 1992.

Smith, Lewis Worthington. "The Drift Toward Naturalism." *South Atlantic Quarterly* 22 (October 1923): 355–69.

Stone, Edward. *What Was Naturalism? Materials for an Answer.* New York: Appleton-Century-Crofts, 1959.

Stromberg, Roland N., ed. *Realism, Naturalism and Symbolism: Modes of Thought and Expression in Europe, 1848–1914.* London: Macmillan, 1968.

Sundquist, Eric J. *American Realism: New Essays.* Baltimore: Johns Hopkins UP, 1982.

Thompson, G. R., and Eric Carl Link. *Neutral Ground: New Traditionalism and the American Romance Controversy.* Baton Rouge: Louisiana State UP, 1999.

Walcutt, Charles Child. *American Literary Naturalism, A Divided Stream.* Minneapolis: U of Minnesota P, 1956.

———. "Naturalism and Robert Herrick: A Test Case." In *American Literary Naturalism: A Reassessment,* Yoshinobu Hakutani and Lewis Fried, eds. Heidelberg: C. Winter, 1975: 75–89.

x. ed. *Seven Novelists in the American Naturalist Tradition.* Minneapolis: U of Minnesota P, 1963.

Watt, Ian P.. "Realism and the Novel Form." *The Rise of the Novel: Studies in Defoe, Richardson, and Fielding.* Berkeley and Los Angeles: U of California P, 1957.

Westbrook, Perry D. *Free Will and Determinism in American Literature.* Madison, N.J.: Associated University Presses, 1979.

Wilson, Christopher P. "American Naturalism and the Problem of Sincerity." *American Literature* 54.4 (December 1982): 511–27.

Winn, Ralph B. "Philosophic Naturalism." In *Twentieth Century Philosophy: Living Schools of Thought,* ed. Dagobert D. Runes. New York: Philosophical Library, 1943.

Ziff, Larzer. *The American 1890s: Life and Times of a Lost Generation.* New York: Viking Press, 1966.

Index